WORKS ISSUED BY
THE HAKLUYT SOCIETY

————

THE TRAVEL JOURNAL
OF ANTONIO DE BEATIS

SECOND SERIES
NO. 150

ISSUED FOR 1976

THE TRAVEL JOURNAL OF
ANTONIO DE BEATIS

GERMANY, SWITZERLAND,
THE LOW COUNTRIES,
FRANCE AND ITALY,
1517–1518

Translated from the Italian by
J. R. HALE and J. M. A. LINDON

Edited by
J. R. HALE

THE HAKLUYT SOCIETY
LONDON
1979

ISBN 0 904180 07 7

Printed in Great Britain at the
University Press, Cambridge

Published by the Hakluyt Society
c/o The Map Room,
British Library Reference Division
London WC1B 3DG

CONTENTS

LIST OF ILLUSTRATIONS

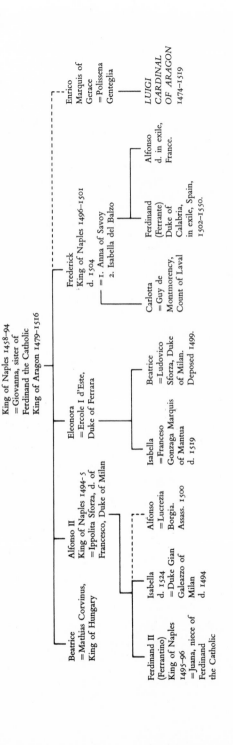

Neapolitan House of Aragon
Simplified Family Tree

PREFACE

In the spring of 1517 Luigi of Aragon, a bastard but one of the most wealthy, cultivated and well connected of Italian cardinals, left Rome for a long northern tour. His itinerary was affected by his desire to make himself known to the great rulers of his age, the Emperor Maximilian, the young King of Spain, Charles V, Francis I, Henry VIII, to make contact with the exiled members of his family, the Neapolitan branch of the royal house of Aragon, and to visit the tombs of those who had died abroad. But it was also, largely in its route and almost wholly in its mood, a pleasure trip.

For this it was well timed: during a lull in the international tensions that repeatedly discharged themselves in the Wars of Italy, and on the eve of Reformation bitterness. And the Cardinal, too grand to keep a record of his own movements, was well served by his chaplain and amanuensis, Antonio de Beatis, who day by day kept a steadily enthusiastic record of the scenes they passed among.

For an unsophisticated man almost untouched by the impress of Humanism, the range of de Beatis's interests was quite remarkably wide. His descriptions of landscapes, towns, of whole regions and the characters and customs of their inhabitants, of churches, palaces, relics and works of art provide one of the clearest impressions we have of the quality of life in north-western Europe in the Renaissance.

This range owes something, of course, to the company he kept. Without the Cardinal he would not have had the organs played in the churches they visited, would not have watched Raphael's tapestries being woven in Brussels or met Leonardo da Vinci at Amboise. But it owes still more to traditions which by 1517 suggested not only what a curious traveller should look at but the way in which he might organize his impressions and express them in writing. For this reason I have devoted most of the Introduction

ix

to explaining how the writing of such a travel record as de Beatis's had become possible.

The journal was first published, in a critical edition based on three manuscripts, by the great German church historian Ludwig Pastor in 1905.[1] He also provided a synopsis (fullest for de Beatis's account of Germany). In 1908 an enthusiastic essay in the *Revue des Deux Mondes*[2] brought its qualities to the attention of a wider public and a somewhat unreliable French translation followed in 1913.[3] Though frequently quoted by scholars, especially art historians,[4] the work has neither been reprinted nor translated into another language until now.

The present translation is made from Pastor's text. This was based on a manuscript in his own possession (now apparently of unknown whereabouts), collated with one equally full manuscript and another with numerous small omissions, both in the Biblioteca Nazionale Vittorio Emanuele III in Naples; respectively MS. x.F.28 and xiv.E.35. The former (N. 1) is illustrated in Plate 1, the latter (N. 2) in Plate 2.

A comparison of N. 1 with Pastor's text confirms what his own collations suggest; that the differences are minor and that he was vigilant to note any discrepancies. A feature of N. 1 not carried into the present edition is the richness of key words and phrases underlined in the text and repeated in the margins. These were gathered into an index of (for the time) unusual length: 56 sides as compared with the text's 282. Entries under each letter follow the foliation of the text rather than an alphabetical order, and are divided into sections: 'In Italia', 'In la Magna Alta', 'In Fiandre', 'In Picardia et tucte le altre provintie di Franza confuse' and (for the return journey) again 'In Italia'. Within each letter the entries are typically miscellaneous, 'Cales' (Calais) and 'Casale' appearing amid the less helpful 'Caverna dove la Imperatore ha posto un crucifixio di mano proprio' (see below, p. 64), 'Conte di San Bonifacio', 'Corpo del beato Simone' and 'Contra Sodomite'. Text, marginal notes and index are in the same hand.

[1] Op. cit in bibl. It had been previously described by L. Volpicella in *Archivio Storico per le Provincie Napoletane* (1876) 106–17.

[2] 15 September. It was reprinted by the author, Teodor de Wyzewa, in his *Excentriques et aventuriers* (Paris, 1910) 45–70.

[3] Op. cit. in bibl.

[4] E.g. Sir Ernst Gombrich, 'The earliest description of Bosch's Garden of Delight', *Journal of the Warburg and Courtauld Institutes* (1967) 403–6. Reprinted in *The heritage of Apelles* (London, 1976).

Both Pastor's manuscript and N. 1 are described as transcriptions (*transcriptione*) made by de Beatis, the former dated 29 May 1521, the latter 21 August 1521. The former has a dedication addressed on 20 July 1521 by de Beatis simply 'to his lords and good friends' (perhaps the chapter of a cathedral or abbey), the latter is addressed to Antonio Seripando (see p. 58, note 1).

N. 2, also in quarto format, is undated, unattributed and unaddressed. The manuscript, which contains 238 numbered sides of text and eight unnumbered sides of index, has, unlike the other two manuscripts, a title page. Written within an elaborate calligraphic frame is: 'Viaggi, et Itinerario di Mon. R.mo et Ill.mo il Cardinal' de' Aragona incominciando dalla Città di Ferrara. Anno M.D.XVII. Mense Maij.' While many phrases and some descriptive and historical passages are omitted, and a few figures are changed (Leonardo da Vinci's age appears as 'more than sixty' instead of 'seventy', the number of hearths in Brussels as '6,000' instead of '8,000') the text is identical with that of the other manuscripts save for the entry for 26 January 1518 (see note to text). Unlike N. 1, the index is not divided into sections within each letter, and the arrangement – from 'Abbatia di S. Barbara' to 'Usanza delle donne di Fiandra mentre conciano il lino' (see below, p. 102) – is alphabetical, not according to page number. N. 2 also differs from N. 1 in having very few marginal entries.

The description of Pastor's manuscript and N. 1 as transcriptions, the omission of matter of general interest from N. 2, and the fact that the drawing of the Holy Shroud only appears in N. 2 and the print of François de Paule only in N. 1, suggest that while all depend from de Beatis's original journal, none was designed for publication.

De Beatis did not add a consolidated itinerary, so one has been provided for this edition. While attempting a faithful rendering of de Beatis's prose into English, we have at times felt the need, or, perhaps, surrendered to the temptation to ease the reader through some particularly staccato passages. Place-names have been modernised (de Beatis's spellings are given in the Index) as have personal names. Forms of address (r.^{mo} et ill.^{mo}, etc.) have been simplified and long entries paragraphed. De Beatis only names the month on its first day; it has been added to each date. He gave distances at the end of each entry; they have been retained only when part of a sentence and all have been transferred to the

Itinerary. This should be borne in mine, for these figures, plus the underlining of place names and the marginal note 'per acqua' when his party took to rivers, emphasize in the appearance of N. 1 the preoccupation with day-by-day movement.

My gratitude to my co-translator and colleague, John Lindon, extends to the generous interest he has shown in the preparation of the edition as a whole, and I am indebted to the careful and questioning scrutiny this volume has received from Dr E. S. de Beer. During the preparation and revision of the typescript Christine Cavanna was sorely tried and never failed in patience or skill.

J. R. HALE
UNIVERSITY COLLEGE,
LONDON

INTRODUCTION

1. *The cardinal and the canon*

On 17 March 1517 the Venetian ex-ambassador to Rome read to his colleagues in the Senate a series of pen portraits of the outstanding cardinals in the papal capital. Among them was Luigi, the Cardinal of Aragon, 'descended from that royal house and addressed as "most reverend and illustrious". He is highly eccentric. His income is 24,000 ducats. The Pope does not get on well with him because though he was one of those responsible for making him pope, he has so far only been given 4,000 ducats from the Abbey of Chiaravalle...He is an enemy of the French and shows affection for our government.'[1] Within a week, the ambassador's successor was reporting on the Cardinal's movements. He has left Rome for good out of dissatisfaction with the pope...No, he has now returned. Now (22 April) he is off again, 'bound for Ferrara and then, it is said, he is going to the Catholic King.[2] He has left ill content with the Pope and it is put out that he is going to Flanders to obtain financial aid for his relatives from the King.' On 9 May the Venetian secretary wrote from Milan that 'it is rumoured in the Kingdom of Naples that the Cardinal of Aragon has gone to His Majesty[3] about the return of lands to the Angevin interest' and from Naples itself the Venetian consul repeated the opposing theory that he had left, at odds with the Pope, to visit King Charles.[4] And in fact it was on 9 May that the Cardinal left Ferrara on a journey that was to lead to meetings with both Charles and Francis I, the journey to which this volume is devoted.

It is true that the ears of diplomats were particularly attuned to gossip about cardinals that spring and early summer. The plot

---

[1] Eugenio Albèri, *Relazioni degli ambasciatori veneti al senato* (Florence, 1839–63) ser. II vol. iii, 57.
[2] Charles I, King of Spain from 1516 and Duke of Burgundy. Emperor, as Charles V, from 1519.
[3] Francis I, King of France.
[4] *I diarii di Marino Sanuto* (Venice, 1879–1903) xxiv, cols. 144, 151, 182, 228, 276.

to assassinate Leo X that came to be associated with its leading instigator, Cardinal Petrucci, was brewing. Its discovery shortly after Luigi had left the country led to the conviction that he had been implicated and, at the last moment, had lost his nerve. But the theory was difficult to sustain when, on 15 March 1518, the Venetian representative in Rome reported that 'this evening the Cardinal of Aragon returned after a year's absence in France and Spain [sic], and he went at once to His Holiness and dined with him'.[1] And that the Pope was not merely waiting to pounce is shown by a report of 29 April that Leo had been hunting with Luigi who is 'one of the leaders among the whole court in entertainments and the chase'[2] and by a letter of 1 May describing how 'Messer Agostino Chigi gave a fish banquet in his house in Trastevere[3] where, amid the most lavish preparations costing 1,700 ducats, the Pope dined with Monsignor of Aragon and many other cardinals.' It also contains the unforgettable picture of Leo, during a hunt organized by the Cardinal, moving in on foot to kill a stag caught in the nets 'with his spear in one hand and his spectacles in the other'.[4] It is a letter doubly precious. Not only does it confirm that Leo saw nothing suspicious about the Cardinal's long absence, but it is one of the very few documents yet found in the hand of Antonio de Beatis, the author of the record of his journey. And it gives a last intimate glimpse of the Cardinal before his death on 21 January in the following year.

The extravagance and mondainity of Chigi's hospitality have become part of our vision of Rome's Golden Age before the sack of 1527, and of that age in general the Cardinal of Aragon was no mean representative.[5] Very much a prince of the church, his father, Marquis of Gerace in Calabria, was the illegitimate son of King Ferdinand I of Naples. [See Table, p. viii.] Born in 1474,

---

[1] Ib., xxv, col. 305. And the conclusion of Fabrizio Winspeare, *La Congiura dei cardinali contro Leone X* (Florence, 1957) 146, is that 'non era colpevole' but wished to avoid contamination from those who were.

[2] Ib., col. 385.

[3] The Villa Farnesina, built for the banker Chigi and decorated by Baldassare Peruzzi and Raphael.

[4] A. Luzio and R. Renier, 'La cultura e le relazioni letterarie di Isabella d'Este Gonzaga' (part 6), *Giornale Storico di Letteratura Italiana* (1902) 205. The part describing the hunt is in Pastor, *Popes* (op. cit. in the following note) viii, 473.

[5] There is no full biography. Short accounts of his career are given by Pastor in his edition of de Beatis (pp. 1–11) and by G. de Caro, *Dizionario Biografico degli Italiani*; and for scattered references see Ludwig Pastor, *The history of the popes...* (36 vols., London, 1891 seq.) vols. vi–viii. For church preferments, C. Eubel, *Hierarchia catholica*, iii (Monasterii, 1910) 6.

Luigi, at the instance of Ferdinand and Pope Innocent VIII was married in 1492 to the Pope's niece, Battistina Cibo, as symbol of the new concord between Naples and Rome. Two years later the marriage was annulled by Innocent's successor Alexander VI to enable Luigi to represent a still closer rapprochement by joining the papal court; in May 1494, at the age of hardly 20, he was appointed cardinal, with Santa Maria in Cosmedin as his titular church, and ceded his rights to the marquisate to his younger brother.

In the following years, which saw first the expulsion of the Neapolitan House of Aragon by the French and then their supplanting by the main Aragonese line represented by King Ferdinand II the Catholic, the Cardinal went on diplomatic missions on behalf of his uncle Frederick and his grandfather's widow, Giovanna to Spain and then to France.[1] Back in Rome in 1503 for the conclave which elected first Pius III and then, on his death a few weeks later, Pope Julius II, he in both instances supported the French candidate, Georges d'Amboise, but was shortly to become one of Julius's most trusted collaborators during one of the most violently active of all pontificates. Though related to the Este family, for instance, he supported Julius's campaign against the Duchy of Ferrara in the winter of 1510–11, riding with the Pope as he accompanied his army and laid siege to Mirandola. In 1512, when Julius was concerned about the power of the Spanish army he had called in to defeat his ex-ally of Cambrai, France, it was rumoured that he was intending to break with King Ferdinand and re-install the Neapolitan Aragonese with Cardinal Luigi as king. Such a move would have fitted with Julius's plan to rid Italy of the undue influence first of France and then of Spain, but there is no firm evidence for it. Grandson of one King of Naples, nephew of two others (Alfonso II and Frederick) and cousin of a fourth (Ferdinand, known as Ferrantino), Luigi was also connected through his family with the ruling houses of Savoy, Milan and Ferrara as well as with the powerful clans of Orsini and Sanseverino. Rich, influential and so well connected, all the Cardinal's journeys, to Venice, to Naples, to Ferrara, quite apart from his expedition to Flanders, were attended by rumours that more than mere pleasure or the ties of kinship was involved. All

[1] L. Volpicella, *Federico d'Aragona e la fine del Regno di Napoli nel MDI* (Naples, 1908) 17–20.

3

that is clear is that his closeness to Julius was followed by intimacy with Leo X, who became Pope on Julius's death in 1513, and this in spite of Leo's initial hope of gaining French assent to the enfeoffment of his brother Giuliano with the Kingdom of Naples and, when rebuffed, his decision to confirm Ferdinand II's investiture.

Wealthy as he was from an inheritance of 40,000 ducats (left to him by his aunt Queen Beatrice) and from the accumulation of benefices a centrally placed churchman could expect almost as a matter of routine, it is not unlikely that he occasionally expressed a grievance that he had not been made even richer. Whether or not the Venetian ambassador was correct in attributing to Leo X the remark 'since God has given us the papacy, let us enjoy it', it is a sentiment that perfectly expresses Luigi's reaction to his cardinalship. His return to celibacy was taken lightly. A liaison with the famous courtesan Giulia Campana was taken for granted from 1505 to 1515, and her daughter confidently drew attention to it by accepting the appellation Tullia d'Aragona.[1] His youth and the splendour of his accoutrements made his disguise easy to penetrate as he rode among the street dances and horse races of the Roman carnival or took part in mounted bull-fights at Monte Testaccio. And more matter for the news-letters from Rome lay in the lavishness of the receptions he gave in his Palazzo San Clemente. As a patron he supported Giangiorgio Trissino, author of the classicizing tragedy, *Sophonisba*, the poet Marcantonio Flaminio, the classical scholar Giovanni Paolo Parisi of Cosenza, and Pietro Martire di Anghiera who dedicated to him two books of the first history of Spanish exploration and settlement in the New World, the *Decades de orbe novo*. He was a close friend of Baldassare Castiglione, and though only mentioned in *The Courtier* as the leading spirit in an egg-throwing carnival jest, was most probably in Urbino at the time (1507) in which the conversations in the book were set.[2]

Lacking a full-scale study, we can then imagine Luigi in the context of Paolo Cortese's portrait of the ideal cardinal in his *de Cardinalatu* (1510) with its fusion of secular habits (riding and the

---

[1] Georgina Masson, *Courtesans of the Italian Renaissance* (London, 1976) 32, 89–90.

[2] Vittorio Cian, ed., *Il libro del Cortegiano* (Florence, 1947) 279. And see D. S. Chambers, 'The economic predicament of Renaissance cardinals', *Studies in Medieval and Renaissance History*, iii (1966) 289–313.

chase) and splendour (a household of 140 officials and servants) with ecclesiastical functions, or of *The Courtier*, with its portrait of Ippolito d'Este as the model of the worldly and well-born cardinal. Or we can turn to the connoisseur-cardinals with whom Benvenuto Cellini chaffered in his early days in Rome. But at least between the foreground of fact and the stage setting of imagination and analogy we can set the Cardinal's role and interests as they emerge from the pages of de Beatis, a man happily unencumbered by too much mental baggage and vulnerable to the infection of his master's cultural enthusiasms.

For what promotes this journal to the status of an important source for our imaginative liaison with ways of life and thought in early sixteenth-century Europe is its being in effect a work of collaboration. On the one hand we have its author; canon of Molfetta (on the coast between – and overshadowed by – Barletta and Bari) and conscious of his inability to meet the purist standards set for a correct latinity or a vernacular castigated to a limpid Tuscan.[1] On the other hand we have the journal's raison d'être: the wealthy 42-year-old Cardinal, already widely travelled and intellectually abreast of whatever Rome, then the cultural centre of Europe, had to offer. What de Beatis had to offer was a steady enthusiasm for observing the people and places he encountered and – as will be suggested – an awareness of the ways in which visual experience could by then be ordered and expressed in a narrative of travel. But as a provincial travelling with a cosmopolite, a humble cleric with a prelate and patron, he had much to absorb. We can see this process in its most elementary form when he notes his master's purchases: an organ at Brixen, ingenious clocks at Nuremberg, flutes and fifes at Ravensburg, hunting crossbows at Malines, a 'royal litter' at Blois and, elsewhere in France, horses and dogs, musicians and mountebanks. De Beatis on his own would doubtless have visited churches, noted the different ecclesiastical administrations through which he passed, examined relics. But his attitude to relics, the mixture of uneasy cynicism and eager devoutness with which he reviews the

---

[1] See 'Postscript'. A host of apologies in early sixteenth-century Italian books for not hewing to linguistic norms suggest a covert regional pride. The letter from Calais referred to in note 1 (p. 11) suggests that he could compose a letter in adequate Italian, or, at least, take one from dictation. Denys Hay has recently pointed out that 'The current language of inter-departmental business in the offices of the curia was Latin by the end of the fifteenth century.' *The church in Italy in the fifteenth century* (Cambridge, 1977) 42.

problem of encountering identical heads and limbs in different places,[1] this surely reflects the easy-going orthodoxy of a prince of the church who finds amusement where others would avoid the issue or cry scandal. It was because of the Cardinal that he tells us so much of organs and clocks, visits libraries, is able to draw on the confidence which could praise a reliquary by 'judging it to be of the highest craftsmanship' or pronounce that the Raphael tapestries being woven at Brussels 'will be the finest in Christendom', in order to produce descriptions of works of art on his own that have been valued by art historians; is helped by the tone of a man he acknowledges to be a judge of gentlemanly physique and behaviour to give roundness to his portraits of the notables they encountered. For it is clear that while de Beatis's reverence and affection for the Cardinal became deep and enduring, the Cardinal found no cause to snub or distance someone he had chosen to accompany him, presumably on grounds of congeniality and common sense, as his private chaplain and amanuensis. It is the alliance between the chaplain's curiosity and the Cardinal's taste that makes this journal uniquely expressive of the long moment dubbed the Renaissance.

This collaboration (though neither the social distance between the two men, nor the prime role played by de Beatis's own brightly naive intelligence should be underplayed by the term) was encouraged by three factors. The trip was expensive, but the Cardinal could afford the 15,000 ducats it cost, and his entourage, with its core of 35 courtiers, household officials and servants, was large enough to make matters comfortable without slowing progress. Europe was – astoundingly, by the standards obtaining since the international participation in the Wars of Italy and their Cisalpine offshoots since 1494 – peaceable: the journey was incommoded only by local squabbles in the Palatinate and along the Guelderland–Holland border, and by the return of French troops from the mini-war of Urbino which marooned the travellers for two weeks at Avignon. And in the third place, their itinerary, as can be seen from the map, had both the overall symmetry and the excursion-like eccentricities (visits to Nuremberg, The Hague, Paris) that suggest the lineaments of a pleasure trip.

[1] See pp. 152–4.

De Beatis is explicit on this point. Introducing his narrative he explains that the Cardinal had resolved that 'not being satisfied with having several times seen the greater part of Italy, nearly all Baetica[1] and the furthest parts of Spain, he would also get to know Germany, France[2] and all those other regions bordering the northern and western ocean and make himself known to so great a variety of people'. This is amply born out in the text, which conveys a strong atmosphere of holiday. Though the party maintained a smart pace, they were industrious sight-seers. Revisiting Malines, 'to make up for the first time, when we simply stayed for a meal and then went straight on, we examined practically the whole town'. And no overtly political motive appears from the Cardinal's making himself known to the members of the exclusive club of cardinals, archbishops and bishops from whom he received so much hospitality and with whom, as aristocrats and, many of them, appointees of Julius and Leo, he must have had much in common. However, de Beatis's rank excluded him from much of their conversation; on the only occasion on which he appears to have been promoted to dine in grand company the talk he records consisted of swapping yarns about miracles, spiced by the rivalry between the family of the host, Guy de Laval, Governor of Brittany, and that of the broadly acred and beneficed Rohans. Guy had married into the Neapolitan house of Aragon, and there is little doubt that among the pieties, if not the purposes, of the Cardinal's visit was to make contact with the exiled members of his own family or, as at Tours, with the places associated with them. Indeed, not the least interesting aspect of the journal is the number of exiles who were met en route, either employed, and sometimes – like the Sanseverino – in positions of high trust, or simply waiting for better times. But there is no suggestion that the Cardinal was angling for a following: if he had been, de Beatis, who though usually placed below the salt, handled the Cardinal's correspondence, would surely have let some hint appear in his uncensored and in no way guileful account.

He does say that the Cardinal set off 'under the cover and excuse of meeting Our Lord the Catholic King, his kinsman', that is

---

[1] See note, p. 57.

[2] De Beatis uses 'France' in the sense of the 'true' France: the Ile de France and the territories to its south, omitting Picardy, Normandy and Brittany.

Charles, King of Spain since 1516 and only waiting for the resolution of conflicts in the Netherlands (where he was Archduke) before sailing to rule there. The Roman Habsburg-watchers had been right about this. Luigi had wished to meet in Frankfurt Maximilian I (whom Charles was to follow as King of the Romans in 1519), who as well as being one of the age's most glamorous potentates was one of its chief curiosities. But at Worms, 'when news came that his Imperial Majesty had left for Augsburg, the Cardinal, though most anxious to meet him, was reluctant to turn back so far, especially as there was a possibility that the Catholic King would sail for Spain, and to meet and get to know him was the chief objective of his journey. If he had left, he would have to follow him, so he decided to continue to Flanders'. That is why the party passed through Malines so quickly the first time: to get to Charles before he sailed from Middelburg.

The meeting there, as de Beatis (and Vital, Charles's own chronicler[1]) described it, was both ceremonious and friendly but apparently without political significance. Perhaps if the Cardinal had not died so soon after his return to Rome some line of policy would have emerged that would enable us to correct this impression. But it is doubtful. The ties of lineage, the respect for the titular heads of the complex international clans that make genealogy so essential a component of the study of the Age of the Individual, the role of the clientage systems they fostered: these are matters whose importance it is unwise to underestimate. Those whose job it was to swell the files on subversion guessed too narrowly; thus when the Cardinal later on reached Rouen the Venetian diplomatic agent there reported (erroneously) that he had been in England and (equally erroneously) was now on his way to 'the court of the Catholic King to see about the release of his relative the Duke of Calabria who is in a castle in Castile in Spain'.[2] Luigi may have put in a good word for the exiles among his own family, but it would have been entirely in keeping with the still quasi-feudal and respect-oriented mood of the time if his dominant motive was to show himself to and to be recognized and remembered by the young man who, if not yet an emperor, was the greatest chieftain in the West.

[1] See p. 26.
[2] Sanuto, op. cit., xxiv, col. 582. His nephew Ferdinand (Ferrante) had been captured after defending Taranto from the Spanish commander Gonsalvo da Cordoba in 1502 and in 1517 was imprisoned in the castle of Jàtiba.

With this meeting in mind, de Beatis noted in his Postscript, the Cardinal had taken along the robes of his office. He changed into them from his pleasant (and not altogether unecclesiastical) mufti of pink silk and black velvet sash only on one other occasion: his meeting at Rouen with King Francis I.

He had, in the meantime, planned to visit England. In 1509 he had written from Naples to congratulate the young Henry VIII on his marriage to 'my relation and Lady' Catherine of Aragon. Now he wrote from Bruges to advise Wolsey of his intention to meet the King in person, and arrived in Calais on 5 August 1517 to cross the channel. Three days later, de Beatis noted that after being told by the Deputy, Sir Richard Wingfield, of the seriousness of the epidemic of sweating-sickness then raging in England, 'his reverence cancelled his journey, and decided to join the Most Christian King, who was at Rouen'.

It is worth pausing for a moment to see what lay behind this laconically recorded incident.

From correspondence with Andreas Ammonius, Henry VIII's Latin secretary, the Cardinal had derived the impression that the King might be disposed to help Frederick's widowed queen Isabella, exiled – as a potential irritant to the status quo in the Kingdom of Naples – both from Spain and France and living in genteel distress in Ferrara. But the last thing Henry, or Wolsey thinking on his behalf, wanted was to resurrect the Neapolitan issue. The Cardinal arrived in the Netherlands at a moment when Wolsey's plans for a peace treaty between all the major European powers, which culminated in the Peace of London in the following year, were being tried out, and when the important detail of the cession back to France of Tournai had reached a point of great delicacy. Henry's agents in Flanders, Cuthbert Tunstall, bishop of London, and Sir Thomas Spinelly, were much perturbed. Who was this cardinal who had impressed Charles V so much that he wanted Henry's support in detaching one of Luigi's benefices for the sake of one of his, Charles's, dependants? – who arrived to take part in the giving of the hat to the young Cardinal de Croy with an entourage of 40 horse, and then was seen in a cloak, and with a sword at his side, trying out the paces of a horse (from which, Spinelly hopefully wrote to Wolsey, 'your grace, may conjecture what manner of man he is')?

Playing safe, Wolsey gave instructions that the Cardinal was to

be prevented from coming to England. Accordingly, Spinelly
wrote to Wingfield at Calais that if he turned up there he was 'to
be colourably detained', perhaps 'under colour of the weather',
and asked Charles's Chamberlain, Guillaume de Croy, for his
advice. De Croy believed that the Cardinal was not going to
England with official letters either from Charles V or from the
Pope. This forced Spinelly to ask him to think of some way of
dissuading him, it 'not being known by what manner the said
Cardinal was departed from Rome, or how he stood with His
Holiness; showing also the suspicion [that] might be had in him
by reason of the demeanour of divers other cardinals and the
special regard Your Grace [Wolsey, to whom he was writing]
must have particularly for the honour and reverence of the Holy
Church'. To this de Croy said that he would ask the Cardinal's
special friend the Bishop of Badajoz to find some reason to
represent the unwisdom of the visit, adding that he would do this
although he personally would 'be very glad of his departing, for
he is a marvellous man that hath importuned us of many things'.
It would have been natural enough for any churchman to use the
gathering of statesmen and ecclesiastics about Charles to push
claims for preferment for himself and his kin (Wolsey's tenure of
the bishopric of Tournai was one of the stumbling-blocks in the
current negotiations), but it was this that seems to have determined
the conclusion of Spinelly's letter. 'The said Cardinal's profession
is rather of a temporal lord than spiritual, and as I am informed
upon the great bruit that reigns of the King my master his
liberality, he was moved to his coming supposing to have some
excellent reward.'

Whether or not the Bishop of Badajoz spoke to him on the
subject, on 5 August the Cardinal duly arrived at Calais. To
Wingfield's embarrassment the weather was fine. The alternative
device he resorted to, the planning of hunting expeditions, could
not remain 'colourable' for long, and he was relieved when on
the 7th a letter arrived from England describing the effects of the
sweating-sickness. This, 'knowing how much Italians are afraid of
coming into a place where there is danger of health', he read to
the Cardinal whose courage, he noted, was 'greatly abated'. And
in fact the Cardinal there and then wrote to Wolsey to say that
he was reluctantly having to give priority to 'the health of myself

and my dependents' and to beg him to make his excuses with the King. He was going across France to Spain, he wrote, and hoped to see Henry and Wolsey on his return. He expressed the same hope to Wingfield.

The Cardinal arrived at Rouen on 13 August, and while there sent his chamberlain, Antonio Scaglione, to Calais. Wingfield reported to Wolsey that this was because he had changed his plans. Instead of proceeding to Spain he had to hasten back to Rome. Scaglione was to explain this to the King and to Wolsey and also to purchase horses and greyhounds and obtain licences for their export. Wingfield suggested that at least the latter might be presented to him, as he was 'so noble and potent a prelate'. And on this note of obvious relief the incident of the missed visit to England closes.[1]

What are we to make of it? Not too much. It is chiefly a reminder of the anxious scrutiny that was brought to bear on any traveller of importance at a time of diplomatic uncertainty and endemic intrigue. The Cardinal *could* have been agitating for the expulsion of the Spanish governors of Naples and the reinstatement of his own line. He *could* have represented the faction in the College of Cardinals that wished to depose the Pope. Why he told Wingfield and Wolsey that he was off to Spain (a tale picked up, as we have seen, by the Venetian agent at Rouen), why he claimed that he was forced to hurry back to Rome: this is unclear. He must have been as conscious, as de Beatis was absorbedly unaware, of the spies and rumour-mongers who kept up a steady murmuration of conjecture about his movements. He may have decided to mislead. But there is no evidence that he had a political aim deeper than to make useful acquaintances, to seek favours, and to divert himself. Fate (as he thought) barred access to Henry VIII, so he turned, without undue haste, to call upon the King of France. Like other monarchs, Francis travelled widely to let himself be seen and known; for a prince of the Church, and one of royal blood to wander through his kingdom without paying his respects would

---

[1] *Letters and papers, foreign and domestic, 1517-18*, nos. 3398, 3472, 3556, 3647, 3566 [Spinelly's letter quoted from British Library, Cotton mss., Galba B.V. 297 r-v], 3559, 3571, 3572, 3610. The Cardinal's letter of apology is Cotton, Vitellius, V. iii, 231. On returning to Rome he wrote to Henry on 20 March and 25 May and to Wolsey on 12 November 1518, expressing his desire to serve them at the curia; B.L., ib., 201v and 216v, and *L. and P.*, no. 4578.

have been a gaffe. Duty, as well as curiosity and pleasure suffice to explain this meeting with the head of what was widely known to be the most entertaining of European courts.

For making such a journey for pleasure, and over such a route, there was a precedent, and a remarkably close one. In 1494 Cardinal Giovanni de'Medici, son of Lorenzo the Magnificent, was exiled from Florence along with his cousin Giulio when the city rebelled against the power of the Medici and restored a more open form of republican government. In 1499, reconciled to the fact that the new government was stable enough to endure, at least for some time, and having found no support elsewhere in Italy for bringing it down by force, the cousins collected a small group of friends and servants, 12 horses in all, and set off incognito for Germany from Venice, taking it in turns to settle each day's destination. Travelling in this way, 'judging it not waste of time nor unuseful to acquire the knowledge gained from observing the habits and customs of different peoples in far places', they crossed Bavaria to Ulm and proceeded up the Rhine to Flanders. There, on the recommendation of Maximilian I (to whom they had been sent by the authorities in Ulm as suspicious strangers) they were entertained by Charles's predecessor as archduke, Philip. They intended to go next to England, but the sight from Nieuwpoort of the heaving seas deterred them, and there began a tour which led them to Rouen (where they were imprisoned until their identity was established by letters from Venice from Giovanni's brother Piero) and thence home, early in 1500, via Marseilles, Savona and Genoa.[1] It is tempting at least to speculate that Luigi's choice of route was not uninfluenced by nostalgic conversations with the Pope he knew so well and who, while he could find many ways of enjoying the papacy, had had to forsake the pleasures of foreign travel.

2. European travel and travel accounts

The importance of travel in the life of early sixteenth-century Europe needs little emphasis. The members of the guilds of inn-keepers which existed in every major town earned a steady income (and a varying reputation) from merchants on their way to trade fairs or the foreign branches of international concerns,

---

[1] Scipio Ammirato, *Opuscoli* (3 vols., Florence, 1639–40) iii, 59–60, and Paolo Giovio, *Le vite di Leon Decimo et d'Adriano Sesto* (Florence, 1549) 77–81.

petitioners en route to secular or ecclesiastical courts, lawyers, stewards, diplomats, army recruiters, courtiers, couriers and pilgrims. Quite apart from the major enterprises of Compostela and the Holy Land the pilgrimage impulse was at its height. In addition to the perennial, as well as the Jubilee attraction of Rome, there were (to mention only relic-centres visited by de Beatis) Aix-la-Chapelle, Mont-Saint-Michel, Sainte-Baume, Grenoble and Chambéry. More occasional guests were wandering masons, journeymen on their Wanderjahre, students, tumblers, pedlars, between-wars soldiers: all those who could from time to time afford to alternate living rough with the hot food, tight roof and servant-girl cuddles afforded by the sign of the Woolpack, the Lion or the simple bush. The formidable itinerancy of Erasmus, from patron to patron, printer to printer, was part of a pattern followed by other scholars and by artists: Cornelius Agrippa roamed after teachers and protectors through Germany and Burgundy, France, Spain, Italy and England, the Estonian painter Miguel Zittoz worked in Denmark, the Netherlands, England and Spain, the Flemish composer Heinrich Isaac left the influence of his talent in Austria ('Innsbruck, ich muss dich lassen'), France and Italy. It is not just that whoever had to travel, did, but that whoever wanted to, could, and at a speed determined for pedestrians by blisters and exhaustion, for riders by the lungs and shoes of their horses; a traveller merely impatient could average 29 miles a day, a professional courier, riding post and under pressure, could get near to 90.[1] The pace of de Beatis's party was that of the reasonably energetic tourist: an average of 24·5 miles a day while on the move, or just over 39·5 kilometres.[2]

The problem of finding accommodation along a chosen route was not a major one. The Cardinal's party travelled in some style. He took his own bed. There were two harbingers to ride ahead to book accommodation and secure provisions, two cooks to supplement the deficiencies of local kitchens, grooms to look after the horses. Though forced on occasion to split up or to travel further than they had wished because all the available accommodation had been taken by other parties, his own was never without a roof over their heads. Indeed, though even more illustrious travellers had to put up (as Pope Pius II did near Nepi)

[1] George B. Parks, *The English traveller to Italy...to 1525* (Rome, 1954) 498–9 and 504.
[2] See note, p. 188.

with 'a small chamber just large enough for a bed', or with sheds and hovels in inn-less hamlets when veering from main routes, it is very rare to read of anyone being benighted in the open. Or, indeed, in spite of the warnings supplied by heavily tenanted gibbets, of their being robbed en route; the danger was there, and travellers tended in certain areas to wait in order to ride in collective clusters or share the cost of hiring counter-cutthroats, but the records of late fifteenth- and early sixteenth-century travel do not give much colour to the notion of the 'lawless roads' of Europe. As far as robbery was concerned, the conventional villain was the landlord and his prices, not the brigand or the outlaw. De Beatis had a bag stolen, at a village near Gaillon, and the loss coloured his whole view of the non-aristocratic French. But at the time of the theft he was snugly ensconced in an inn.

As for chosing the route to be taken on a long journey, this was perfectly possible, at least in outline, with the maps then available. Writing from London in c. 1498 a Venetian noted that 'the Kingdom of England is situated in the island named Britain, which, as your Magnificence has seen, is in the Ocean, between the north and the west'.[1] And when the news of the disastrous Venetian defeat in 1509 at Agnadello was received in the capital, a group of senators were standing in front of a wall map from which they could at once read off its strategic significance.[2] The Cardinal could have used the fairly widely distributed 'Cusanus' copper-plate map of 1491, which showed the whole of his route until he left Flanders for France, and his return journey once he neared Marseilles. Similar coverage was given by the smaller but more useful wood-cut map of central Europe issued by Erhard Erzlaub in 1500, more useful because it crammed in more than 800 names of towns and indicated the main roads (at least those leading to Rome, for it was primarily intended for pilgrims) by dots each in theory a German league apart; the slightly extended version of 1501 went as far west as Calais.[3] Then thanks to successive editions from 1477 there were by 1517 several thousand copies of Ptolemy's *Geographia* in circulation. Heavy folios, these were books for scholars and the cultivated rich. They varied in

---

[1] *A relation, or rather a true account, of the Island of England*, ed. and tr. C. A. Sneyd (Camden Soc., 1847) 7.

[2] Sanuto, *Diarii*, viii, col. 247.

[3] O. B. Durand, 'The earliest modern maps of Germany and Central Europe', *Isis*, xix (1933) 486–502.

usefulness as new maps were introduced or left out, but the Rome, 1507, edition had a 'Tabula nova Italie' which covered the Cardinal's route from Ferrara to Bolzano; Bolzano to Bruges was covered by a 'Tabula moderna Polonie, Vangarie, Boemie, Germanie, Russie, Lithuanie' and the rest of his route was included in the 'Tabula moderna Francie'. Still better for his purpose was the edition produced at Strasbourg in 1513. The wood-cuts were cruder, but there was a new 'Tabula moderna Germanie', reaching from the Brenner to Dordrecht, and a 'Tabula nova, particularis provincie rheni superioris', and though many of the place-names were printed upside down, requiring the constant twirling of a massive tome, there were many more of them. Given such sources it is unlikely that the Cardinal would have found much assistance in the maps in Francesco Berlinghieri's Ptolemaic *Geographia* (Florence, ?1480) or the best-selling *Libri cronicarum* ... (Nuremberg 1493, 1496, 1497, 1500 etc.) of Hartmann Schedel though they covered all the route save western France; they were clumsier and less accurate and, in the case of the former, place-names were crowded out by the exuberant conventions used for mountains and water.

De Beatis does not mention a map. Nor does any of the travellers to be mentioned in the following pages. But they must have been used. There are many indications: the preoccupation with rivers (always exaggeratedly large on maps) rather than roads (seldom shown save on the Erzlaub maps) and the ability to describe where they rose, with which others they connected and where they ran into the sea; the nonchalant use of Latin place-names in otherwise severely vernacular narratives and the non-use of them when they did not feature on maps; the confident awareness of passing from one geo-political region to another. But all these maps were of restricted practicality. They were double folio or smaller and the information they contained, while adequate to the overall planning of a route and, to a lesser extent, to timing it, was of little use for day-to-day direction-finding purposes.

No regional maps for sections of the Cardinal's route have survived. That they existed, at least for parts of the route through Germany, may with some confidence be conjectured from the sketch-map of *c.* 1495 known as the Koblenz Fragment.[1] The

[1] Leo Bagrow, *History of Cartography*, revised R. A. Skelton (London, 1964) 148.

bird's-eye view by Konrad Türst of *c.* 1496, showing the lakes, rivers, hills and villages of the country between Schaffhausen and Constance may represent a fairly common type.[1] On a larger – and thus even more useful – scale were veritable route maps like the engraved map of *c.* 1500 by Giovanni Pontano. This covers part of the northern border of the Kingdom of Naples, from Viesci (a hamlet north of Rieti) to the mouth of the river Tronto at Porto d'Ascoli, showing road, river, mountains and villages with a table of distances from one village or town to another.[2] The more useful a map, the more likely it is to perish in the course of being used. But while these examples suggest what may have been available, conjecture should not extend to the Netherlands or France, where cartography was less advanced than in the German-speaking lands or in Italy.

And route maps, in any case, were not necessary to the traveller. He found his way, as he had done for centuries, by asking. By 1517 the development of the 'new' Ptolemaic map and the Türst-like regional views had done more to foster the traveller's ability to generalize about his whereabouts and to describe the main features of the landscape through which he passed than to assist him in finding his way. For that an itinerary, a bare list of place-names, still sufficed. Two years before the Cardinal and his party passed from France back into Italy, Jacques Signot had published in Paris a traveller's handbook with a very promising title, *La totale et vraie description de tous les passaiges, lieux et destroicts par lesquelz on peut passer et entrer des Gaules es ytalies.* He described the goal graphically enough: 'The land of the country of Italy, according to the configuration in the maps of Ptolemy, seems to be placed in the shape and semblance of a man's boot, so that the Duchy of Milan is situated in the middle of the thigh, the city of Rome at the knee, Apulia in the heel and Reggio at the tip of the foot.'[3] But the ten routes there that he offered were simply strings of place-names.

It was entirely typical that a map-less Machiavelli, passing through Geneva on a diplomatic mission to Maximilian I in 1507 should have found out how far away Constance was by asking

---

[1] E. Imhof, *Die ältesten Schweizerkarten* (Zürich, 1939).

[2] Bagrow, op. cit., 145.

[3] Sig. Bir–v. The Cardinal's route, Nice–Savona–Genoa, was Signot's ninth alternative.

an Italian merchant.[1] Trade had created communities on a scale sufficient for Fernand Braudel to dub 'a second Italy' the German towns of Augsburg, Ulm, Ravensburg and Nuremberg. There were Italian merchants centred on Innsbruck. Elsewhere they were to be found (to mention only places visited by the Cardinal) at Trent, Geneva, Antwerp, Paris, Lyons and Avignon. The thread of a common language was, however, but a series of useful fragments. In the gaps, and where there were insufficient men of education to respond to Latin (though in theory every European parish contained an information centre in the person of the priest), the traveller could find himself at a loss. Travelling on the same mission as Machiavelli, but independently, Francesco Vettori described how 'it was with great difficulty that we got to Partenkirchen. As we had sent our Germans in advance to engage lodgings, we became lost because none of us could ask the way and we had forgotten the name of the town we were bound for. We came to a bridge which is on the road to Munich. And at last I remembered the name which I pronounced as well as I could and engaged a guide to take us to Partenkirchen.'[2] At Ueberlingen he had at least been able to communicate with the parish priest who had 'a feeble grasp of Latin'.[3] And it was at least in part because of the feeble Latinity of the theoretically educated classes of Renaissance Europe that rich travellers took interpreters with them to aid the harbingers and mediate at princely tables. The 'herald who knows seventeen languages' who was lent to Rozmital by Duke Philip the Good of Burgundy in 1465 was doubtless of thoroughly exceptional competence,[4] but though the Cardinal's party could have found their way without the interpreter they took with them, the richness of de Beatis's narrative must owe much to him, the Cardinal's Spanish being of limited use[5] and there being no indication that he was master of the age's second *lingua franca*, French.

The interpreter must also have been present during the party's bouts of sightseeing. That this proclivity was already well developed is clear. De Beatis's remark about the second visit to Malines echoes that of Piero Casola on his return visit to Verona: 'we went

[1] *Legazioni e commissarie*, ed. S. Bertelli (3 vols., Milan, 1964) ii, 1064.
[2] Op. cit. in bibl., 211.   [3] Op. cit., 105.
[4] Op. cit. in bibl., 39.   [5] See below, p. 89.

about the city to see the things we had not yet seen, until supper-time'.[1] His impulse to climb bell towers as a prelude to visiting the sights had been anticipated by Isabella d'Este's account of her visit to Venice in 1502: 'directly after lunch we went to S. Marco, hoping to find very few people at that hour, but we were mistaken, as there were a good many, and then, so as not to leave anything undone and to see this marvellous city well, we climbed the Campanile of S. Marco, where we greatly enjoyed the beautiful view and examined the noble buildings on all sides'.[2] When they could, travellers enlisted resident compatriots as local guides (and one can imagine the sighs of the busy merchants of Venice's Fondaco dei Tedeschi as yet another eager German pilgrim arrived in Venice with time to spare before his galley sailed for the Holy Land);[3] in addition, there was the patter of the custodians of individual buildings to absorb.

For by now curiosity was widely accepted as one among, if not the chief of the reasons, why a man might travel. Some moral disapprobation could still attach to travel undertaken purely for motives of pleasure, as in the story by Thomas More that begins: 'Now was there a young gentleman which had married a merchant's wife. And having a little wanton money which him thought burned out the bottom of his purse, in the first years of his wedding he took his wife with him and went over the sea, for none other errand but to see Flanders and France, and ride out one summer in those countries.'[4] But the old outcry against the 'curious' pilgrim[5] had dwindled into a thin pipe of complaint (only Erasmus re-scored it for a full orchestra of denunciation in de Beatis's generation), and though Humanism had brought again to light Plato's proscription of unnecessary travel in the *Republic* and the *Laws* together with Plutarch's description of Lycurgus's ban on it, these were messages from the past his generation was not attuned to receive. Among pilgrims to Jerusalem, Casola in 1494 essayed a long description of Venice 'solely to amuse myself during the time I had to spend in such a great port',[6] and in 1515

[1] Op. cit. in bibl., 343.

[2] Julia Cartwright, *Isabella d'Este* (2 vols, London, 1903) i, 220.

[3] See von Harff, op. cit. in bibl., 50–1.

[4] Quo. P. S. Allen, *The age of Erasmus* (Oxford, 1914) 229.

[5] Christian K. Zacher, *Curiosity and pilgrimage. The literature of discovery in fourteenth-century England* (Baltimore, 1976) passim.

[6] Op. cit., 125.

Peter Falk of Freiburg was industrious in bringing his guide-book to the Holy Places up to date.[1] Non-pilgrims were by now content simply to recommend their narratives as interesting, useful, and possibly character-forming. Three may be quoted as suggesting the background against which de Beatis's Postscript may be read.

Setting down in *c.* 1451 his somewhat jejune reminiscences, the much travelled Gilles le Bouvier explained that 'since a number of men of various nations and countries take pleasure and delight, as I have done in time past, in seeing the world and the different things that are in it, and also because several want to know without travelling and yet others intend to go and see for themselves, I have begun this little book (according to the little understanding I possess), so that those who see it might know the truth about the manner, the form and the character of the things that exist in all Christian Kingdoms and in the other kingdoms I have visited: their breadth, the mountains there, the rivers that traverse them, the nature of each country and its inhabitants, and other unfamiliar things which will hereafter be disclosed'.[2]

Writing a description of a journey from Trent, followed by a period of residence in England, the Italian Andreas Franciscius claimed in 1497 to the friend to whom he sent it that 'the result of seeing such a variety of things and disparity of customs is that even men of low intelligence soon become quick-witted and clever. In fact there can be scarcely anyone who, by picking out the best and worst of all he sees, will not quickly form sensible habits of life and improved virtues. And so...I have decided to compile a little book containing descriptions of every town or fort[ified place] that I visited, together with the ways of life and government characteristic of them.... I want you to read it over and over again; for, if you have not had the opportunity to see for yourself and study all that this report describes, you may get the same pleasure from reading it as if you had been on the spot with us.' And he concludes by saying, very much as de Beatis does, that 'I have avoided the use of any art in the writing, or beauty of style. I merely jotted down daily, while on my journey, a few remarks, as I did not want you to miss anything'.[3]

Vettori, summing up his months in Switzerland and Germany in 1507, was mainly concerned with the conditions that could

[1] Allen, op. cit., 230.   [2] Op. cit. in bibl., 29.
[3] Tr. in C. H. Williams, *English historical documents, 1485–1558* (London, 1967) 187.

make travel thoroughly enjoyable. 'Among the honest pleasures that men can experience, the pleasure of travelling is in my opinion the greatest. He who has not come into contact with many men and seen many places cannot be perfectly wise. However, to profit from journeys several factors must combine: a good and robust constitution, wealth, and companions of a cheerful and relaxed character. If one of these is missing, travel is no longer a pleasure, but a delusion and a weariness... And, in addition, a man must be without business concerns, be free, be able to stay in a place for a fortnight at a time, to travel by land or water and not to be at the mercy of any delays.'[1]

Like the great majority of travel narratives, none of these three was published, being compiled only for the benefit of the authors' friends. But at least it can be said that when de Beatis set off there was a recognizably modern philosophy of travel in the air.

This did not mean, of course, that more than a very small proportion of those who travelled set down any account of their experiences. Most men did travel on 'business affairs', too fast or too uncomfortably for them to wish to add writing to their burdens. The anonymous Milanese[2] author whose manuscript is discussed below was unusual among merchants in showing almost as wide an interest in the scenes through which he passed as did de Beatis. Vettori was rare among diplomats, whose dispatches and reports seldom refer to the process of getting from one place to another, let alone to any pleasure that might be involved. Far more typical was another traveller in 1507, Ulrich Bertsch, who went to Geneva and Bologna on ecclesiastical business for the Cathedral Chapter of Strasbourg at a rate of between 35 and 65 kilometres a day, stopping only for rest, during storms or when troop movements in northern Italy made the roads perilous.[3] From him and other such men we receive little more than jottings about distances covered and the expenses incurred, stage by stage. Yet others joined the great majority of the silent because the act of travelling held no appeal for them, prompted them to nothing save the wish that it were done with. Erasmus, who could have given us an unparalleled record of people and places, self-consciously

---

[1] Op. cit., 203–4. And see the explanation offered by the scholarly cleric Diego López de Stunica, op. cit. in bibl., Dedication.

[2] See below, pp. 53–5, and bibl.

[3] Francis Rapp, 'Ce qu'il en coûtait d'argent et de démarches pour obtenir de Rome la confirmation d'une élection épiscopale', *Revue d'Alsace* (1962) 106–15.

rejected the call of curiosity. Crossing the Alps to Italy in 1506, 'in order to beguile the tediousness of the ride...I got this poem ['De fuga vitae humanae'] done, noting it down from time to time upon the saddle, in order not to lose any part of it, as new ideas are apt to drive out the old. When we came to the inn, I wrote out from my notes what had thus taken birth.'[1] Again, he told More that he had drafted the *Praise of Folly* 'on my journey back from Italy into England, in order not to waste all the time that must needs be spent on horseback in dull and unlettered gossiping'.[2] And when in 1518 he followed de Beatis's route from Strasbourg up the Rhine to Cologne and on to Louvain, the account he gave comprised little more than a series of moans about bad food, dishonest blacksmiths and innkeepers, wretched roads, jolting carriages, hovering (if unseen) brigands: in sum 'incredible and almost unendurable discomfort'.[3] Apart from the elements of hypochondria and of resentment that a man of his intellectual calibre should be forced out of his study and on to the road in search of a living, Erasmus's attitude is instructive. He was willing to select incidents from his travels to make a moral point or even, as in the colloquy on inns, to entertain, but he apparently did not believe that the record of a journey, however discursive, was a respectable literary *genre*. It is, indeed, probable that this view was widely shared, and accounts for the fact that apparently few travellers sought to print their narratives.

Reputability continued to inhere in publishing the record of a pilgrimage to the Holy Land; the voyages of discovery were already beginning to preoccupy the press;[4] but travels in Europe, which did not take their authors in the footsteps of Christ or reveal peoples who lived without the benefit of His teaching, were, perhaps, in addition to the modesty of their chroniclers, not yet considered by printers to be of sufficient interest to a public reared on the headier itineraries of a knight errant among the paynim or Sir John Mandeville among the anthropophagi. Indeed, taking this attitude into account and allowing for the sheer literary energy required to sustain descriptions of places and buildings as de Beatis

[1] F. M. Nicholls, *The Epistles of Erasmus* (3 vols, London, 1901–17) i, 416–17.
[2] J. Huizinga, *Erasmus of Rotterdam* (London, 1952) 209.
[3] Ib., 223–8.
[4] The *Columbus letter* appeared in 1493; Peter Martyr's *Decades* from 1504. The first, very short, accounts of Portuguese voyages, began in 1505. None of these was relevant, in form or scope, to the development of the European travel journal.

does (Dürer thought it enough to refer to the printed description of Charles V's coronation which he witnessed at Aix-la-Chapelle in 1520),[1] and how many a diarist gave up with a 'my pen is not equal to describing it', not only is his achievement impressive, but so is his determination to essay it. Both can only be appreciated by reviewing the various traditions which, blending together, enabled a traveller not only to notice what he saw and to wish to record it, but to find the appropriate words.

3. The sources of the Renaissance travel journal

While not suggesting that by the early sixteenth century anything like a standard form of travel journal had been (or ever would be) established, it was then that a number of features tended to be more habitually present than had been the case hitherto. They include: dated entries, the giving of place-names where the mid-day meal was taken as well as where the night was spent; a note of the distance travelled each day; descriptions of important isolated buildings and of the countryside, accounts of the walls, streets, squares, houses, monuments and inhabitants of towns; extended essays on the most notable human and physical features of whole regions; pen portraits of notable persons encountered en route. All are present in de Beatis's journal. All represent what a traveller's friends at home might have wished to hear about. Indeed, in some measure and with no system, several were present in the most widely circulated accounts of medieval travels outside Europe, those in particular of Marco Polo. Yet neither these marvellous exotica nor the curiosity of stay-at-homes appear to have influenced the way in which journeys within Europe were recorded. And such records, rarely printed or widely distributed in manuscript, grew to maturity by drawing far less on one another than on a number of independent genres.

The basic traditions which helped to shape the developed travel journal were quite unliterary. One was the late medieval passion for compiling lists. It is the early fourteenth-century Giovanni Villani's almost remorseless listing of the republic's sources of income and expenditure down to 'pasta' for its symbolic lions[2] that makes his chronicle so valuable to the economic historian of Florence. In the following century another chronicler, Benedetto

---

[1] Op. cit. in bibl., 107.   [2] See below, p. 42.

Dei, abruptly introduces two lists of names, one headed 'these are the friends of Benedetto Dei', the other 'these are the proven enemies of Benedetto Dei'.[1] Brought up on lists, on statistics *avant la lettre*, travellers absorbed them or sought to create them. In Bruges, one of the chroniclers of Rozmital's journey, Schaseck, remarked that there were 525 bridges in Bruges, 'at least so it is reported', and his other chronicler, Tetzel, noted that 'it is said that there are 170,000 churches in France, and some 60,000 castles and towns with markets'.[2] In Venice, Casola wrote 'I wanted to count the wine shops of every kind, but the more I counted the more I became confused, for they are indeed innumerable', and, again, 'I fatigued myself very much by trying to find out if possible – and with the aid of people very familiar with Venice and the surrounding places – the number of all the ships, both large and small, to be found in Venice...I commenced the work; but, although the days were long, because it was the month of May, I found it was no task for me any more than for Saint Augustine – as they recount – to write about the Trinity, for the number is infinite.' This is the strain that leads de Beatis to estimate the number of castles and villages that can be seen along the Rhine and to count the number of steps in bell towers; it was one of the essential moulds that helped to give shape to a traveller's curiosity.

Another was the itinerary, the bare list of place-names and the distances between them that enabled a traveller to ask his way from one end of his route to another. The diffusion of itineraries can be judged from the late fifteenth-century compilation known as the Bruges *routier*, which contains 95 of them. To traveller and stay-at-home alike this form of list exerted a great fascination. Sanuto included a number in his *Diarii*, giving in 1513, for instance all the places where Andrea Gritti, Venice's senior military proveditor, stopped for lunch and dinner on his return from a period of captivity at Blois.[3] But before this, in 1483, Sanuto had shown how the armature of an itinerary could be filled out with miscellaneous information into something like a gazetteer. As a young man of 17 he had accompanied three patricians charged with investigating complaints and reporting on the condition of the Venetian terra ferma. His first draft[4] combined little more than

---

[1] I owe this reference to Dr Mark Phillips.
[2] Op. cit., 41 and 70. [3] Op. cit., xvi, cols. 457–60.
[4] 'Frammenti inediti dell'itinerario in terraferma di Marin Sanudo', ed. R. Fulin, *Archivio Veneto* (1881) 1–62.

names and distances and means of transport (horses or boats), the names of gates and of the Venetian officials they encountered, with an occasional classical citation, as when he quoted Pliny's *Natural History* on Lake Garda. In revising it, however, he added further clusters of information, producing a fairly full description of the city of Verona and a genial portrait of the countryside around it: 'very beautiful, made pleasing by gentle hills, pastures, places for fishing, hunting and bird-snaring, rich with grain and heavily cultivated; it yields excellent wine in abundance...large quantities of oil and apples of every variety'.[1]

Equally susceptible to expansion was a third non-literary activity, the keeping of household accounts.[2] Travel was expensive. Moving fast and with only one servant, Ulrich Bertsch's journey from Strasbourg to Bologna and back cost seventy florins at a time when a well-to-do prebendary of the cathedral had an income of 100 or less. Travellers were constantly changing from one currency to another and working out equivalences: Dürer, en route from Nuremberg to Antwerp, was successively handling pfennigs, florins, white-pfennigs, hellers and stivers. The cashing of bills of exchange could involve much haggling. In accounting for expenditure on the move, information was perforce included that verged upon the keeping of a richer form of journal. Though primarily a record of expenses, Dürer's diary reveals much more as he shopped for food and painting materials, expressed relief at getting toll-free through a customs point, noted gambling debts and bought presents and souvenirs. The point that what men buy illuminates what they do needs no labouring. Without the household accounts of Henry Earl of Derby's expedition to Prussia in 1390 we would have no hint of a revealing aspect of medieval *luxe*: the desire to make each stopping place a replica of the traveller's home by deploying the familiar tapestries, silver-ware, bed and escutcheon.[3] Our understanding of the lifestyle of an Imperial Commander-in-Chief during the Italian wars would be thin without the daily accounts of the Prince of Orange's expenditure on couriers, watch-repairs, surcoats, banners and liveries for his troop of light horse and pages, perfume for his

---

[1] *Itinerario...per la terraferma veneziana*, ed. Rawdon L. Brown (Padua, 1847) 96.

[2] For a contemporary example, see *Anton Tuchers Haushaltbuch (1507 bis 1517)*, ed. W. Loose (Stuttgart, 1877).

[3] Grace Stretton, 'Some aspects of medieval travel', *Transactions of the Royal Historical Society* (1924) 77–97.

handkerchiefs, debts incurred by wagers on cards, dice and tennis, and by tips to the instrumentalists and singers provided by his hosts at every place of note he passed through.[1] More to our purpose is to emphasize the stimulus of account-keeping to a narrative. To note mileages and stopping places, purchases and the cost of accommodation, and to seek statistical information under the stimulus of 'listomania': the bare ingredients of a journal are already there, awaiting a flavour imparted by another set of traditions or conventions, each separate from but contributory to the mature journal as represented by that kept by de Beatis.

Four of these share a common characteristic: the desire to commemorate.

By 1517 the practice of keeping records of prestigious events by heads of families both to celebrate important moments in their own lives and to inform and instruct succeeding generations had become commonplace. Among such moments journeys figured prominently: journeys to clinch an important business deal, to select a suitable wife for an heir, to carry out a diplomatic errand or, through pilgrimage, an act of devotion. Regardless of their purpose, long journeys were important because of their costliness, so the days spent on them were granted a special emphasis.[2] In this sort of family memoir (ricordanze) Italy was particularly rich.

A second convention was the logging by comptroller-chroniclers of the progresses undertaken by monarchs to show themselves to their subjects. Beginning as a bare record kept to justify the expenditure of the court as it moved about offering and receiving hospitality, this too was a formula susceptible to accretion, a process most readily demonstrable from the progresses, or voyages of the rulers of Burgundy and the Netherlands.

The account of the Duke of Burgundy's voyage of 1464–5 gives little more than dates, names, expenditure and the names of those entertained by the Duke.[3] That of Maximilian of Austria's voyage from Wiener-Neustadt to Bruges in 1477 cites the gifts made to him, usually oxen and wine, by the townspeople en route, and the jousts and banquets he offered in return, but there are also a few brief descriptions of places. Thus 'Louvain is one of the chief

[1] A. D. Pierrugues, Giornali del Principe d'Orange nelle guerre d'Italia dal 1526 al 1530 (Florence, 1897).

[2] For a good example, see Das Reisebuch des Familie Rieter, ed. R. Röhricht and H. Meisner (Tübingen, 1864).

[3] See the extracts given in the introduction to Antoine de Lalaing, op. cit. in bibl.

cities of Brabant. It has a university of about 3,000 students'. Or Ghent 'is a large city, a good half mile greater in extent than Venice'.[1]

Richer again is the account given by the comptroller Jean de Vandenesse of Charles V's *voyage* to take up his Spanish inheritance in 1517. Though his chief responsibility was to check expenditure on the household and stable, to organize the linen and utensils carried with the court and to make sure that courtiers did not surreptitiously load their own belongings on to the monarch's sumpter mules, Vandenesse gave so full a picture of entries, festivities, meetings and discussions as to amount to a vivid social diary of Charles's peripatetic public life. There was still very little about the places he visited. But progresses were not sight-seeing tours. The time was devoured by formalities: church services, receptions, audiences. The prince was the sight and the comptroller's job was to enable him to be seen. All the same, Vandenesse was working up the records kept as part of his job into something which, however fraily, had a literary purpose. Dedicating his account of this and later journeys of Charles to Cardinal Grandville he said that his purpose was to produce agreeable souvenirs for the lords who had been in Charles's entourage. And at least 14 manuscripts of his work have been traced.[2] The real extension of the household record into something near to a travel journal, however, was made by another court official who accompanied Charles on the same *voyage* of 1517, Laurent Vital, his *aide de chambre*. He, too, wrote up his account from notes of what Charles was doing and whom he was seeing from day to day (including his meeting with the Cardinal of Aragon at Middelburg), but he also includes observations of his own on the places he visited and regional descriptions which embrace some of the topics dealt with by de Beatis: agricultural products, the *mores* of the inhabitants, including their dress and physical appearance.[3]

Though the works of Vandenesse and Vital have the special interest of being exactly contemporary with de Beatis's journey, the way in which the *voyage*-narrative could verge into the travel journal is shown most clearly by an earlier account, that of Duke Philippe le Beau's journey to Spain in 1501 written by his

---

[1] H. van der Linden, ed., *Itinéraires de Marie de Bourgogne et de Maximilian d'Autriche (1477–1482)* (Brussels, 1934) 121–4.
[2] Op. cit. in bibl., 53–4.   [3] Op. cit. in bibl.

chamberlain Antoine de Lalaing. On the outward trip Lalaing sticks to the details of his master's ceremonial life. Thus nothing is said of Paris but the services Philippe attended and his meetings with representatives of the city, the parliament and the university. On the way back, however, Lalaing broke off with a few companions to visit Marseilles, where two members of his family were buried. Free at last from duties with the ducal household he describes, very much as de Beatis was to do, the harbour and the great churches of Saint-Lazare and Saint-Victor. Then, moved doubtless by piety in this region of the Magdalen but also, one suspects, by a certain holiday feeling, he visits La Baume and St Maximin, and having acquired the habit of a daily stint of words, describes the chapels and relics fully and firmly. And thereafter, even after re-joining the Duke and his train and taking up again his record of their ceremonial progress, he henceforward includes descriptions of the towns they passed through. 'Cologne', he begins, in a style he has now mastered, 'is an archiepiscopal and metropolitan city in Germany, rich, powerful, heavily populated, rich in commerce, well paved, well guarded with thick walls and strong and thick fortified towers; it has very fine, well-built and sumptuously decorated houses, is as large as Bruges, or larger, and is situated on the great river Rhine in good, fertile and level country.' And he proceeds to describe the churches, not omitting to note that Albert the Great was buried in that of the Jacobins: 'he was formerly bishop of Ratisbon not, as some say of Cologne; he left his bishopric to go to study, out of his love for theology, at Paris and then at Cologne, where he died in the monastery belonging to his order, and where you can see him whole, through a grille, clad in his chasuble'.[1]

While the *ricordanze* commemorated significant events in the author's life, the *voyage* convention (best represented in Italy by the diaries of papal masters of ceremony like Johan Burchard and Paris de Grassis) commemorated the public life of others. In this it was allied to a third commemorative *genre*, the biographical eulogy.

Lalaing explained at the beginning of his manuscript that his aim was to perpetuate the memory of his natural lord. Great men relied on others to commemorate their journeys along with their

---

[1] Op. cit. in bibl., 131–3, 272–4, 334–5. Cf. below, 77.

other outstanding actions. No person of substance described his own travels – except in the special case of Pius II[1] – any more than he set down an account of his own heroism in battle. Thus we know about Baron Rozmital's impressive wanderings from the accounts of two subordinate members of his train, his squire Scheseck and Gabriel Tetzel, whom he recruited in passing through Nuremberg probably with this function in mind. The account of Graf Gaudenz von Kirchberg's pilgrimage to Jerusalem in 1470[2] was written by his attendant Friedrich Steigerwalder, as was Philippe De Voisins, Seigneur de Montaut's[3] of 1490 by his squire and Sir Richard Guylforde's of 1506 by his chaplain.[4] Two years before de Beatis set off with his Cardinal, Riccardus Bartholinus published an account of a journey undertaken by his master the Cardinal of Gurk (Mathius Lang) from Salzburg to Vienna to discuss a crusade against the Turk with Maximilian I.[5]

All these three conventions are chiefly concerned with commemorating the traveller. A fourth was devoted to commemorating not persons but places: the civic eulogy. This was particularly true in Italy and Germany, where in so many cases the city represented, visually and emotionally, the region it dominated. Patriotism as well as mere civic pride expressed itself naturally through elaborate urban word portraits. With the ancient Roman surveys and the example of the medieval *Mirabilia* to build on, by 1288 Bonvesin della Riva was able to produce in his *De Magnalibus urbis Mediolani*, a description of his native city of Milan that became in its turn a model for others. Formidably statistical, from the consumption of foodstuffs imported from a fertile hinterland to the number of bells in the city's *campanili*, what chiefly contributed to the work's influence was its systematic plan, for Bonvesin divided his material into eight sections: *ratione sytus, habitationis, habitantium, fertilitatis et omnium bonorum* (spiritual as well as material) *affluentie, fortitudinis, fidelitatis, libertatis* and *dignitatis*.[6] The masterpiece of the *genre*, however, was Leonardo

---

[1] See below, p. 46, n. 1.   [2] Ed. R. Röhricht (Innsbruck, 1905).
[3] Ed. Ph. Tamizey de Larroque (Paris, 1883).
[4] Ed. Sir H. Ellis (Camden Society, 1851).
[5] *Odeporicon idest Itinerarium...D. Mathei Sancti Angeli Cardinalis Gurcensis...* (Vienna, 1515). Mainly concerned with the Cardinals's movements and meetings and speeches, this clumsy work has only two descriptions of any detail: the cathedral at Ratisbon and the Castle at Salzburg.
[6] J. K. Hyde, 'Medieval descriptions of cities', *Bulletin of the John Rylands Library* (1966) esp. 327–9.

Bruni's *Laudatio Florentinae Urbis* of 1403–4,[1] so perfect a blend of historical and patriotic feeling with an almost scientific approach to topographical description as to daunt rivalry. All the same, it is not uninteresting to note that the civic eulogy became a form used not only by proud citizens but by visitors to flatter their hosts. Thus in 1489 the Florentine Franciscan Bernardino Barduzzi, by way of thanking those who had invited him to preach in Verona, published there a short but glowing tribute to the city's wealth, beauty and classical associations.[2] The Bruni of Germany was Conrad Celtis, whose detailed Latin description of Nuremberg, its buildings, inhabitants, occupations, government and countryside, was published in 1494 and reprinted in 1502 and 1518.[3]

Cities, with their safety and comfort and reassuring bustle, the brimming markets that followed scarce provender along the road, their places of worship and residences of wealthy or politically important men, were of such compulsive interest that the civic eulogy was not needed as the sole inspiration of that staple of the travel journal, the description of a town. To some extent townsmen themselves offered a matrix for the organization of their visitors' impressions. The admission charged for ascending belltowers – Dürer paid a stiver at Antwerp – suggests that these were exploited as popular vantage points from which to begin a tour. There were cliché phrases and hints to pick up and use. Tetzel's 'Avignon has three remarkable things, a fine bridge, a fine circuit of walls, and a fine palace' sounds like such a remark. Pius II noted that 'the admirers of Florence... mention the bridges... and the shops of all sorts and the great estates and splendid villas near the city... and finally the quick wits of the citizens'. The references to towns in chronicles, or simply the habit of bringing back verbal accounts to please stay-at-homes, account for such workmanlike accounts as this description of Novgorod in 1413 by the terse soldier-diplomat Ghillebert de Lannoy: 'The city of Novgorod is a wonderfully large city, situated in a fair plain, surrounded by great forests and lying in low ground where there are lakes and marshes. A very large river, called Wolosco [Wolchow] runs through the middle of it. But the city is enclosed by wretched walls made of

---

[1] Printed in Hans Baron, *From Petrarch to Leonardo Bruni*... (Chicago, 1968) 232 seq.

[2] *Epistola reverendissimi magistri Bernardini florentini*..., reprinted (Verona, 1976) with an English translation.

[3] A. Werminghoff, ed., *Conrad Celtis und sein Buch über Nürnberg* (Freiburg-im-Breisgau, 1921).

turves and earth, though the towers are of stone. And it is a free city with a self-governing commune. They have a bishop who is like a ruler for them . . . And within the city there are 350 churches. And they have a castle beside the river where the chief church of St Sophia is situated, and their bishop lives there.'[1]

All the same the eulogy, the specialized description of a town, did by its example encourage range, methodical organization and an attempt at vividness, and acted as a stimulus to description at length. A literary impulse beyond mere record lies behind this description of Basel in 1434 from the *Commentaries* of Pius II, then Cardinal Aeneas Silvius Piccolomini: 'The roofs of the churches are made of many-coloured glazed tiles, and when the sun strikes these they sparkle brilliantly. Since a good many private dwellings are also tiled, a beautiful spectacle rewards one who views the city from a nearby eminence. These roofs are very steep because the great weight of the winter snow would cave them in if they were not. The roof tops are inhabited by storks who build their nests there. People do not molest them because they have a superstition that if the birds are deprived of their young they will set fire to the houses.

'The interiors of the homes are exceedingly well appointed, much like Florentine apartments. They quite gleam with cleanliness. Each house has its garden, also a well and a courtyard. Each has a chamber which may be heated, and in this one room they are accustomed to eat, live, and often sleep. The windows in these rooms are of glass and the walls and floors of pine. Caged birds add their trills to the general merriment. Walls are papered, and carpets cushion the floors.'[2]

There is nothing inconsequential about the way in which Casola's lengthy description of Venice in 1494 is planned: first the main distinguishing characteristic of the city, its means of transport, boats and canals, then, in order, an estimate of its size; descriptions of the ducal and then of other palaces; squares; commerce and warehouses; shops and markets; churches and monasteries; the arsenal; the character of the patricians; the status and dress of women.[3] There is no reason to believe that this, or other town

---

[1] *Œuvres* . . ., ed. C. Potvin (Louvain, 1878), 32–3.
[2] Quo. Gerald Strauss, *Sixteenth-century Germany: its topography and topographers* (University of Wisconsin Press, 1959) 15.
[3] Op. cit., 124–54.

descriptions of the late fifteenth and early sixteenth century (including de Beatis's) were affected by the increasing number of woodcuts that represented, or purported to represent, individual towns.[1] The ordering of such accounts was determined not by what had been seen but by what had been read.

Turning to another staple of the mature travel journal, the summary description of a whole geo-political region, its appearance and products, its inhabitants and their characteristics, we turn to another genre of writing which, if travelling was necessary to produce it, lay well aside from the main stream of travel literature, though waiting to be used by it: topography or chorography.

Dependent on the re-awakened Humanist interest in such authors as Ptolemy, Strabo, Ausonius and Pausanius (and on the topographical flair of historians like Caesar and Tacitus) and therefore arising later than the civic eulogy, the fifteenth-century descriptive geographers were not untouched by the desire to commemorate the land of their birth. While not indifferent to its urban heart they were primarily concerned with the whole skeleton, the digital bays and estuaries, the backbone of mountains covered with forest or snow, the arteries and veins of rivers and streams. And while a Bonvesin or a Bruni was chiefly interested in merchant and magistrate and the headdresses of their women-folk, the topographer, convinced of the formative influence of climate and terrain, sought more generalized insights into human nature and included the populations of the countryside, peasants, shepherds and boatmen.

As practised in the mid-Quattrocento, notably by Flavio Biondo in his widely read *Italia Illustrata* of 1453 and Pius II (when he was still a cardinal) in his *Cosmographia*, topography was a subject of considerable miscelleneity, including the etymology of place names, history ancient and recent, folk-ways and odd customs as well as descriptions, often exact and first hand, of the features and products of the land. Thanks to Pius's inclusion of a long section on Germany (with the polemical aim of proving that rural prosperity and urban civilization had been fostered by Christian and not classical influence) the areas of Germany crossed by de Beatis, notably Bavaria and the Rhineland, had been

---

[1] As, for instance, those in Hartmann Schedel's *Liber chronicarum...* (1493 and subsequent editions), where Nuremberg, Strasbourg and Cologne, at least, are represented with considerable accuracy and detail.

described in the sort of detail that could readily stimulate a traveller's own powers of observation. Among the works influenced by Pius, for example, was the *Descriptio Sueviae* of Felix Fabri. In the course of following the Rhine from Lake Constance Fabri noted the defiles through which the growing river had to cram itself. 'You observe this especially at Schaffhausen where the Rhine falls in a headlong descent and with such force that no one can think of proceeding by boat. Below the town of Laufenburg a narrowing of the rocky bed compels the river to squeeze through with impatient rage so that you see no water at all, only white foam. In this region boats are emptied of passengers and cargo and are guided over the cataracts by means of ropes. A few skilled boatmen, however, manage to lead their craft down without the help of ropes. But the people thereabouts say that the church denies the Holy Eucharist to these pilots because they expose their lives to danger for the sake of money.'[1]

As with the civic eulogy, however, the topographical works (contact with which could be made not only directly but through their absorption into more accessible historical writings) should be seen as providing models for the organization of observations and a stimulus to their expression, rather than as second-hand substitutes for them. A French contemporary of Biondo and Pius, the unscholarly but much travelled herald Gille le Bouvier, could do much the same sort of thing on his own, and to emphasize this point, and to show how far a traveller of de Beatis's generation might be expected to include regional descriptions as a matter of course, it is worth quoting the account of Bavaria in Le Bouvier's *Le livre de la description du pays.*

'The country is good land, fertile with vines and grain and with farm animals large and small and excellent horses. The nobles are fine men, and blond, and they ride steadily and well and go lightly clad. The labourers and commonalty are rude and unwashed and are great eaters because their country is cold, especially in winter, and all those in cold countries are heavy eaters. The men are good crossbowmen both on horseback and on foot, shooting with bows of horn or sinew which are good, accurate and strong, for they never snap...Because of the cold of the winter in Germany they have stoves which keep them warm in their rooms and in winter the craftsmen pursue their trade there together with their wives

[1] Quo. Strauss, op. cit., 68–9.

and children and they seldom lack wood to heat them. And the nobles, soldiers and others who are at leisure similarly gather round them to gamble, sing, eat and drink and pass the time, for they have no fireplaces. The Germans are a cheerful race and flavour their food heavily with spices and saffron and often go to the baths. And they take great pleasure in singing and gambling.'[1]

Chronologically nearer de Beatis, the influence on this sort of hotch-potch of impressions of the more sophisticated humanist topography can be seen in the genially assured portrait of Friuli by the young aristocrat-soldier Luigi da Porto. Dispatched to this theatre of the war between Venice and Maximilian I in 1510, he arranges his material with nonchalant expertise. First he describes the province's frontier in terms of the Alps, rivers and the sea. Then follows a comparison of its capital, Udine, with Padua (better known to the relative he is writing to), a description of the hills, valleys, streams and scattered castles of the countryside, its dimensions, the character of its men and the dress (affected, he points out, by the proximity of Germany) of its women, its natural products, foodstuffs and animals.[2]

In what has gone before it has been assumed that the traveller, though his eyes are open for the same time each day at all periods, chiefly records what past convention and current fashion suggest is worth looking at with attention and expressing in words. The act of travelling could be spontaneous: we have only to read the early pages of Benvenuto Cellini's *Autobiography* to be convinced of this; but writing about travel never was. Any form of expression, whether committed to paper or paint, is historically conditioned. Writers on the literature of travel assume that a journal was a natural concomitant of a journey. But no form of writing was less natural. Why, tired from horseback, baffled by an unfamiliar tongue, nauseated by strange and often clumsily presented food, itching from the attentions of a new strain of bugs, should the traveller scratch not himself but paper under a trembling rushlight when all about him – from the stamping in the adjacent stables to the bare legs of the maids – were appeals not to the mind but to the senses?

This is why we have been looking at narrative and descriptive

---

[1] Op. cit. in bibl., 62–3.
[2] *Lettere storiche...*, ed. B. Bressan (Florence, 1857) 178–80. These were not published in his lifetime, and there is a possibility that he revised them before his death in 1529.

forms which, taken together, stimulated conscious observation and methodical record. And this study of supportive genres is all the more necessary in that the travel writer was very seldom moved by either the urge for self-expression, the communication of individual thought or feeling, or by the desire to give an original literary shape to his record. With very few exceptions, travel journals, though necessarily reflecting something of the personality and interests of their authors, were neither confessional nor experimental.

Among the exceptions are works in which the day by day record is supplanted by a more broadly selective desire to communicate an especially interesting period in the author's life in a relaxedly autobiographical vein. Such a work is the Spanish soldier Pedro Tafur's account of his travels in 1435–9.[1] Writing it considerably later, probably in the mid-1450s, Tafur names only the places that lingered most clearly in his memory and the topics – crafts and trades, the important people he met and the military actions he took part in – that interested him most. There are formal descriptions, but these may include some cherished personal memory as when, recalling how coins were tossed for some girls into the public baths at Basel, where both sexes bathed together, 'one can imagine what it was they held in the air when they put down their heads'. Or there is Johannes Butzbach's account of his reluctant travels in Germany and Bohemia between the ages of 10 and 16 as the servant first of a wandering schoolmaster and then, after fleeing from him, of a number of other unsatisfactory employers.[2] Written again somewhat later in life, this too contains formal descriptions of places and peoples, but in both the record of travel is subordinated to the depiction of self.

More strictly a variation on the journal form is the account of Vettori's journey of 1507 to which reference has already been made. Here an accurate descriptive itinerary is interspersed with invented anecdotes and Boccaccesque *novelle*; misadventures, chiefly sexual, which purport to have befallen his fellow guests with servants and innkeepers' wives. Some of these Vettori represents as having been recounted after dinner, others he claims to have witnessed. Thus he and a friend visit a darkened chapel

[1] See bibl.
[2] See bibl. and Malcolm Letts, 'Johannes Butzbach...', *English Historical Review* (1917) 22–33.

in a church at Ulm where the body of a woman lies in a bier. While the friend kneels to pray as an automatic act of piety, Vettori hears a light groan. A friar brings a candle. The woman proves to have merely been in a coma. The populace identifies the 'miracle' with the friend's prayer and pursue the new saint with such clamant devotion that he is forced to flee the city. Vettori was well aware that this mixture of fact and fiction was a novelty and, against a critic of the first instalment, defended the proposition that the author of a journal was as free to follow the prompting of his imagination as was a poet.[1] A comparable exploitation of the travel journal was the tedious record kept by the pedant Francesco Grassetto of the voyages he made on a Venetian galley, probably as ship's chaplain. Here almost every description of ports entered or cleared is prefaced by some high-falutin' description of the weather designed to display his knowledge of classical mythology. Leaving S. Vito (on the Apulian coast near Monopoli) for instance, 'Phoebus had already yielded place to the o'ershadowing night in which Proserpina drooped towards her Pluto, revealing her light to mortals, and the rounded stars gleamed in every quarter of the heavens.' In every storm he invokes either St Mark and St Nicholas, or Eolus and Neptune. And his flat and unevocative record of places visited is interspersed with poems of his own or long quotations (seldom apposite) from Dante, Petrarch or – and this is the main interest of the work – popular songs, some of them unrecorded elsewhere.[2]

More successful, and more interesting because it deals with some of the places visited by de Beatis, is the humanist Mario Equicola's account of a pilgrimage he made in 1517 with Isabella d'Este to Marseilles and the shrines associated with the cult of the Magdalen.[3] Here, though the mingling of historical and philosophical reflections with the itinerary is, in Julia Cartwright's words, 'more with the object of showing his learning than of recording facts of interest',[4] is the germ of the reflective and self-revelatory travel record first established as a genre in its own right by the *Itineraria* (1532–3) of the poet Johannes Secundus of Malines.[5]

[1] Op. cit., 124–5, 84–6. The stories and anecdotes were published separately as *Novelle di Francesco Vettori* (Lucca, 1857).   [2] See bibl.

[3] Op. cit. in bibl. This very rare work is discussed in Domenico Santoro, *Il Viaggio d'Isabella Gonzaga in Provenza* (Naples, 1913).

[4] Op. cit., ii, 133.

[5] First published by Heinsius in 1618.

These exceptions have been cited to reinforce the dependence of the travel journal on the conventions we were discussing previously. Two more remain to be taken account of.

The first is the example set by diplomats; professional, if often reluctant travellers, and professional reporters of their actions and impressions. Here a clear distinction must be made between correspondence, the dispatches sent frequently, at times daily, while the ambassador was en route or *en poste*, and the final report he submitted, reports so much a Venetian speciality at this time that they are habitually called by their Venetian name *relazioni* or relations. Dispatches contained either nothing, or very little, about the process of travel or the experiences garnered on the way. The journal kept by the Florentine Francesco Guicciardini while en route to Spain in 1512, and which we shall look at when considering the nearest contemporary parallels to de Beatis's narrative, was quite exceptional.[1] The only travel news usually reported was the quality of the reception granted to ambassadors by cities or princes as they passed along, whether they were greeted by trumpeters, for instance, or whether the local lord had their rooms at the inn hung with his own tapestries; for these details enabled the government to assess the repute in which its representatives were held. And once *en poste* an ambassador's dispatches were almost entirely concerned with reporting on negotiations, meetings, political news, and with commenting on letters received.

Observations about the nature of the country visited were stored up for incorporation into the relation. The first Venetian *relazione* that has survived is that of 1492 by Zaccaria Contarini on France.[2] (It is possible that hitherto they had been delivered orally.) His relation contains two elements that were to become characteristic of these reports. One was a sceptical examination of the information handed out to him. He was, for instance, told that from 25,000 to 30,000 students attended the university of Paris.[3] But he pointed out that if you deducted children, friars, priests and all those others who enrolled themselves solely to gain privileges, you were left with only 5,000–6,000 genuine students.

---

[1] For another, much shorter example, we have to wait until 1524 when Sanuto copied out the itinerary kept by Carlo Contarini (? or his secretary) on a mission to the Archduke Ferdinand. Op. cit., xxxvi, cols. 573–81.

[2] E. Albèri, *Relazioni degli anbasciatori veneti al senato* (1839–63) ser. i, vol. iv, 1–26.

[3] Cf. below, p. 117.

In the second place, his pen-portraits of the young Charles VIII and his Queen began a notable series of such descriptions.

'His Majesty the King of France is twenty two years old, small and misshapen as to his body, ugly of face with bulging pale eyes that make his vision poor. His lips are also very large and he keeps them continually open, and he makes certain nervous movements of his hands which are very unpleasant to watch, and he speaks haltingly... The Queen is seventeen years old. She too is small and meagrely built. She is noticeably lame in one foot, though she wears shoes with platforms to conceal this. She is dark and has a very attractive face and for her age is very astute, so that she gets her way to everything she fancies either through laughter or tears. She is jealous and excessively attached to His Majesty the King, so much that since she has been his wife she has let few nights pass without sleeping with His Majesty, and has managed so well in this respect that she is eight months pregnant.' There is no doubt that this and later relations were illegally circulated in manuscript form, but before assuming their influence on de Beatis's pen-portraits of Charles V and Francis I and their womenfolk it is worth bearing in mind another source, admirably illustrated by the careful description of Lorenzo de' Medici's future wife Clarice Orsini which was sent to his father by his mother, who had inspected her in Rome.[1]

In 1506, reporting on his embassy to Burgundy[2], Vincenzo Querini defined the purpose of *relazioni*: 'Nothing... is of greater benefit to a well founded republic than a detailed understanding of the methods of government, the power and the attitude of all the great lords and princes of the world, and the nature of their lands and of the people who live in them.' Much of this detail was irrelevant to the travel diarist, being concerned with constitutions, court officials, armies, income, attitudes to Venice and other powers. But they may have helped the traveller to summarize information and impressions when embarking on a regional description. Here is Querini on the Burgundian Netherlands.

He names the provinces concerned, 'among all of which there are in sum 143 walled towns, including small ones which are really large castles, and three are so large that they lack nothing but a bishopric to be called cities. Among them the middle sized have

[1] Janet Ross, ed. and tr., *Lives of the early Medici*... (Boston, 1911) 108.
[2] Albèri, op. cit., ser. 1, vol. 1, 1–30.

3–5,000 hearths, the large from 6–25,000. Bruges has 25,000, Antwerp from 20–25,000 and is richer in merchandise than any other one can think of: Ghent has 20,000, Brussels 12,000, Boisleduc and Malines 8,000 and Louvain 10,000. Arras and Amsterdam in Holland have 6–7,000...And there are, in addition in these lands, 1,500 villages and hamlets. There is always enough grain, but not enough wine, as an insufficient number of vines grow there. In these lands three things are of the highest quality: very delicate and lovely cloths in Holland, very beautiful storiated tapestries in Brabant; and the third is music, which without any doubt can be called perfect.' Moreover, he goes on, there are products which may be called 'the four elements', namely, beer, salted butter, herrings and peat. 'The people of all these provinces are good natured, loyal to their lord, good Christians. They are not vainglorious either in conversation or dress. The men all devote themselves to trade, frequent taverns from time to time, and indeed take no pleasure in carnal satisfaction so much as in eating and drinking...The women wear a black cloak over the head in the style of those of our Franciscan tertiaries...[1] [after marriage] they live virtuously, both because they are carefully guarded and because the women of these provinces are frigid and disinclined to sexual indulgences far beyond those of any other country I have known.'

Again, however, the influence of the regional descriptions contained in *relazioni* must not be assumed. They follow in time those of the topographers. The need of governments for information about their own domains (illustrated by the party of inquisitors the young Sanuto accompanied) and of great landowners about their more scattered possessions, had created a habit and a technique of description, as had the strategic needs of governments: in 1432–3 Bertrandon de la Broquière travelled widely in the Middle East amassing information that would be useful for Duke Philip the Good's crusading plans,[2] and in the 1490s Conrad Türst explained his topographical work on Switzerland as being carried out because 'I have been asked to describe the regions of our Confederation and their environs so that you may realize how useful such a description is to all those princes who are about to

---

[1] Cf. below, p. 100.
[2] Margaret Aston, *The fifteenth century: the prospect of Europe* (London, 1968) 108.

take the field with their armies'.[1] Machiavelli's description of Germany contains a number of the points made by de Beatis: the way towns amassed stores of foodstuffs and the fuels and the raw materials for industry that made them self-sufficient in time of siege, the universal custom of shooting practice, but there is no suggestion that this, or his description of France and the French, were part of his diplomatic duties or influenced by any access he might have had to Venetian *relazioni*.

Irksome as such caution must be in the interest of emphasizing that the influence on such a journal as de Beatis's were multiple, vague, but cumulatively determinative, it must be repeated when dealing with the last: the influence of the literature of pilgrimage.

Before setting off for Jerusalem in 1483 Felix Fabri described how 'I read with care everything on this subject that came into my hands; moreover I collected all the stories of the pilgrimages of the crusaders, the tracts written by pilgrims, and descriptions of the Holy Land...and roved through pretty nearly all the Canonical and Catholic scriptures – I give you my word I worked harder in running round from book to book, in copying, correcting, collating what I had written, than I did in journeying from place to place'.[2] It is probable that the literature of travel to Jerusalem was more copious – certainly it was as far as printed works were concerned – than that of travel in Europe. What is not clear is how far it was read by travellers in Europe who had not themselves contemplated a pilgrimage to the Holy Land. Its relevance as a model was in any case lessened because most descriptions of pilgrimages only started, after the barest of European itineraries, with Venice and the preparations to be made there for the voyages. Casola was among few exceptions. Moreover, because once in Venice the pilgrim became part of a group, and then was in the hands of guides in Palestine as well as during the side-trips some hardier spirits made to Sinai and Cairo, the experience of successive parties had enough in common to justify a plagiarism[3] that does not characterize the more ad hoc

---

[1] Strauss, op. cit., 88.

[2] *Jerusalem journey*, tr. and ed. H. F. M. Prescott (London, 1954) 69–70.

[3] Thus William Way's *Itineraries* (1458 and 1462) were the basis of the anonymous *Information for pilgrims unto the Holy Land* (c. 1498) and the narrative of Sir Richard Guylforde's *Pilgrimage* (1506) liberally exploited Breydenbach's *Peregrinatio in terram sanctam* (1486). And Sir Richard Torkington (1517) in his turn exploits Guylforde, while

and independent journeys made in Europe. In any case, the richest pilgrimage journals, like those of Casola and Fabri, post-date narratives like those of Rozmital's scribes as well as the developed forms of the conventions that continued to feed the form and subject of the European travel journal. If influence there was, it is more likely to have been of the latter on the former than vice-versa.

Finally, in spite of the example of such superb letters as that of Pliny the Younger which describes his new villa and its environs, the correspondence of humanists contained little that might have been suggestive to the travel writer. Poggio Bracciolini's letters to his friends about the classical monuments he inspected in the 1420s are thin and unatmospheric. When the young Cardinal Francesco Gonzaga was following Pius II's peripatetic court in 1462, his tutor, Bartolomeo Marasca, wrote frequently to his mother in Mantua. His letters are typical in their concentration on personalities rather than places, news rather than views. Only one exceptional passage shows that he could describe nature as charmingly as could the Pope himself. Near Pienza the party rode through 'a wood of chestnut trees that goes on for more than six miles. The trees reach up as far as you can see and are as thick as three men could span. Underneath the grass is as trim as a mown meadow. There are many clear-running springs and there is always a light breeze moving through the wood so that you are not oppressed by the heat.' In all the letters written by the humanist (and dramatist) Cardinal Bernardo Dovizi da Bibbiena during his 1518–19 legateship in France there is only one expression of his reaction to a place: at the recently completed Château du Verger, near Angers, he remarked abruptly 'this is the finest thing I have seen, or think I ever will see'.[1]

It is not that men like these did not look about them and appreciate what they saw. Doubtless, when they returned home they spoke of what they had seen. But letters, especially at a time

---

the editor of Santo Brasca's *Viaggio in Terrasanta* (1480) has pointed out that 'it is very likely that Brasca had with him the *Itinerary* of Gabriel Capodilista [1458] which he certainly used when he wrote up his own narrative'. Ed. A. M. Momigliano Lepschy (Milan, 1966) 32.

[1] *The letters of the Younger Pliny*, tr. Betty Radice (London, 1963) 75–9; refs. in Roberto Weiss, *The Renaissance discovery of classical antiquity* (Oxford, 1969), 63; D. S. Chambers, 'The housing problems of Cardinal Francesco Gonzaga', *Journal of the Warburg and Courtauld Institutes* (1976) documents, p. 48; G. L. Moncallero, *Epistolario di Bernardo Dovizi da Bibbiena* (2 vols., Florence, 1955) ii, 118.

when they were frequently handed about, copied and (since the influential example of Petrarch) thought of as publishable, were a form of literary expression governed by conventions as to their content. And, save fitfully, those conventions had not yet expanded to include any but the most laconic references to the visual experience of travel.[1]

4. Influence and originality in the journal of de Beatis

De Beatis cites no models. His aim, he says in the Dedication, is to provide a 'true account of things, either seen by me or reported by persons of great authority and worthy of all trust and belief', and in the text, apologizing for spending so short a time in Cremona that he cannot provide an adequate description of it, he makes it clear that he wishes his account to be not merely a record of the Cardinal's movements and meetings but to be as informative as possible. He refers to his presentation manuscripts as transcriptions, and in spite of some evidence of later editing (as when he anticipates features of a place he has not yet reached) and two references to features he has to trust to memory to describe, it seems likely that they are largely derived from notes written on the spot, day by day. And his remark that he wrote one of the regional descriptions, that of France, 'weary as I am', suggests that these essays, too, were at least reasonably complete before his return.

It is unlikely, then, that he either prepared for this journey by a course of reading as Fabri did, or worked up his notes to any great extent before making his transcription in 1521. Prepared by the conventions we have outlined as to what he might expect to write about and how it should be set down, once en route we must imagine him supplementing his own experience by absorbing information from the Cardinal and the members of his entourage, from those they were entertained by and conversed with, from innkeepers and fellow guests, from the priests, monks and ushers who acted as guides to churches and palaces, from Italian merchants and exiles who could not only act as escorts but had matured their

---

[1] Thus even two of Petrarch's most remarkable letters do not appear to have been found suggestive, neither the quasi-allegorical 'Ascent of Mont Ventoux' (trans. in Cassirer, Ernst et al., eds., The Renaissance philosophy of man (Chicago, 1948, 36–48) nor the delightful description of the route and means of transport by which a friend might travel from Tivoli to stay with him at Vaucluse (Tatham, E.H.R., Francesco Petrarca...life and correspondence ii, 101–3) a reference I owe to Ms. Gray Standen.

own impressions of the populations among whom they had come to live. Some of the details or points of view he includes may have come from books but it is more likely that they reached him by word of mouth: when he does quote from a book (as at Mont-St-Michel) he says so. Apart from its fullness, its breadth of alert inquiry and the contact it gives with an engaging character, one of the chief attractions of the journal is the sense it gives of sharing the interests and opinions of others. Much of it has, for the historian of interests and attitudes, the strong appeal of unoriginality.

Like earlier travellers, de Beatis uses objects and places in his own country for purposes of comparison. Thus the St Christopher in Notre Dame in Paris is 'almost the size of Marforio', the antique statue in Rome; the old women of Flanders wear mantles pleated 'like the ones worn by our women in the region of Bari'; Antwerp is compared in size to Bologna, the canal leading from the Rhine into Strasbourg to the Venetian Grand Canal, the lions of Ghent to those of Florence; it is clear that at least he had not passed all his life in the backwoods of the Melfitana. And in spite of the heartfelt 'Italia Bella' with which he heads the concluding section of his journal, de Beatis is almost free from national prejudice. He does say of German green cheese that 'no Italian would eat it' and is moved by the theft of his travelling bag to exclaim against all lower class Frenchmen. He is perhaps patronizing when he writes of the Count of Nassau's garden that it is 'so well laid out that it could have been in Italy'. But he consistently compares religious life in the north to the disadvantage of his own country, and whether praising or blaming features of other peoples' characters is dispassionate and objective.

In this he resembles other temporary observers of foreign manners. It is usually the reluctant emigré who speaks with bitterness, such as Tommaso Vincidor whom de Beatis may have met when he was in Brussels helping to supervise the weaving of Raphael's tapestries: 'I have much to bear', wrote Vincidor, 'away among foreign barbarians.'[1] De Beatis's observations often draw on the brisk market in national and urban stereotypes that was, and had long been, available. Thus Ulrich von Hutten, in one of his *Letters of Obscure Men* (1515–17), can say – in a passage I much

---

[1] *Italian art, 1500–1600: sources and documents*, ed. R. Klein and H. Zerner (Englewood Cliffs, 1966) 49.

shorten: 'I send you more salutations than there are thieves in Poland, heretics in Bohemia, boors in Switzerland...pimps in Spain, topers in Saxony, harlots in Bamberg, children of Sodom at Florence, sailors in Zeeland, artisans in Nuremberg, herrings in Flanders.'[1] When de Beatis writes that in the Low Countries 'nearly all the women have bad teeth, caused by the butter and beer they consume', he is tapping a tradition expressed by Butzbach's remark that 'in Holland three or four women are accustomed occasionally to drain a whole keg of beer mixed with butter in a day or a half day'.[2] Before de Beatis noted the appetite for food and drink and the neatness of the houses of the Dutch, Erasmus had given wide circulation to these traits in his *Adages*.[3] That the Italians were sexually jealous and the English xenophobic were propositions endlessly propounded, yet the author of the anonymous 'relation' on England of *c.* 1498, while repeating this and other charges, could write with objective admiration of the goldsmiths' shops in the Strand, that 'if all the shops in Milan, Rome, Florence and Venice were put together I do not think there would be found so many of the magnificence that are to be seen in London'. De Beatis makes a similar remark of the goldsmiths of Paris. While there was plenty of latent, and formulated, prejudice abroad, de Beatis is a useful reminder of how little this affected contacts in time of peace.

That de Beatis should refer to the appearance of women as he moved from region to region is but natural; travel literature irresistibly reflected after-dinner conversation. Returning across Italy from his pilgrimage to Jerusalem in 1499 Arnold von Harff wrote 'it seems to my feeble understanding that I saw there the loveliest women in all my travels, and in Venice the richest, in Cologne the proudest and in Moabar the blackest'.[4] The formula echoes that applied to towns, 'Barcelona la ricca, Saragosa la harta, Valentia la Hermosa' – and so on[5] and is an aspect of the 'listomania' referred to above, but de Beatis is more considered, perhaps reflecting the opinion of dais rather than tavern. Though he was a cleric serving a cleric, there was nothing professionally

[1] H. Holborn, *On the eve of the Reformation: "Letters of Obscure Men"* (New York, 1964).
[2] Op. cit., 63.
[3] Ed. of 1508, in M. Mann Phillips, *The 'Adages' of Erasmus* (Cambridge, 1964) 211.
[4] Op. cit., 255.
[5] This example is from Andrea Navagero, *Il viaggio fatto* [in 1524–8] *in Spagna et in Francia...* (Venice, 1563) 5 v.

celibate about the functions at which they were entertained (or, as we know, about the Cardinal's personal life). Beatis also, on one occasion, at least, relied for information on the party's servants when he opined that German women 'are libidinous in spite of being temperamentally cold'. But as interesting as his appraisal of their beauty is the tolerant approval with which he notes the more active role in running inns, tending stalls and other aspects of economic life played by northern women – though he can almost be heard to gulp when recording that they were entrusted with the custodianship of altars.

As an ecclesiastic, with an eye sharpened for the niceties of clerical dress, de Beatis can be expected to take an interest in clothes. But the constant railing of preachers and moralists against indecent or vainglorious costume, the attempts of governments to enforce sumptuary laws, the importance of clothes in defining occupation, age and status, all ensured that travellers remarked on them. Like others he only comments on women's clothes (though men's fashions changed more frequently), and though he encountered nothing so intriguing as the headdresses in Esturias which Vital delicately likened to 'the things with which men make children', his descriptions are so neat and clear as to have something about them that would suggest the man-tailor, were there not similar descriptions with which they can be compared.[1]

In the company of an ecclesiastic we can, too, expect to hear much of churches and their relics and other matters of devotional as well as professional concern. Yet apart from comments on the conduct of religious communities, the way in which services and the attention paid to them differed from those of Italy, there is little to suggest de Beatis's status. He is careful to note the diocese in which towns and some of the larger villages or abbeys lay, but such was the power of church courts and the role in secular as well as ecclesiastical affairs of bishops that most travellers informed themselves on this point. Nor is the diet of churchgoing particularly heavy, let alone sanctimoniously undertaken. It behoved the Cardinal to visit churches and examine relics, but this was Luigi of Aragon who in Avignon was entertained with 'dancing until

[1] Cf. Celtis, op. cit., 157: 'Incessus autem et habitus matronalis et qui pudorem vultu gestuque insimulet, peplo parum in fronte rugato septuplo aut decuplato ob frigoris asperitatem capita involutae, plerumque etiam velo, quod insigne matronarum est, lato et sinuoso plicisque retorto et circa tempora bicorniculato, quod non omnibus gestare concessum est, si infamia aliqua notantur, velo illis interdicitur.'

midnight with unconstrained merrymaking and amusement', and de Beatis is on his guard against over-credulousness. The attention to relics is, then, neither more nor less than that paid by secular travellers. The emphasis first of the preaching orders and then of the secular clergy on urging congregations to imagine the circumstances of Christ's life as vividly as possible had affected the attitude to the lives of saints and martyrs: what could bring their lives and holy deaths more immediately to the imagination than bits of their bodies and clothing? There are times when de Beatis's wish to believe everything genuine is at odds with his common sense, but this was nothing new. San Bernardino himself had announced from the pulpit that 'all the buffalo cows of Lombardy would not have as much milk as is shown about the world' as the Virgin's. Tafur at Nuremberg was shown the lance that had pierced Christ's side, 'but I said that I had seen the real one in Constantinople, and I believe that if the great people had not been with me I should have been in peril from the German people for what I said'. Faced by a second body of St Matthew in Padua, von Harff shruggingly remarked, in the vein adopted at one point by de Beatis, 'the blunders of priests I leave to God to settle'. Credulity varied (and in front of pieces of the clothing of Charles I or Marie Antoinette still varies) between acceptance and disbelief according to education and experience. At one extreme was – as reported by de Beatis – Cardinal d'Este's setting a jeweller to test the genuineness of the Holy Grail in Genoa (paralleled at the same time by the Venetian government's testing a piece of the True Cross sent by the Sultan by heating it in a crucible),[1] at the other the naive wish to believe in the heroic physical stature of the Magdalen and of those other friends of Christ whose boat had been wafted by miraculous breezes from Palestine to the shores of Provence. Both strains are movingly present in this journal. Of particular interest is the careful description (with an accompanying drawing – see plate 2) he gives of the Holy Shroud, then at Chambéry. Here he felt no doubt: 'it can be said to be the most venerable and wonderful relic in Christendom'.

The book is a useful reminder, too, that even for educated Italians – and de Beatis owed his place on the expedition to his competence as a Latinist – erudition and antiquarian fervour were not the norm. Libraries were examined, at least as one of the sights

[1] Sanuto, *Diarii*, xlix, col. 73.

45

in princely houses, but only a glancing notice was paid to the existence of universities. A patron of classical scholars the Cardinal may have been, but there was no attempt to include classical monuments – like the famous amphitheatre at Arles – in his itinerary, and those that were encountered were described with no special enthusiasm.

The only hint that such a thing as Humanism existed (let alone would find its name attached to the period as a whole) is the preference expressed for the ancient as against the new. When appraising in general terms, de Beatis can appreciate work in progress, especially on churches, and can praise buildings of comparatively recent date, like the Certosa of Pavia, 'the finest, loveliest and most resplendent church we have seen anywhere in our journey'. But writing at a time when Renaissance Italian influence was beginning to affect the styles of the north (as in the tomb for Maximilian he saw in the making outside Innsbruck) de Beatis can say of a monument in the Augustinian priory in Pavia that 'no modern master can achieve such an effect' and of the coffer at Aix-la-Chapelle containing the body of Charlemagne, it 'is carved with figures and horses in perfect relief: you can judge from this that it is antique'.

Like the great majority of his contemporaries, de Beatis when judging works of art was working with few and clumsy linguistic tools; the terminology of appraisal had not yet worked its way from such sources as Alberti's treatises on painting, sculpture and architecture into everyday speech; hence the unremitting use by every traveller of 'bello', 'bellissimo' or its foreign equivalents. What had come through from Humanist studies was the simplest of classical aesthetic opinions: that good art should be lifelike. This was the criterion wielded in the mid-*Quattrocento* by Pius II when describing the sculptures on the façade of the cathedral at Orvieto; 'the faces stand out from the white marble as if alive, and the bodies of men and beasts are so well rendered that art seems to have equalled nature. Only speech is lacking to make them live.'[1]

The same approach underlies de Beatis's well-known description of the Van Eyck altarpiece at Ghent and leads to his judgement that 'one has no hesitation in saying that this is the finest painting in Christendom'.[2] But in 1495 Hieronymus Münzer had written

[1] *Memoirs of a Renaissance pope. The Commentaries of Pius II.* Tr. F. A. Gragg (New York, 1959) 163. [2] Below, p. 96.

an account of it which by using the 'lifelike' criterion was as long and enthusiastic as de Beatis's: 'Et omnia illa sunt ex mirabili et tam artificioso ingenio depicta, ut nedum picturam, sed artem pingendi totam ibi videres. Videntur quasi omnes ymagines vive...O quam mirande sunt effigies Ade et Eve! Videntur omnia esse viva.'[1] It was the Cardinal who expressed admiration for the tapestries being made from Raphael's idealizing cartoons; de Beatis, faced by another example of High Renaissance art, Leonardo's Last Supper, sought to bring it within a naturalistic formula: 'the figures in the painting are portraits, from life and life-size, of various court personalities and Milanese citizens of the time.' It is not a hint art historians have felt inclined to pursue.

Had Dürer's watercolours illustrating some of the natural features he saw on his journey to the Netherlands not survived, it would have been impossible to guess from his thoroughly burgher-like diary that he had the remotest feeling for landscape. Though not alone in his wish to record the countryside for its own sake – the beginnings of the pure landscape are to be seen among contemporaries like Leonardo and the Germans Huber and Altdorfer – Dürer surpassed in paint the ability of nearly all contemporary authors to transcribe their observation of nature without recourse to cliché or to filtering their response through ready-made phrases from the pastoral poets of antiquity. Among prose writers, Pius II in his *Commentaries* supremely expresses an exuberant sense of pleasure and well-being when passing through the country, but though his descriptions of nature can be full and accurate they, too, repeat conceits like 'never-failing streams'. And even he finds it easiest to respond to nature when tamed by man. Entirely typical of his (and de Beatis's) day is the passage in another work in which he explains how even the landscape of Germany has improved since Roman days. 'As for the beauty of the landscape, who does not know that this is now much greater than formerly? Everywhere there are cultivated fields, fallow-lands, vineyards, gardens, flower beds, orchards, farms and villas filled with every pleasurable thing, charming villages, castles on the summits of mountains, most splendid cities...'[2]

This urban viewpoint, which screens out the dangerous, unproductive or unoccupied elements in a landscape, is very much de

---

[1] Op. cit. (ed. Goldschmidt) in bibl., 347–8.
[2] *La Germania*, tr. G. Paparelli (Florence, 1949) 39.

Beatis's. For him and his contemporaries, mountains and forests, heaths and marshes and sea-shores are features occasionally to mention, never to express pleasure in. But de Beatis, though somewhat leadenly conscientious about enabling the reader to imagine the lie of the land he rides through ('all those towns and places, in whatsoever kingdom or province, which I do not describe as being in the mountains should be assumed to be in level country'), does draw attention more frequently than most to prospects he considers pleasing. What we might expect to find from a cleric so constantly out in the open and in the saddle, but seldom do, are references to the weather (save one retrospective remark about the rain in Germany), to discomfort (save when his boots froze to his stirrups when riding north from Genoa), or (except in Provence and on the Riviera) to the state of the roads; here too his reticence is part of a stoic tradition and is a last reminder that the great majority of men do not express a sensation unless there is some literary warrant for putting it into words.[1]

5. *The travel journals of de Beatis's contemporaries*

Before leaving the reader with de Beatis's text, its appraisal may be helped by a brief review of the travel journals kept during the previous 25 years that are most akin to it.

Of particular interest because of the closeness of method to the journal of de Beatis is the account kept in 1492 by Andrea de Franceschi, assistant (*coadjutore*) to the secretary who accompanied two Venetian ambassadors into Germany on a mission to the Emperor Frederick III and his son Maximilian.[2] In his diary, clearly kept (at least in note form) from day to day, the 19-year-old Franceschi noted the distances covered and the places (frequently naming the inns) where the ambassadors ate, stressing the reception accorded them at each town of any note, sometimes gifts of wine and food, almost always a musical entertainment with lutes, drums, rebecks, flutes, fifes, singers and sometimes dancers and tumblers (at Ulm the dancing 'ended by being extremely lascivious'). He noted that the women of Innsbruck were 'very

[1] The voice of the minority is represented by Jacques Le Saige, a silk merchant of Douais, much preoccupied with the habits and health of his horse and with the occasional pleasures and many trials of the traveller, as when on going to the kitchen to inquire about his supper he found the innkeeper's wife bathing nude in the copper. Op. cit. in bibl.

[2] Op. cit. in bibl. They were to congratulate them on the peaceable conclusion of the recent war in Bavaria.

beautiful and courteous in the highest degree'. Like de Beatis he mentioned whether towns were free or imperial, whether or not they were the centres of episcopal sees. And when he praised a work of art, he used the criterion with which we are familiar. A carved reredos in Landsberg contained figures 'which are just like those in nature', and in the painting which hung above it, the man dragging Christ along with a rope 'resembles the Venetian patrician Giacomo Bembo totally and explicitly'. The way in which this young man described the cities they visited shows the extent to which de Beatis inherited a formula. Thus Ulm 'lies in a most pleasing and delectable site in a fine plain which has some very gentle small hills...It is a noble and most worthy free city with many very rich merchants, Venetian and from other countries. The streets are wide, and have gravel spread on them. Trades of all sorts are practised and there are very pretty fountains. The houses are very impressive and are constructed in the German manner, that is with the walls divided by beams and other timbers which are fixed together not with iron but with wooden pegs.' The journal ends with an itinerary tabulating places and distances, including a *summa summarum* of 1,296 Italian miles.

Hieronymus Münzer who, though a doctor, fled the plague that attacked his native city Nuremberg in 1494, wrote an account of his travels in that and the following year through the Low Countries, France and Spain.[1] As a humanist scholar he wrote in Latin, enthused over classical monuments that de Beatis passed by without mentioning, and devoted considerable space to the universities he visited. He showed a gentlemanly disregard for daily distances and costs. In the company of three wealthy younger friends (he was 57) his route was determined chiefly by the pleasurable anticipation of broadening his knowledge of the world – so much so that he included a somewhat laborious defence of the benefits travel brought to the wise and reflective man – and by a piety that led him to Santiago and to the centres of the Magdalen cult in Provence.

Münzer was an amateur geographer of considerable standing. He assisted Schedel with the preparation of his *Chronicle*, for instance. Yet though some of his descriptions of towns were considerably longer than those of de Beatis their subject matter

---

[1] See bibl.

was the same: trades and markets, streets and fountains, churches and their relics, palaces and walls. As de Beatis was to be, he was a great climber of bell towers, counting the 380 steps at Bruges, the 388 at Notre Dame. His interest in people was weaker, he seldom described either their costume or physical appearance. His appraisal of landscape was more narrowly bounded by a preoccupation with fertility than was de Beatis's, and his regional descriptions were much briefer. Nor was he any freer from accepting the formulae suggested to a visitor by the inhabitants themselves. Thus at Avignon 'tria miranda vidimus: pontem superbissimum...; secundo palatium apostolicum cujus simile in toto orbe credo non esse...ut quasi laborinthum et Dedali opus crederes; est tertio murus, ambiens civitatem...similem non vidi.'[1]

In 1497, 'Andreas Franciscius'[2] wrote the account of his journey from Trent to London whose prefatory paragraphs we have already glanced at.[3] Travelling probably as secretary to the Venetian ambassador to Henry VII, Andrea Trevisano, his route corresponded with de Beatis's at times very closely, taking him through Bolzano, Ulm, Speyer, Worms, Mainz, Coblenz, Cologne, Aix-la-Chapelle, Diest, Antwerp, Ghent, Bruges, Nieuwpoort and Calais. And though he wrote in Latin, and included one or two classical commonplaces (men get more civilized as you move westwards from Germany; men who live in the plains are milder mannered than mountain people), his tone is as undoctrinaire and his interest almost as wide-ranging as de Beatis's. Crossing Germany he noted the wide paved streets, timber-framed houses, steep pitched roofs and the use of slate. Sailing down the Rhine from Mainz, with his party's horses following in another boat, he reacted almost lyrically to the scene. 'Along the banks of the river we saw many castles, towns and villages, sometimes quite close to each other owing to the benefits

---

[1] E. Déprez, 'Jérôme Münzer et son voyage dans le midi de la France en 1494–95'. *Annales du Midi* (1936) 62.

[2] See bibl., ed. Malfatti. The English section is re-printed in C. H. Williams, *English historical documents 1485–1558* (London, 1967) 187–92. I put the author's name in inverted commas because it seems not unlikely that he was identical with the Andrea di Franceschi we have just been discussing, and who accompanied other Venetian diplomatic missions as secretary, including one to Constantinople and Cairo in 1513. Op. cit., 279, note. It is perhaps a difficulty that the 1492 journal was kept in Italian, that of 1497 in Latin. The identification also opens the authorship of the anonymous *Relation...of England* (cited above, p. 14) to discussion, but this is an issue to be pursued elsewhere.

[3] Above, p. 19.

to be had from a situation near the river, which greatly increases the prosperity of the district. All the hills around are covered with vineyards, and I cannot say that I have ever seen more gay and delightful country than this region on the banks of the Rhine.' He noted the beauty of the women in the Netherlands, and that their independence was such 'that they walk about the town late at night, even unescorted, and yet no one dares to insult them', adding that 'in Germany nearly all the men and most of the women and children are very dirty; in this country such a condition is strongly disapproved of'.

He paid little attention to relics, apart from the Virgin's nightgown at Aix-la-Chapelle ('beatae Virginis nocturna vestis quam vulgo camisiam nominent'), but noticed organs and praised the musical taste of the Netherlanders. 'Most people are fond of music', he recorded in Bruges; 'this art is highly appreciated.' Again, at Antwerp 'everyone goes in for music, and they are so expert at it that they play even handbells so harmoniously and with such full tone that the handbells themselves seem to sing. There are real experts at this particular art who, by shaking six or seven handbells very cleverly and skilfully, can, without any accompaniment, play on them any tune they wish.' And in Calais he commented, as did de Beatis, on the snugly guarded lives of the citizens. 'Every day in the afternoon, when the inhabitants take their rest, the gates are closed; and this also happens on holidays, only, instead of once, as on working days, it is done twice, the first time when services are being held in the churches, and the second time, as before, when the people are having lunch. At these times sentries and guards keep watch from the town's walls on all sides, so much so that I never heard of a guard being kept anywhere else with such care.'

Two more examples will suffice to show, as the narrative of Franciscius does so clearly, how naturally an interested traveller could, by 1517, draw on a habit of describing his journey and on the traditions that determined what matter should be included in his account.

One was written by the greatest of all Italian historians, Francesco Guicciardini. As a young man of 28 he was sent in 1511 on his first diplomatic mission from Florence to Spain.[1] His

---

[1] Op. cit. in bibl.

account of the journey he undertook with a small staff was kept for his own interest only, or perhaps to pass with his other autobiographical writings to his successors as a record of his first important public service. Most of the entries are short. He was traversing on average between 40 and 50 kilometres a day and much of the route was barren and sparsely populated; lodging was often in peasant hovels that were not conducive to meditative composition. For much of the route he did little more than note distances and where he ate, with a word or two about the nature of the terrain and the authority into whose jurisdiction he had passed. Under orders to travel fast, he only allowed himself two whole days of sightseeing, one at Montpelier, the other in Barcelona. Of the latter he wrote that it lay in level ground beside the sea. 'It is a site well adapted for trade which does not, however, flourish as it did in the past; it is not in the prosperous state it used to be in mainly because the court is now in Castille. It is a beautiful and well populated city, without very splendid or outstanding buildings though the houses, and those in every district, are fine... The cathedral church, dedicated, if I remember aright, to Santa Eulagia, is small, but is fine and well designed. It has an altar richly and elaborately made of silver and a very wealthy sacristy with many relics, among them one of the Holy Innocents who from the head down is very well preserved; each individual limb can be made out... There is a large hospital with large numbers of sick in fine and well decorated rooms. As far as I could see they were well cared for. In the same hospital they care for foundlings, and lunatics are there too.' After describing the chief convent and the customs of the merchant community he summed up: 'Taking all together, the city is fine and impressive for its houses, for the sea which comes right up to the loggia of the merchants, for streets which though narrow, are clean, for the pleasure given by beautiful gardens and many orange trees, for being well populated and still rich and, were it not for its inhabitants' own feuds, very peaceable. All the same, if affection does not delude me, it is not a city that can be compared to Florence.'

Later on he essayed his only regional description of any length. Two miles from Lerida 'we entered Aragon, and because on that day we changed provinces I will briefly describe Catalonia, that is, the part I rode through. I do not know whether the part I did not traverse, especially that along the coast, is different from what

I saw which is mountainous, savage and very barren, with here a village there a farm, each cultivated for a small space around it, and then you cover leagues of barren ground. All the same where the land is cultivated it produces grain, wine and oil; there is little other produce...The men all go armed, everyone on the road carries a sword, many have staff-weapons or crossbows. They are all violent, with a reputation for being proud and warlike; this is the essential trait of their character, even if in the towns they employ an infinity of ceremonies and courteous manners...The logdings one encounters are bad because the hosts are all peasants and the innkeepers can provide nothing but shelter and cater for the needs of horses. You have to buy bread in one place, wine in another, vegetables in another: this is the custom and law of the country.' He concluded with a discussion of the considerable legal independence Catalonia enjoyed vis-à-vis the crown of Aragon.

The last example to detain us is the closest to de Beatis of all as far as the places visited and the scale on which they are described are concerned. It is almost exactly contemporary, a record of journeys undertaken between 1516 and 1519 and roughly conflated into what is, in effect, the first comprehensive guidebook to Western Europe – The Netherlands, France, England and Spain (but not Switzerland or Germany) – ever compiled. It is anonymous, though clearly of Milanese origin, and unpublished.[1]

The author appears to have been a merchant, and the long string of itineraries and distances he includes at the end are those of the most used commercial routes. He gives the dates of the four annual trade fairs at Lyons, but also a detailed pilgrim itinerary from Milan to Santiago and – evidence of a residual 'listomania' – the names of the notables of Castille 'cum suis redditibus'. Such latinisms occur sporadically in his text as currants in the very plain duff of a rebarbatively regional and unliterary vernacular prose. But it is precisely this unlettered quality that provides such impressive evidence of the traditions available to help even the culturally naive traveller sort out and express his impressions and determine to write them down.

There is little reference to landscape. This is essentially a guide to the chief objects of interest in towns. The author notes the state of their defences, the diocesan authority to which they belong, the

---

[1] Op. cit. in bibl., Anonymous Milanese.

length and number of arches of the bridges across which they are reached. He repeats what we can now recognize as the clichés handed out by local informants: that Paris was divided into three parts, the university area, the original city and the larger, more recent, residential zone; that the exterior of the town hall at Brussels was finer than the interior and that the great bed was the major curiosity in the palace of the Count of Nassau; that the gates of Calais were shut while the townsmen took their lunch. He could describe a great man, King Charles, whom he saw in Barcelona, as 'about twenty two years old, very tall and rather thin than otherwise; he has a rather long and cadaverous face and holds his mouth a little open. He and the whole court were in mourning for his grandfather.'

He did essay regional descriptions, though in the form of undigested snippets of information. Thus reviewing the Netherlands he names the chief towns and the courses of the main rivers, describes the use of peat, the construction of houses, the 'sanctuary' significance of kerchiefs on doorknockers (as de Beatis does), women's dress, the types of drinking vessels used in inns, how oxen were harnessed to carts and whores protected from harassment by the law. Scattered through his accounts of towns in the Netherlands are other pieces of general information such as the beauty of the women, the habit of even the poorest men of carrying arms, the preference for travelling by cart rather than on horseback.

His forte, however, was the description of towns, several of which were allocated considerably more space than de Beatis gave them. More revealing of the descriptive impulse than his accounts of trading or administrative centres like Lyons, Paris, Antwerp or Brussels is his treatment of Gaillon, a place of the scantiest concern to merchants save as a stage on the route from Rouen to Paris.

'It is small and has a fortress-like palace which was built by the Cardinal of Rouen, and they say that for a place of no outstanding size it is the finest in France, and even in Italy there is nothing so fine of its sort...Its walls, inside and out, are of cut stone of the very white kind that is used in this region instead of marble. They bear the figures of emperors and other great Roman and Greek and foreign captains carved from the same stone and very fine...In the middle of the courtyard there is a large and very beautiful fountain of pure marble topped by carved marble children, and it throws water continuously from more than ten spouts, and when a certain channel beneath it is plugged the water leaps straight up for more than nine *braccia*. [1]

'Upstairs there are many rooms with ceilings of wood wonderfully carved and gilded. Most of them are panelled with wood carved into very beautiful figures, and there is a very fine library with about 200 books all written by hand and all bound in velvet or brocade. But best of all there is, also upstairs, a small church made entirely of marble with innumerable carved figures in fine marble which makes a very beautiful impression. And on entering the church on the right there are the members of the house of Amboise who have been churchmen, and on the left those who have been soldiers, all carved in fine marble. And all the windows, upstairs and down (and they number over 150) have beautiful glass on which is painted the whole of the Old and the New Testament. And all the doorways, about 100 of them, are of wood and are carved with beautiful figures. And to sum up, there are so many fine things that even half cannot be described. And it is thought that were another like this to be built it would cost [*blank in text*].

'The garden and wall of the park adjoining this palace includes a garden, very fine and as large as the courtyard in Milan. It is walled with thick high walls with very beautiful gates in each side. And in the middle there is a very beautiful building with a very lovely fountain all carved out of marble. And on one side of the garden there is an enclosed space of about 200 *braccia* long and about 30 *braccia* wide where there are birds of all the sorts that there are, except for raptors. Then you leave this garden through a gate and go into a walled park about two miles in extent. It contains dense groves and little thickets and lawns and pools, all for the benefit of the animals; there are roe and fallow deer, both wild and tame, and all the other animals of the earth. In the centre is a fine building for the person in charge of it. [Altogether] it is a very fine place and is twenty leagues from Paris and nine from Rouen.' To compare this description of Gaillon with that of de Beatis[2] is to judge the extent to which a slightly higher level of education and the presence of an important and widely cultivated patron could modify the raw material of an already established genre.

---

[1] The Milanese *braccio* was 60 cm.   [2] See below, pp. 112-4.

Accompanying de Beatis, as we are about to do, we shall be not only in a sympathetic presence but in contact with the whole range of conventions whose fusion formed a process dubbed by Jacob Burckhardt 'the discovery of the world' but is better, because less subjectively, called the discovery of how to describe the world.

THE JOURNAL

Don Antonio de Beatis, canon of Molfetta, to his lords
and good friends, greeting and perpetual felicity.

My most reverend and illustrious master the Cardinal of Aragon
of immortal memory (as you are aware) having resolved, under
the cover and excuse of meeting Our Lord the Catholic King, his
kinsman and lately elected invincible King of the Romans,[1] that
not being satisfied with having several times seen the greater part
of Italy, nearly all Baetica[2] and the furthest parts of Spain he would
also get to know Germany, France and all those other regions
bordering the northern and western ocean and make himself
known to so great a variety of people – *Quoniam modicum et iam
videbitis me et iterum modicum et non videbitis me, quia vado ad patrem*[3]
– he decided to take with him no more than ten of his gentlemen
and some officials, as can be seen in more detail at the end of this
book; and this was not out of avarice (for if ever there were a
generous and liberal clerical or secular gentleman it was he, and
during the journey he spent some fifteen thousand ducats, part on
food and drink but mostly on presents to many and on purchases
of little luxuries and objects that pleased and satisfied him) but
solely in order to move swiftly with a sufficiency of servants.
Among the officials it pleased fate that I, though the humblest,
should have been numbered, so that no more for my good master's
glory than out of the respect and service due to my lords his
friends, and for their pleasure, I could obey his sacred desire that

[1] Charles V of Habsburg. King of Spain (hence the title 'the Catholic King' granted
by Alexander VI to his predecessor Ferdinand) since 1516, elected Emperor after the death
of Maximilian I in 1519 but with the subordinate title King of the Romans until his
coronation at Aix-la-Chapelle in 1520. Even then his official title was 'elected Roman
Emperor' until his coronation in 1530 by the Pope.
[2] De Beatis has 'La Bectica'. The Latin name for Andalusia-Catalonia; i.e. 'nearer', as
opposed to 'further' Spain.
[3] John, XVI, 16: 'A little while, and ye shall not see me: and again, a little while, and
ye shall see me, because I go to the Father.' A quotation so famous, and used in so many
contexts (e.g. Dante, *Purgatorio* xxxiii, 10–12) that it must not be read here as implying
a direct comparison between the Cardinal and Christ.

from our leaving Ferrara for Germany I could take on the task and burden of accurately describing, day by day, place by place and mile by mile the cities, towns and villages we rode through successively, with particular reference to all the things we found worthy of notice. This, with God's aid, I have done, from the beginning to its appointed end. And because among other friends and lords it is you to whom I am chiefly obliged, I have judged it proper to send you a copy of this entertaining itinerary and journey written in my own hand which I beg and beseech you as earnestly as possible to accept, read and re-read with a calm and tranquil mind, forgiving me if you find it neither in style nor arrangement a composition worthy of your learned and sensitive ears. For since I have not wished to write in the Latin language, both because it is not understood by everyone and because I would have fallen far short of deserving praise by so doing, and since being born in Apulia I have never mastered Tuscan, to express myself I have not been able to give up my own tongue and idiom, such as it is. All the same, neither you[1] nor any other reader who wishes to inform himself will find in all this number of well-filled pages anything but true accounts of things, either actually seen by me or reported by persons of great authority and worthy of all trust and belief.

And even if quasi-miraculous matters are included (as, indeed, they are), you are not to impute this to the writer but to the variety and the divine origin and nature of the world. Though as well as saying the Divine Office with Monsignor my most illustrious Lord of eternal memory, and preparing for mass every day and sometimes celebrating it, I was extremely busied in writing many letters in his name between night and morning, I did not wish to omit the laborious, detailed noting down of so long a journey because of the pleasure, understanding and wisdom you will acquire in looking through this book. And more than this I do not ask or desire as recompense and thanks for all my vigils and pains, save that you should often remember and commemorate

---

[1] The ms. owned by Pastor did not name an individual dedicatee. Nor does N. 2. The fuller of the two Naples manuscripts is dedicated to Antonio Seripando (1494–1539) who was described by the Cardinal of Aragon in a letter dated 11 July 1516 as 'our secretary'; while headed 'To the reverend Antonio Seripando health and eternal happiness' the dedication itself is identical; there is no suggestion, therefore, that Seripando was taken on this journey, though cf. E. Nunziante, *Un divorzio ai tempi di Leone X* (Naples, 1887) 93–4. He was the brother of Cardinal Girolamo Seripando and a close friend of the poet Jacopo Sannazzaro.

the happy bones and divine spirit of my good, just, pious, holy, generous and most gracious master. Farewell.

In the city of Molfetta, on the 20th of July, 1521.

The itinerary of my most reverend and most illustrious Lord the Cardinal of Aragon, begun in the month of May in the year of Our Saviour 1517 from the city of Ferrara and described with all possible care and accuracy by me, Don Antonio de Beatis, canon of Molfetta.

May 9. From Ferrara we went to lunch at Ficarolo, 15 miles away; we spent the night at Melara, an unfortified place in the Ferrarese. 30 miles in all.

May 10. From Melara to lunch at Isola della Scala, a distance of 21 miles. Three miles beyond Melara and on the Po is Ostiglia, a very important town belonging to the Marquis of Mantua.[1] From Isola della Scala we went on to spend the night in the city of Verona. 33 miles.[2] This city lies on level ground with one side against the hills. Full of life and beautiful with its streets, piazzas and palaces, it has an almost intact theatre.[3] Well populated and wide in circuit, Verona is divided in the middle by the river Adige.

May 11. From Verona to lunch and dinner[4] at Borghetto, 24 miles away. Half way, after 12 miles, is the gorge of Chiusa. Only a stone's throw wide, the aforesaid[5] Adige running through it, with crags and extremely harsh mountains of bare rock jutting straight up towards the sky it is a very strong site. From the German side it is impossible to take, especially with the Venetians guarding it as well as they do with a garrison and, in certain casemates built into the naked rock of the mountain itself, many pieces of artillery. From the Verona side it is not so well defended. The way through for those wishing to go to Germany lies to the right. It is barred with a gate and the path, which is simply cut

[1] Gianfrancesco II d'Este, Marquis 1484–1519.
[2] From now on bare self-contained statements of mileage, whether in the course of an entry or at its end, are omitted. The distances noted at the end of each day's record of travel by de Beatis will be found in the Itinerary on pp. 190–2; for a note on the measures of distance used by de Beatis, see p. 188.
[3] The Roman amphitheatre known as the Arena. De Beatis only pays laconic attention to the monuments of antiquity he encounters.
[4] 'Pranso et cena', the formula habitually used, is thus translated without implying that the latter was always the heavier meal; in spite of its cooks and harbingers the party was at the mercy of what they could procure at each stopping place.
[5] In the interest of readability de Beatis's repititious use of 'el dicto' has been henceforward suppressed. Chiusa is Chiusa di Rivoli.

in the rock, is so narrow and awkward that only one horse at a time can manage it, and then not without danger. There is no pass on the left side because the river flows against the side of the mountain which rears up at its highest and steepest at that spot. It should be noted, however, that among these extremely rugged mountains it is possible to ride continuously along very flat valleys. From Borghetto begins the jurisdiction of the Emperor,[1] though the inhabitants are Italians.

May 12. From Borghetto, which is an unfortified place or, rather, staging post, we went on to lunch at Rovereto, a strongly walled town 13 miles away. From there we went on to spend the night at Trent, 12 miles farther on. In all, 25 miles.

May 13. Trent is a very fine city lying in level ground and is well supplied with streams which run through it. We lunched in the castle with the Bishop[2] who has both spiritual and secular charge there, in order to see the body of the Blessed Simon and the Emperor's artillery which is numerous and of great beauty, especially as far as the large pieces are concerned. Thence we went to dinner at Salorno, three German miles away (note that each of these miles is the equivalent of five Italian ones). You enter Germany a German mile from Trent, after crossing a bridge over a river that runs into the Adige by a church dedicated to St Ulrich. He was a bishop of Augsburg who, falling gravely ill in Italy and desiring to return to Germany, begged God to preserve his life until he reached there. Arriving at this spot, where the little church was built in his name, he died. In Salorno my master was called on by the Duke of Bari, brother of Massimiliano Sforza the son of Il Moro – though he is of a different nature from his brother being, indeed, a nobleman of high cultivation, very prudent and of firm character.[3]

May 14. From Salorno we lunched and dined four miles away

[1] Maximilian I of Habsburg, succeeded Frederick III in 1493. After long contention between emperors, Venice and independence-seeking bishops of Trent, the boundary between Venetian and Austrian territory was fixed here in 1487 and confirmed in 1517.

[2] Bernhard II von Cles, bishop from 1514.

[3] Ludovico Sforza, nicknamed Il Moro, was expelled from the duchy of Milan by Louis XII of France in 1499, dying a prisoner in France in 1510. With the expulsion of the French in 1512 Massimiliano was installed, buttressed by Swiss and Imperial support. He resigned his title after the new French conquest under Francis I in 1515. He died in 1530. Another French defeat in 1521 led to the installation of his brother Francesco as duke. The duchy of Bari had been ceded to the Sforza by the King of Naples in 1464 and continued to be a title adopted by Sforza's younger sons.

at Bolzano, a walled town of over 700 hearths[1] belonging to the bishop of Trent. The water supply is good, with many fountains, and it is well built. There are two fine churches. Half a German mile before the town one leaves behind the river Adige to one's left, because the route to Merano turns up a valley which reaches into Swiss territory, where the river has its origin. And at that place a river called the Eisack flows into the Adige. The German etymology signifies 'sack of snow', and so, in effect, it is: it only reaches its full size when the snows melt. It flows past Bolzano. The valley one rides up from here on is named after the Eisack.

May 15. From Bolzano to lunch and dinner at a walled town called Chiusa four miles away. It belongs to the bishop of Brixen.

May 16. From Chiusa to lunch and dinner at a staging post called Eisack four miles away. Half way is the city of Brixen which though not very large is populous and well laid out. There my lord left a deposit for a small organ which is to be made by a man who is highly reputed as a master in the making of such instruments.

May 17. From Eisack to lunch and dinner at Steinach, a distance of five and a half miles. Two miles away from Eisack is a village called Sterzing which consists of one very long street. And at a place called Brenner there are two small lakes at the foot of a mountain; the Eisack flows out of one of them, and out of the other a stream called the Sill which runs towards Innsbruck, and from this it can be seen that from here the way begins to descend. Neither river is large, and where they begin they are extremely small. In Steinach is a lodge belonging to the Emperor where he stays when he comes to hunt chamois and deer; they drive them off the mountains and down into a stream that runs in front of the lodge and there they kill them with cross-bows and hand-guns. And to commemorate this there are six magnificent pairs of stags' antlers hung inside the lodge, their bases gilded and with the coats of arms of the noblemen who killed them. The same has been done with chamois horns.

May 18. Three and a half miles from Steinach to Innsbruck for lunch. Half a mile from Steinach is a village called Matrei which

---

[1] All de Beatis's population estimates are given in terms of *fochi*, fires or hearths, because hearth taxes were more or less ubiquitous and provided the most readily available estimate of population. Roughly one hearth meant one household, or family – on average 3·5–4·0 persons.

has a fine street with houses and acceptable lodgings. The city of
Innsbruck is built on level ground and is of no great size but is
populous, strong, cheerful and pleasant. The Emperor likes to
come there and it is said that he has often stayed with six thousand
horse. They make armours of the utmost perfection there which
are proof not only against cross-bows (as we saw from those My
Lord had made there) but also against gunshot. I do not know
whether this is due more to their craftsmanship or to the iron itself
and the tempering of the steel in water. The houses look very
attractive built as they are with the roofs, windows and façades
in a style of their own. The streets are wide, and there are many
streams and fountains in the city. The river Enus, colloquially
known as the Inn, flows by the walls, and thence comes the
German name Innsbruck, that is, bridge over the Inn. If not very
large, it is a fine looking river. The city lies in the diocese of Brixen.
Here we saw an artillery park larger, if anything, than the one in
Trent, besides such a supply of hand-guns, cross-bows, lances and
corselets that 30,000 infantry could easily be equipped from it. In
the chief church[1] there is an organ which, while not particularly
large is most beautiful, with many stops which produce the purest
tone representing trumpets, fifes, flutes, cornets, crumhorns,
bagpipes, drums, and the choruses and spring songs of various
birds with so much naturalism that they cannot be distinguished
from the real thing (which is most pleasing and ingenious); indeed,
of all the many other organs we saw in the course of our whole
journey, this was pronounced the most perfect.

Here the Cardinal called upon the two Queens in the Emperor's
quarters, which are very beautiful and contain many suites
constructed in the German manner. The Queens gave us audience
in a room one side of which was entirely occupied with ladies of
the court to the number of more than fifty, beautiful, and well
dressed in the German fashion. One of these queens, called Anna,
is the sister of the King of Hungary[2] and is fourteen or fifteen years
old; she is to be married to Ferdinand, brother of the Catholic
King. She is very lovely and most amiable, with lively eyes, and
her complexion is such that she seems to be all milk and blood.
She was dressed in black velvet and wore a cap of the same

---

[1] St Jacob's. The organ had been restored in 1497.
[2] Louis II (ruled 1516–26). The marriage took place, and from 1521 Ferdinand and Anna
ruled over the Habsburg lands in Germany and Austria.

coloured velvet on her head. The other, sister of the Catholic King and betrothed to the King of Hungary,[1] is 10 or 11 years old, dusky and not very good looking to my eyes. She was dressed in the same style but in silk of another colour than black, though with a man's cap of black velvet. In the same house is a room belonging to the Emperor filled with pretty curiosities and objects of iron made with great ingenuity. There are also fine and beautiful suits of armour, among them the one belonging to the King of Scotland which was captured when he was killed in battle in England by the English while the English king was encamped with the Emperor before Tournai.[2] His consort having sent the armour there after the victory, His Majesty gave it to the Emperor, and he sent it to be kept in this room in Innsbruck. There is also a hare with six horns on its head, a picture of a pig six palms high and another of a stag as big as a horse killed by one of the great lords of this place. The whole room, as well as some of the others, is decorated with huge stags' antlers in the way I mentioned at Steinach. Among them is one of thirty-six branches, the finest that could be seen.

A mile down the river Inn from the town, on the left bank, the Emperor is having twenty-eight metal statues made of his ancestors of the house of Austria and their kin, both men and women. We saw eleven there that had been finished; they were about nine spans[3] high. They are also making 128 metal statues of three spans each. In the place where they are working on them we saw some that had been finished; they were of various saints. According to the craftsmen and the gentlemen of Innsbruck, the Emperor intends to place them, together with the large statues, in a chapel which he plans to build, and indeed when this project is completed it will be very fine, and worthy of the large-mindedness and greatness of His Majesty.[4]

[1] Mary, five years after the death of Louis II, became Charles V's regent in the Netherlands.
[2] James IV, killed at Flodden in 1513, the year in which Henry VIII and Maximilian I won the Battle of the Spurs before taking Tournai.
[3] The *palmo* varied in size from place to place. If de Beatis is using the Neapolitan *palmo* it was about 26 cm. Other Italian *palmi* were shorter, from 22 to 24 cm. But it is most likely that he was using the span of his own hand, from tip of thumb to tip of little (or of second) finger. 23 cm. would be a reasonable assumption.
[4] Maximilian had ordered work to start at a number of foundries outside Innsbruck on these figures for his own tomb as early as 1502. His intention was that it should be set up in the Burgkappelle, Wiener Neustadt, but this proved impractical for technical reasons, and when the vast complex was eventually finished – not until 1583 – his grandson Ferdinand had it installed in the nave of the Hofkirche, Innsbruck.

The Cardinal stayed until the 21st, Ascension Day, with the greatest satisfaction.

May 21. After lunch we left Innsbruck to dine at a village called Seefeld, three miles away. About a mile from Innsbruck, in a mountain of sheer rock[1] and at a height I would put at about 50 or 60 *passi*[2] is a cave to which the Emperor climbed and fixed with his own hands a crucifix which can be seen from the road. A mile farther on is a populous village called Zirl.

In Seefeld, which does not have many inhabitants, the parish church[3] contains a miraculous host, seemingly of flesh and blood, which has been in a tabernacle since 1384. In that year one Oswald Milser, a noble and prefect of certain guilds, believing there to be a difference between the large and the small consecrated wafer, and wishing to communicate on Maundy Thursday, requested the parish priest or rector that on that day he would not give him communion with the small host, as he did the ordinary congregation, but should give it him with the large host used by the clergy. The priest answered that once consecrated there was no difference between wafer and wafer, large or small. The prefect, however, insisted that the priest should give him communion with the large one and out of fear the priest let him do so. And when the body of our Lord Jesus Christ entered his mouth it immediately turned to flesh and blood, and the ground at the corner of the altar where he was kneeling opened and began to suck him in. Terrified by the magnitude of the miracle and feeling himself sinking he clutched the corner of the altar with his right hand, where by God's will the stone, although extremely hard, yielded to his fingers just as though it were wax, as can clearly be seen today. So the priest, taking the body of Christ from his mouth put it with due reverence in a tabernacle of crystal decorated with silver, which the Cardinal and the rest of us saw with our own eyes. Brought to repentance, the prefect led an austere and virtuous life until his death. It is said that this reliquary has always caused miracles, and does still. As far as this village, which is in the diocese of Brixen,

---

[1] The Martinswand. The feat de Beatis described was part of the 'instant folk-lore' Maximilian's propagandists fostered to emphasize the Emperor's prowess and devoutness and his being under the special protection of the Deity.

[2] Literally a 'pace', the *passo*, like the *palmo*, varied from place to place, averaging something over one and a half metres.

[3] The Oswaldskirche. In a note, Pastor (p. 33) quotes authorities to show that de Beatis took the story that follows from an inscription on a painting commemorating the miracle.

stretches the county of Tirol which belongs to the Emperor and, as ancient writings show, and no memory contradicts, has always been under the house of Austria.

Swabia [1]

May 22. From Seefeld to lunch at Mittenwald, which is a small village three miles distant, and thence to dinner at Partenkirchen, another three miles. This is in the diocese of Freising.

May 23. From Partenkirchen to lunch and dine at Rottenburg, a monastery of Augustinian canons regular belonging to the Friesing diocese, dedicated to the blessed Virgin. Its chief festival is celebrated on the day of her birth. There is a capacious guest house belonging to the monastery, which has temporal and spiritual jurisdiction over five German miles around. And a mile from Partenkirchen we came on a Benedictine monastery in a part of the country which had once been occupied by brigands. There is a large and ornate church built on a round plan with a fine cupola supported in the centre with a pillar. [2] This monastery was built by the Emperor Frederick IV as an *ex voto* to thank God for bringing him back safely from Italy, and the site was revealed by an angel which appeared to him in the Benedictine habit, such as the monks there wear. The monastery is named after the Madonna of Eype. [3]

May 24. From Rottenburg to lunch and dinner at Landsberg, five miles away. On a low hill a mile from Rottenburg is a pleasant walled town called Schöngau which belongs to the Duke of Bavaria, and further on is another belonging to him called Schönach; a river of the same name flows past its walls. Landsberg belongs to the same duke and is in the diocese of Augsburg. A river runs past the gate where there is a fine bridge, made, as are all the others in Germany, of wood; none is made of stone. The river, which is neither small nor of any great size, has its source near the monastery of the Madonna of Eype and in Latin is called Licus, in German Lech. A waterfall within the town makes it run with furious speed.

[1] The heading is de Beatis's (*Svevia*).   [2] The Alte Kirche St Martin.

[3] An example of de Beatis either mishearing at the time or misreading his notes; for Frederick IV read Louis IV (emperor 1314–47) and for Eype read Ettal. Louis of Bavaria was in Italy 1327–30 vainly trying, against increasing political odds, to force Pope John XXII to recognize his claim to the empire. The church was comparatively recent: 1476–92.

May 25. From Landsberg to lunch and dinner at Augusta, called Augsburg by the Germans. The distance is six miles, and these we covered leaving mountains and woods behind us, and from Landsberg riding over a plain as wide and bare as that in Apulia.

This city is large, populous and built entirely on the level. With its squares, streets, houses and churches it makes a most beautiful, cheerful and civilized impression. A great number of fountains are spread throughout it. Their water comes neither from local springs nor from a source piped in from a distance as is usual elsewhere, but comes from a certain device in a tower at the edge of the city. Wheels force water from a stream which runs into the tower up to a high level and it then flows away through underground conduits to supply the many fountains in the squares and streets. They throw it to a really considerable height. The Cardinal went to see this tower and pronounced it to be a costly and ingenious device. We saw the Fugger palace, among the finest in Germany. It is highly decorated with marble and variegated stone, and the façade facing the street has painted scenes which employ the most perfect colours, including much gold; the roof is entirely made of copper.[1] Among the German-style rooms are some done most beautifully and expertly *all'Italiana*. In the Carmelite monastery the Fuggers have made a chapel at the end of the nave of the church.[2] It is raised on some eight steps, is excellently painted, is floored with marbles and mosaics and has a highly decorative tapestry worked in gold and azure and other rich colours. The screen which occupies almost the whole façade contains the most perfect marble figures which strongly resemble those of Antiquity, and inside there are oaken choir stalls, highly individual in style and with full relief figures of prophets and sybils done with the finest craftsmanship. There is also an organ which for such a chapel is very large and fine. According to Jacob Fugger, who is the oldest member of the family and who had it built, the cost of the chapel together with all these embellishments was twenty-three thousand florins. These Fuggers are today among the greatest merchants to be found in Christendom, for without any outside help they can lay hands on three hundred thousand ducats in ready money and still not touch a hair of their property, which is by no means small. This wealth is derived from loans to the great

---

[1] The remodelling had been completed in 1511.
[2] St Anna's. The work on the Fugger chapel was then just coming to an end.

benefices, bishoprics and abbacies of Germany, so that messer Jacob boasted that he has helped every one of the bishops in his lifetime, many of them two and three times, and he is not yet more than seventy years old.[1] In addition, they still make an excellent profit from the gold and silver mines farmed very advantageously to them for many years by the Emperor and the King of Hungary, although the farm fee was raised some time ago and although they reckon that in Germany and Hungary they have to keep ten thousand miners permanently in their pay. Also here are the Welsers, local men of good standing, familiar with Italy and good merchants but in no way to be compared to the Fuggers. Monsignor the Bishop of Gurk[2] is also a son of this city and after he became a cardinal built a fine large house there. These Fuggers entertained my illustrious master with dancing and the company of many beautiful ladies in their garden, which is in a suburb near the city walls; there are fountains, even inside the rooms, with water conveyed by a device of wheels. Besides the episcopal church, which is large and beautiful, there is the church of the Dominicans.[3] This is very splendid and well designed and was entirely constructed, we were told, in three years. Another resident is Paulo Ruzo,[4] a layman, deeply learned in Hebrew and Latin, a great philosopher and on excellent terms with the Emperor and members of his court. Augsburg is an imperial or – it amounts to the same thing – a free city.

May 27. From Augsburg to lunch and dinner at Donauwörth, six miles distant. This place is named after a river which runs through its ditch and is of little account. The Danube, which is of no great size there, passes a bowshot away. Between Augsburg and Donauwörth is a town with a number of good inns called Abessidorf.[5] In the walled town of Donauwörth is a Benedictine monastery called after the holy cross where there is a piece of the cross of our Lord Jesus Christ and a thorn from his crown of thorns, enclosed in a beautiful tabernacle of silver gilt decorated with great pearls and other jewels in the form of a tree containing

---

[1] Born in 1459, he was then 58.
[2] Mathius Lang, formerly secretary to Maximilian I. Born in Augsburg 1496, bishop of Gurk 1505, Cardinal 1511.
[3] S. Mary Magdalen's. Built 1513–15.
[4] Pastor's suggestion that de Beatis meant Konrad Peutinger (1465–1547) is convincing.
[5] Unidentified.

more than fifty very delicately wrought figures. The Cardinal was delighted, judging it to be of the highest craftsmanship.

May 28. From Donauwörth to lunch and dinner at Weissenburg, a distance of four miles. A mile from Donauwörth there is a monastery belonging to the order of St Bernard called Kaisheim which has an annual income of 30,000 florins. It has a large and beautiful church with many good buildings around it. It was built by a count of Swabia and the abbot, who is elected by the monks, has to be a Swabian. Note: beyond the county of Tirol is the province or county of Swabia which is bordered by Switzerland and the bank of the Rhine.

May 29. From Weissenburg to lunch and dinner at Nuremberg: seven miles. Five miles from Weissenburg is a fine and strong walled town which belongs to Ramiro, Margrave of Brandenburg – not the imperial elector but a relation of his.[1]

Nuremberg lies on flat land with a small part on the hills. With its churches, streets, houses and squares it is extremely fine. It is copiously stocked with merchandise and artisans' work, especially objects of iron. Though it does not have any large river, there is one that runs through its centre in which many mills are at work. They manufacture a great deal of iron wares there, especially wire; enormous quantities of this, both thick and thin, are readily made with wheels turned by the water. In the main square is a stone fountain carved with many most beautiful figures in full relief; it is very tall and has more than thirty jets. There are others elsewhere in the town but none so beautiful. The streets, all chained off with extremely strong and thick chains, house merchants of all nations and men of standing. Though not to be compared with those of Trent and Innsbruck, there is a park of admirable artillery, both large and small. Among the lighter firearms are three 'triangles',[2] and the crossbows are numberless. There are stores of everything necessary from horses to pull the guns to stone, balls, powder and pole arms. A large long building

[1] The elector was Joachin I (1499–1535). 'Ramiro' is puzzling; the Margrave was named Kasimir.

[2] In a marginal note de Beatis added: 'Triangles are triple-faced, [mounted] on carts, and on each face there are 40 or more *schioppetti* and fewer arquebuses of metal; and on lighting one they all fire, and when one face is discharged it is turned to the next, and then the next.' Machines based on multiple-fire smallarms were not uncommon in a period when ingenuity was valued at times above practicality, though 'triangles' were more frequently drawn than built, so this is a precious piece of observation.

is kept full of fuel so that in case of a siege the iron works will not come to a halt for lack of it. The city also maintains eignteen establishments constructed as storehouses with three or four rooms full of victuals, that is, oats and rye, because there is little wheat. To judge from one which we saw with the Cardinal, if the others resemble it, as the citizens say, one can judge the supply to be incredible. And we were shown rye that was a hundred years old and more which was still sound. This was also shown to Cardinal d'Este when he was here towards the end of the pontificate of Julius of happy memory.[1] About a hundred or more *passi* outside the town gate, where the river flows, is a plantation of five rows of the tree called linden in Germany, one of which follows the river bank, which is almost level with the water. These trees are very large and their foliage resembles the white mulberry. They cast a pleasant shade and bear a white blossom which smells strongly but produces no fruit. Beneath them is a close cropped turf of a delightful green, containing certain small herbs, and there are four carefully spaced fountains. Altogether I would hardly be lying if I said that I could imagine no lovelier or pleasanter spot. These trees are to be found in all the towns in Germany and Flanders, especially in public places *causa captandi frigus opacum*.[2] In Italy they are unknown, as is another tree called the larch, whose foliage somewhat resembles the fir's but which has smaller branches and is much pleasanter to look at. It grows in great numbers among the woods in mountainous places, though on the lower slopes. In Nuremberg the Cardinal left orders for clocks,[3] and other things of iron and brass which amounted to a good sum of ducats. They show there the crown of Charlemagne, son of Pepin, made all of gold and containing many extremely valuable gems, also his sword with a sheath of red velvet and that of St Maurice which was given him, they say, by the angel. And the master smiths (and I have said how very many there are of them here) cannot decide what metal it is made of. They also claim to have Charlemagne's

[1] Ippolito d'Este (1479–1520), son of Duke Ercole of Ferrara, Cardinal from 1493; Giuliano della Rovere was Pope as Julius II from 1503 to 1513. Ippolito was out of favour until late in 1511, but probably visited Nuremberg during the period of intense diplomatic activity that led to the papal-imperial alliance of November 1512.

[2] 'For taking advantage of the shaded coolness.' Cf. Vergil, *Bucolics*, I, 52.

[3] Nuremberg pioneered the making of small portable striking clocks (even with alarm systems) and pocket watches, the so-called 'Nuremberg eggs'. Intricate and expensive, these were much valued as presents.

orb[1] with its cross, and a thorn from our Lord Jesus Christ's crown of thorns and the point of the lance which pierced his side; they assert that they have compared it with the lance in St Peter's in Rome on the altar where Innocent VIII is buried which lacks this point.[2] Nuremberg is in the diocese of Bamberg and is a free city. They do a thriving trade there in furs from Muscovy and the Baltic: white fox, lynx, ermine and sable. They are often in conflict with their neighbour, the Margrave of Brandenburg, and this has led at times, they say, to pitched battles. And, great lord as he is, though he has laid siege to them he has on occasion had the worst of it and been routed.

On *June 1*, after lunch on the second day of Pentecost, we left Nuremberg, where we had spent two days, for Constance. And turning back into Swabia we dined at Gunzenhausen, a town belonging to the Margrave of Brandenberg, six miles away.

June 2. From Gunzenhausen five miles to lunch and dinner at Nördlingen, a free walled town in the diocese of Augsburg. Three miles from Gunzenhausen is the walled town and county of Öttingen.

June 3. From Nördlingen to lunch and dinner at Lauingen, the home of Albertus Magnus, who is painted – they say from the life – on a façade of a tower inside the town which was built as a memorial to him and was paid for by a countess of Schwabeck called Gisela. When he was elected bishop of Regensburg the house where he was born was turned into a little church dedicated to the Madonna, as you can see today, and masses are frequently said there in his memory.[3] Another native, now living there, is an Augustinian friar called brother Gaspare Amonio, deeply versed in Greek, Latin and Hebrew, who makes fresh translations of many parts of the scriptures.[4] Lauingen now belongs to the Palatinate, five miles away. Formerly it was an imperial town. Past its walls flows the Danube which rises five German miles away at a place called Tanisia.[5] There are many little villages in between and the

---

[1] The crown and orb were part of the imperial regalia; they were taken to Aix-la-Chapelle, for instance, when Charles V was crowned there in 1520. They are now in the Hofburg in Vienna.

[2] De Beatis is more sceptical when he reviews the whole question of duplicated relics; see pp. 152–4.

[3] Born in Lauingen *c.* 1206, the great Dominican theologian died in 1280.

[4] Kaspar Amman (Amonius), biblical translator and Hebrew scholar, died in 1524.

[5] In fact, far to the west; on the eastern slope of the Black Forest. I cannot identify Tanisia.

country is flat. We passed through it somewhat fearfully with a military escort from Augsburg on account of a report that there were fifty mounted bandits in the woods.

June 4. On the bridge beyond the gate through which we left Lauingen are eleven very large and fine windmills and one for iron working, six on each side. We went to lunch and dinner at Ulm, a populous free town in Swabia, a good six miles away, because the same fear made us veer from the normal route. The main church is very large and beautiful.[1] The Danube flows past and fills its ditches. Two miles out of Lauingen there is a walled town called Günzburg which belongs to the house of Austria and has been pawned by the present Emperor to the bishop of Augsburg. Half a mile farther is another town called Leipheim. Ulm is in the diocese of Constance.

June 5. From Ulm to lunch and dine at Biberach, a free town in the diocese of Constance: distance, 4 miles. On the way there are a few little places of no importance. Note: all those towns and places, in whatever kingdom or province, which I do not describe as being in the mountains should be assumed to be in flat country.

June 6. From Biberach to lunch and dine at Ravensberg: 4 miles. It is a free town in the diocese of Constance and half way there lies the town of Waldsee, where the Cardinal ordered flutes, fifes and crumhorns to be made, and left a deposit. These are made extremely well in this place.

June 7. From Ravensberg to dine at Constance, four miles away. We lunched at a place called Meersburg which is on the lake and belongs to the bishop of Constance. There we embarked with all the horses for Constance, which lies half a German mile away. It would have been more than four miles by land.

Here we stopped for two days. It is a very cheerful town, for the most part surrounded by the lake. You enter it over a fine long wooden bridge where the Rhine begins; it rises, however, some five miles above the lake, then flows into it and from the bridge onwards becomes narrower and begins to bear its name. After flowing for a mile it forms another small lake, where there is a little island, and thereafter resumes its direct course. The lake of Constance, which is very beautiful and pleasing, is eight German miles long and about two across. In the city the women are

---

[1] The Münster, one of the largest churches in Germany (5,100 square metres).

extremely good-looking, gay and friendly. In the cathedral, which is being re-built on a large and splendid scale, we saw many reliquaries and precious objects in gold and silver, among them two crosses each about six spans in size of solid gold specie. There are also many golden shrines. There is a casket or ossuary, four spans in size, containing the bones of a martyr; it is of solid gold specie with an infinite number of jewels, some of them precious and of fine quality. The canons there say that the cover of this ossuary is of Arabian gold; of excellent craftsmanship, it cost three thousand florins simply to make. Also there were two altarpieces entirely of silver, each eight spans tall and five wide. There is a fine and large library in the church which contains among other things a superb astrolabe. The canons are having a tin-piped organ made, over thirty spans in size. According to the builder it was to reproduce the tone of thirteen instruments. He showed us the design. The majority of the pipes – there are to be three thousand four hundred of these – are already made, and the largest, which the Cardinal got one of his servants to measure, was about five *palmi di canna* round; he estimated that when finished it would be the largest organ that has ever been made. Yet the builder did not think it would cost more than two thousand ducats; in Italy it would cost ten thousand. Near the chief gate on the lake is the room where the Council of Constance met;[1] now it is used as a warehouse and customs house for goods arriving by water. It is an imperial or free city, which means the same thing. Near the lake gate is a sphere set in the wall marked with the twelve months of the year beneath which are painted the fish which are good in each month – that is, those which are caught in the lake – and they are purchased accordingly.

June 10. We went to lunch and dinner at Schaffhausen, four miles away. It is [the capital of] one of the Swiss cantons, lying on the right bank of the Rhine which we crossed by a fine wooden bridge which leads to the chief gate of the town. It is not large in circumference but crammed together and crowded. There is a Benedictine abbey with the largest crucifix you ever saw; throughout Germany it is referred to in the saying *Magnus Deus*

---

[1] The Council of Constance, summoned to restore unity (at a time when there were three rival popes) to the Church, to quash heresy (notably that of Jan Hus) and propose reforms of ecclesiastical morals and manners, met from 1414 to 1418. It was the conclave which met in the warehouse (the ordinary business of the church having to continue), not the council, which commonly sat in the cathedral.

Schiafusensis. Note: Swiss miles are twice as long as the other German miles. [1]

June 11. Corpus Christi day. We left after lunch and went on to dinner at Laufenburg, four miles away. It is built on both banks of the Rhine, is an imperial city and is in the diocese of Constance. An Italian mile from Schaffhausen the Rhine falls precipitously between savage rocks. A mile farther on is a town called Neunkirch, a mile beyond there is another called Thiengen and three miles from Schaffhausen is Waldshut. We passed through the two last named. Laufenburg is of no great size. The Rhine passes through it in a deep gorge spanned by a stone bridge where there is another waterfall or cascade. This makes a mighty noise because of the great rocks that are there, and rushes most violently. By the bridge you cross to the left bank where the greater part of the inhabitants live. From there the river begins to be navigable all the way to the ocean. From there, too, the salmon fishing begins, fish that are scarcely smaller than tunny, very plump and delicate. We ate two very big ones.

June 13. From Laufenburg, where we stayed for a day to rest the horses, we went on to lunch and dinner as Basel, four miles away. Half way, we came on a town on the other side of the Rhine called Rheinfelden which has a wide and lengthy bridge across the river. Basel is [the capital of] a Swiss canton, large and strongly fortified with walls and multiple ditches. It is on level ground and where there are no walls it is defended by the Rhine flowing past it; there is a wooden bridge crossing the river which is very wide and long and is supported on masonry piers. And around the end of the bridge on the right bank there are many houses and fine streets, though it is a less agreeable district than the city itself; it is called Basel the Less, and is in the diocese of Constance. The city's artillery is good, notably twelve very large pieces of the most ingenious workmanship. The Swiss are very proud of them and guard them jealously, because they were captured from the Empire. But the inhabitants of Constance fear the Swiss much more and guard their city at all times especially since in the past, had the Emperor not been prepared to aid it in person, by the terms of a secret treaty, it would have been taken over by now. The Council of Basel [2] was held in the cathedral.

---

[1] De Beatis does not allow for this when calculating daily distances; he continues to use German miles.   [2] 1431–49.

June 14. From there at dawn, when the sun was hardly risen, we set off down the Rhine with two boats, the Cardinal and the rest of us in one, the horses and their grooms in the other. Towards sunset we arrived at Strasbourg. It is fourteen miles by land and twenty by water because the river winds considerably. We lunched in the boat on food we had bought in Basel.

Strasbourg lies in the plain half an Italian mile from the Rhine, and you enter it along a man-made canal which runs from the river through the middle of the city; this is so wide and so full of water that it almost resembles the Grand Canal in Venice. There are other watercourses as well, notably those that fill the ditches. It is a large and well inhabited city with very fine streets and squares and with houses built for the most part in stone. It belongs to the Empire, has a large and excellent park of artillery and stores of wheat, rye and oats. Most notable is the great cathedral, entirely roofed with lead and very beautiful. It has a large and perfect organ and a campanile, which they call a tower. This is much taller than the cupola of Santa Liberata[1] in Florence, than the Torre dell'Asinello in Bologna or the campanile of St Mark's in Venice or any other building in Italy that I have seen or heard about. And it is most ingeniously secured with iron clamps and, inside, the stonework sealed with lead so that not a scrap of mortar is used. You could not imagine a lovelier or more splendid building. You can climb it easily by spiral staircases at all four corners. The Cardinal climbed half way and some of the rest of us to the very top. We counted more than eight hundred steps of a span in height. We stayed there two days.

June 17. To leave Strasbourg by land it was necessary to cross the Rhine, which at this point broadens out greatly as in many other places, by a wooden bridge half an Italian mile long. We went to lunch and dine at a place called Rastatt, six miles away. On the way are two villages with little in the way of lodgings.

June 18. From Rastatt to lunch and dinner at Speyer, which is eight miles away. An Italian mile from the city you cross the Rhine by boat. Speyer is neither very large nor small, it is well populated and there is a fine cathedral roofed with lead which contains a fine organ with many stops;[2] in the choir is a very beautiful brass chandelier. In the cloister there is a Mount of Olives with Our

---

[1] The Duomo, or cathedral.   [2] Installed in 1505.

Lord, the disciples and a crowd of Jews, carved in full relief in stone. The figures are life-size and the work is as beautiful as it could be. Also eight emperors are buried in the cathedral.[1] It is an imperial city. The bishopric is held by the brother of the Count Palatine.[2] In the sacresty we saw a chalice made entirely of agate which is extremely fine and a book-case containing various works of craftsmanship. Our party stayed there five days awaiting my return from the Count Palatine and from Franz von Sickingen who was in a castle of his called Ebernburg eleven German miles away. I brought back safe conducts from them licensing us to travel securely by land or water.[3]

June 23. From Speyer we went to lunch and dinner at Worms: six miles; in between is a walled town belonging to the Count Palatine, where the Cardinal was met by the Burgundian men at arms who were in Worms on account of the hostilities with von Sickingen. Worms is an imperial city, large and fine, lying at the same distance from the Rhine as Speyer does. We stayed there two days, waiting for news of the Emperor who was then in Frankfurt. When news came that his Imperial Majesty had left Frankfurt for Augsburg, the Cardinal, though most anxious to meet him, was reluctant to turn back so far, especially as there was a possibility that the Catholic King would sail for Spain, and to meet and get to know him was the chief objective of his journey.[4] If he had left, he would have to follow him, so he decided to continue to Flanders. So we wrote to the Apostolic nuncio, Cardinal Campeggio[5] who was then with the Emperor, asking him to make the Cardinal's excuses, and set off on our way forthwith.

June 26. From Worms to lunch and dinner at Mainz, seven miles away. Half way along is a place belonging to the Count Palatine called Oppenheim. Mainz is an imperial city set on the left bank of the Rhine, extremely large and embellished with fine churches,

---

[1] Actually three emperors (Konrad II, Henry III, and Henry IV) and their empresses, Henry V, and the daughter of Frederick Barbarossa.

[2] The bishopric was in fact held by the Count Palatine (George, bishop 1513–20) younger brother of the Elector Palatine Louis V (1508–44).

[3] The territory and silver mines at Ebernburg had been pawned to the Sickingen family in 1482. Five days would give time for de Beatis to go there and to Heidelberg, Louis's capital. The latter's safe conduct was necessary because of the current disharmony between the members of the Swabian League to which the Palatinate belonged, the former's because of Franz von Sickingen's feud with the city of Worms.

[4] See Introduction, pp. 7–8.

[5] Lorenzo Campeggio, 1469–1539, cardinal from June 1517, was the chief diplomatic intermediary between Maximilian I and Leo X.

squares and houses. The streets, however, are somewhat narrow compared with those of the other German cities. The archbishop has both temporal and spiritual authority there. We found Franz von Sickingen who had come with a safe-conduct from the Emperor and the imperial electors, who were to gather here, so that he could justify his hostilities with the men of Worms. He came to call on the Cardinal in his lodgings. Along the side of the river, which in many places from here on is half as wide again as the Po, were an infinite number of boats and covered vessels of a particular shape which are so large that they can carry two hundred *botti* each.[1]

June 27. Taking provisions for lunch with us, we left by water in two boats, as I said when we came on the same river to Strasbourg. We ate on board while passing a town called Koblenz, which belongs to the bishop of Trier; the Rhine passes it on one side and on the other is a wide river which comes from Trier across which is a fine stone bridge. It is called Confluentia *confluxu duorum fluminum.* From the outside the town is very beautiful and impressive; we did not go inside it. We went on to spend the night in a place on the left side of the Rhine going to Cologne, called St Goar.[2] It belongs to the Landgrave.

June 28. From St Goar, on the eve of St Peter's Day, we spent the night in a town on the same side of the river called Bonn. Well fortified and populous, it is under the bishop of Cologne. And as the view of the Rhine from Mainz to Cologne is the most beautiful I have ever seen and ever expect to see along any other river, I think it is appropriate and its due that I should describe it. Both banks of the river are covered with vineyards and from five miles out of Mainz to three Italian miles from Cologne the hills on both sides are planted with vines. Within half an Italian mile on both sides lie two hundred and thirty five hamlets and villages and fifteen walled towns, some of them belonging to the archbishop of Mainz, others to the bishops of Cologne and Trier and to the count Palatine. And there are a number of small castles built strongly on the hilltops as is the German custom. They belong to private individuals.

June 29. The day of the glorious princes of the earth St Peter and St Paul. After hearing mass as is proper, we left Bonn by boat

---

1 See note on p. 170.
2 Pastor's suggestion for the manuscripts' 'Sanghiver'.

and went on to lunch at Cologne, which is four miles away. This city lies in the shape of a half moon on the left side of the Rhine and is more beautiful and more populous than all the others we have seen in Upper Germany, both for its houses, which are commonly large and well built of stone, squares, streets and churches and for whatever else can grace a city. The bishop holds both spiritual and temporal authority. And there are an infinite number of the most beautiful reliquaries, in the cathedral, that is. This is being made very large and beautiful; above the main doorway two towers or campanili have been begun in a most splendid fashion. They display the heads of the three kings Caspar, Balthasar and Melchior which we saw through grills in an iron shrine where they say their bodies are too. And in a very rich sarcophagus made of silver and gold, with jewels and a most beautiful cameo is the body of a martyr. In the church of St Ursula is her body and those of the eleven thousand virgins who were martyred on the spot where the church of the Dominicans now stands. The relics of the eleven thousand virgins, especially the heads, have been divided and distributed among all the churches in Cologne and among many other churches in Christendom. In St Francis, the church of the Minorites, the body of Scotus[1] lies in the middle of the choir; the stone covering the grave is a span high and bears a bronze image of him in half relief. In the Dominican monastery is the body of Albertus Magnus. This lies above ground before the high altar in a sepulchre with two semicircular grills occupying its front. Under the first is a glass plate through which you can see the body dressed in his Dominican habit. The head and the bones, which are still joined, though fleshless, give you an impression of their chief characteristics; Scotus, from what we saw, having been of small stature while Albertus was largely built. In the monastery's library is a *de natura animalium* written in his [Albertus's] hand and the chair from which he taught.

In the Benedictine monastery church of St Pantaleon is the body of the Englishman Albinus, both flesh and bone; according to the fathers there he died in 1200.[2] The Cardinal and all the rest of us

---

[1] The Scottish philosopher-theologian Duns Scotus, the opponent of Aquinas, died in Cologne in 1308.

[2] 1200 is an inaccurate date either for the conjectural English protomartyr St Alban (martyred *c*. 300) or the definitely mythical St Albinus, first heard of in the eleventh century; the two were frequently confused.

saw him, as we did many other relics in the form of heads, arms
and bones of martyrs which are in different churches in this city.
There is also a small hill called the Capitol[1] on which is built a
church dedicated to St Mary which is served by a great number
of canonesses, as happens in many places in Germany and Flanders.
They say their office publicly in the choir. They eat in common
and sleep in their convent, but otherwise they can go out by day,
in pairs, as they please, and they employ servants in a most
gentlewomanly way; if they wish they can marry legally. The city
is said to have more than 15,000 hearths and to be able to produce
18,000 well equipped troops between morning and evening. There
are twelve houses of religion and thirteen parish churches.

And as Cologne is commonly considered to be the end of Upper
and the beginning of Lower Germany, or Flanders, it would be
appropriate briefly to set down the character of Upper Germany.
The chief point to make is that five miles out of Verona (as I have
already said) as far as Innsbruck and then to within a day's journey
of Augsburg, one travels among extremely savage mountains of
naked rock which reach up to the sky, riding through a succession
of very flat valleys, and it is the same with other valleys among
hills we passed through right up to Cologne; you can go
everywhere among them comfortably in carriages. Infinite numbers of these do, indeed, come and go all the time, as it is their
custom to transport everything in four wheeled carts, some of
which are such that they can carry more goods than four of our
Lombardy ones; they are drawn by numerous powerful horses.
Lodgings are good everywhere. Though after leaving Trent no
vines are to be found almost until the Rhine is reached, all the inns
have two kinds of wine, white wines and red, sound and delicate;
some of them are flavoured with sage, elder or rosemary. The
staple in Germany, as in Flanders, is beer. Good veal, plenty of
poultry, excellent bread. Up to Cologne the wine is reasonably
priced and veal so dirt cheap that in some places we consumed
four calves for a gold ducat. The only open fireplace is the one
in the kitchen; in the other rooms they use stoves. In each of these
is a cabinet, carefully wrought in a characteristic style, which
contains a tin vessel for washing purposes. They are very fond of
keeping different sorts of birds indoors in cages made with a high

---

[1] De Beatis uses the Italian term for the Capitoline Hill, *Campidoglio*.

degree of skill and fancy; also some which are allowed to come in and out as they please. Feather mattresses are universal, together with feather coverlets, and you never come across a flea or a bug in them, either because the country is so cold or because the upper and lower feather beds are anointed with some kind of preparation. According to the Germans this is not only noxious to bugs and other pests but conditions the feather cases in such a way that sleeping in them is like sleeping between covers of fine wool. They use this method only in summer. These feather beds are very large and the pillows immense, but they have so many geese that several times in Germany I saw flocks of four hundred. It is true that they put as many beds into a room as it will hold, which is inconvenient and blameworthy, and in the rooms where you sleep there is neither stove nor fireplace to give warmth so that there is too sharp a contrast when you leave the heat and get undressed in such an extreme and excessive cold. But since they get warm as soon as they get between the feather beds they do not worry about it at all.

There are many extensive forests, in which fir and pine are commoner than other trees. Most notable are the forest of the Ardennes and the Black Forest. Though the forest of the Ardennes is regarded as being in France it begins from the banks of the Rhine. The Black Forest begins in Switzerland and stretches along the Danube among many different peoples; it is written that it is more than nine hard days ride across and forty long; where we rode, however, it seemed to us to be patchy and not very wide. There are many cultivated fields, and though they do not grow much wheat and barley they harvest quantities of rye and oats as well as vegetables, apart from chick peas which we never saw. There are many small red cattle, also sheep and pigs, but fewer of these because in my opinion the continual snows make it impossible to rear sheep, and they only eat the flesh of pigs salted. The cheeses are not particularly good largely because the Germans only like cheese that has gone off. They have a high opinion of a green cheese which is flavoured with the juice of herbs so that it is sharp and aromatic; no Italian would eat it. As for fruit, we found good wild cherries and large numbers of apple and pear trees everywhere, though they were not ripe; also some plum trees.

Though the women are clean housekeepers, they are usually extremely dirty as to their persons and dress themselves alike, in the coarsest materials. Still, they are good-looking and pleasant, and according to the men we had with us they are libidinous in spite of being temperamentally cold. As long as flowers are in season the young girls wear wreaths contrived of various coloured ones on their heads, especially on festival days, and so do schoolboys and the boys who serve in the churches. The women go barefoot for the most part, even those who have shoes do not wear stockings. Neither are their skirts, all of them being short and narrow, long enough to cover their legs. They do their hair in braids wound about their heads and over this wear pleated scarves and caps: all this on account of the great cold there. Wealthy and upper class women wear a sort of very wide folded cloth on their heads, and over this a closely woven veil of delicate samite of the purest white over it which is secured and arranged in certain folds giving a most majestic appearance; the veils of those who keep vigil or are in mourning hang three or four spans down their backs. All wear gowns,[1] for the most part of black serge, occasionally of silk. It is their custom to rise to their feet and do a reverence when they see strangers and men of rank passing, especially foreigners. Each inn has three or four young and pretty maidservants. Though you do not kiss them as you do chambermaids in France, you shake hands not only with them but with the hostess and her daughters; you can put your arm round their waists and even give them a hug. They often sit down to drink [with the customers] and use who knows what freedom in their speech, and they let themselves be handled, but only over their clothes. Both women and men go to church frequently, each family having its own pew, so that all the churches are furnished in this way with the pews ranged on one side and the other with a narrow space in the middle as in the public schools. The choir is left free exclusively for the priests. They do not talk business or make merry in church as in Italy; they simply pay attention and follow the mass and the other divine services and say their prayers all kneeling.

Throughout Germany as a whole there are very beautiful fountains and many watercourses which work mills. Fish from lakes and rivers and good trout are always available; there is no innkeeper who does not have one or two fish tanks in front of

---

[1] 'Gonnella': a skirt with bodice attached to it.

his inn, made of wood and locked with a key. The fish are kept alive in them and water from a fountain flows in and out in such a way that they remain alive and in excellent condition for a long time.

The Cardinal was visited by the local authorities and given presents of wine, fish and fodder in all the free states and also in the two Swiss cantonal capitals we passed through; it is, however, their custom to do this with all lords, spiritual as well as temporal, who come by. At intervals of an Italian mile, or perhaps closer, crosses of stone, wood or iron set on well-made columns of stone or wood are set up from Verona as far as Trent. From Trent onwards they place very tall and large crucifixes by all the roads near villages, towns and cities standing in the open air; most of these have the thieves at the sides and induce, indeed, no less fear than devotion. And at short intervals from one another wooden or stone [shrines] have been built with an embrasure containing crucifixes with the two Marys or other symbols of the most holy passion of our saviour Jesus Christ. You rarely see a picture of a saint in Germany which does not contain some reference to the passion. Their houses, although commonly of wood, are beautiful and striking on the outside and by no means lacking in comfort within. It is very common to have very fine bow windows, two or three sided, so that they can easily watch everything passing along the street; these are all painted and covered with coloured tiles bearing coats of arms and figures of saints very finely done. The doors of these houses, notably the main doors opening on the street, are either made entirely of iron or of very strong wood reinforced with many strips of iron painted some in red, some in green, others in blue or yellow. The house roofs, like those of the churches, are steep and very decorative, those of the houses being covered with ordinary tiles and those of the churches with a kind of small clay tile tinted in various colours and highly glazed so that they make a very lovely sight from a distance. The bell towers of the churches are tall and very narrow. They have very beautiful bells and there is no village, however small, that does not have at least one fine church with glazed windows as large, beautiful and skilfully worked as can be imagined. Only important and rich men are buried inside the churches, all the others are buried outside in cemeteries which are open to the sky but closed in with walls. They contain many crosses and some of the graves have a stone carved with letters and brass coats of arms and have posts in the middle with little pots of holy water fixed to them. They pay such attention to divine worship and to their churches and build so many new ones that when I think of the state of religion that obtains in Italy and how many of the poorer churches there are dilapidated and ruinous I feel no little envy of this region and am pained to the heart by the scant devotion of us Italians.

The German men are for the most part tall, well proportioned, strong and fresh complexioned. All from an early age carry arms and there is not a city or town which does not have a place set aside where customarily on every festival day they shoot with crossbows or handguns and practice with pikes and all the other kinds of arms they employ. Everywhere we came upon an infinite number of wheels and gibbets which are no less ornate as structures – for indeed they are decoratively and sumptuously built – than they are replete with hanged men, as well as a number of condemned women. From this you can see that justice is severely administered, which is doubtless most necessary in such regions. For as all the members of the aristocracy live outside the cities in their castles, which are built in extremely strong locations and serve as places of refuge for many scoundrels, if justice were not so strictly enforced life would be impossible there. Yet for all that, outside the county of Tirol there are numerous murders. In this connection it is worth noting that throughout Germany, especially in the free towns, government is in the hands of wealthy citizens of authority while the men of noble blood reside, as I have said, in their castles or in some suitable residence on their lands, coming into town once or twice a month. And the government and justice of the citizens is of so severe a nature that in recent years in Nuremberg, according to what we gathered there, there were two outstanding examples. The first: it is their custom to tax at so much per cent according to the financial situation and needs of the community, and the sum is left, upon oath, to the conscience of each citizen who has to put the appropriate sum in a certain chest reserved for this purpose which has multiple locks. One year the officials in charge came to suspect that one of the richest men, but one who bore a bad reputation, had cheated on his contribution and had thus perjured himself. So they arranged it that in order to betray himself he should be the first to put his contribution in the aforesaid chest. And when the fraud and the perjury were

82

revealed, at once and in public they had his right hand cut off and neither his family connections nor the extent of his riches could delay or corrupt this judgement.[1] The other: Nuremberg being at war with the Marquis of Brandenburg, as I related at the appropriate place, an evilly disposed citizen, prompted by some grievance, openly joined him and on several occasions accompanied the Marquis's men when raiding the city's territories. The then governors or magistrates, anticipating that this evil citizen would be going to a certain place nearby took steps to secure him and when orders had been given to this effect one of the magistrates, who was related to him, warned him by letter or through a messenger that he should avoid being taken or things would go ill for him. When this came to be known to his colleagues, and they had verified it, the magistrate was at once seized and was assigned indefinitely to a tower in the city wall where no one has spoken to him to this day, nor has he seen the light, nor will he. And we were shown the tower which contained his prison.

The torture of the wheel is the one in which two planks stretched on the ground are placed under the arms of a man condemned to death. The executioner or torturer breaks one arm after the other with blows from a wooden wheel and then both legs in the same way, ending by breaking the back in the middle with the wheel. Broken in this way and hoisted on the wheel to the height of a great beam fixed in the ground, the man miserably breathes his last.[2] Such a death is indeed very cruel, for many such unfortunates have been left alive for two or three days to increase the penalty and the publicity of so horrible a spectacle. In one place we found a whole field planted with these wheels, each with its body on top.

From Cologne begins the general use of fireplaces in rooms and large windows suited to the summer, as opposed to the very small

---

[1] This custom was used by Machiavelli (*Discorsi*, lib. 1, c. 55) to prove that in Germany 'the ancient virtue still in great part prevails'. He did not mention Nuremberg in this connection, nor mention the perjurer. Celtis does not mention the custom (see Bibliography). De Beatis's story of the cheat appears to derive from a case that arose in 1469 and may still have been current gossip in 1517 as the exception that proves the rule. It is described in Gerald Strauss, *Nuremberg in the sixteenth century* (New York, 1966) 92.

[2] The interested reader can clarify this account from the detailed description made in 1616 by John Taylor, who witnessed such an execution at Hamburg. Johann Janssen, *History of the German people at the close of the Middle Ages* (17 vols., London, 1896–1925) xvi, 208–9.

ones used in Germany. Different manners and a different tongue; better clothes and great cleanliness. The women and the men are better-looking than in high Germany.

The Imperial electors are six: the three prelates of Mainz, Cologne and Trier; three secular princes, the Count Palatine, the duke of Saxony and the marquis of Brandenburg; and if they do not agree they are joined by the King of Bohemia.

Flanders, Holland and Brabant.[1]

July 1. From Cologne, where we stayed two days, we went to lunch and dinner to a small town called Jülich, a duchy six miles away. On the way there is only a place with a few lodgings.

July 2. From Jülich we went for lunch to Aix-la-Chapelle, four miles away, a town built by Charlemagne and very fine, large and strong. Here there is a church dedicated to St Mary, round in form and surrounded by a pillared and vaulted arcade. This too was built by Charlemagne. It is small but very beautiful. His body rests there under a small arch in the wall on the right side of the high altar, in a marble chest the front of which is carved with figures and horses in perfect relief; you can judge from this that it is antique. It is seven spans long and about four high, with two grills the size of the arch from top to bottom. His statue is above the tomb, with a cross in one hand and an orb in the other. I think it is of a wooden material, but not, I was told, of natural wood. In the floor of the same church there is also the tomb of Henry IV.[2] The head and arm of the aforesaid Charlemagne are in the sacristy, enclosed in silver; they are venerated as relics, and indeed this emperor led a holy life and brought great benefit to the Christian faith. In this sacresty we also saw the horn of Roland.[3] In the church the canons have built a very beautiful semi-cupola or tribune where they have brought the high altar and they have made a most beautiful choir. And in the middle of the space under the dome of the old church they have made a great tabernacle of stone carved with reliefs and

---

[1] Editor's heading.   [2] In fact, of Otto III (d. 1202).

[3] According to the Chanson de Roland, in its eleventh century and subsequent versions, Roland died summoning Charlemagne to assist the Christian army at Roncevaux with this horn. De Beatis's reference to the treachery of Ganelon (who had alerted the Saracens to the weakness of Roland's force) on p. 115 is a second indication of the power the Charlemagne legend still exerted, and its propagation by the custodians of more genuine Carolingian relics.

very beautiful figures. In this they have placed the following relics: the shift of the Madonna; the loincloth worn by our lord on the cross; St Joseph's stockings; and the blood-stained cloth in which the head of John the Baptist was wrapped when it was given to the dancer Herodias.[1] And there are many other relics which are shown every seven years on the day of the seven holy brothers,[2] which is on July 10th., with a plenary indulgence and, as they call it, a jubilee. I gather that this does not have apostolic sanction; Pope Alexander VI[3] had decided to do away with it altogether but the devotion was of such antiquity that it was not possible, and so it continues. As a result, on this septennial there is such a concourse of gypsies that the air stinks for many miles around. This year, in which the septennial falls, we found an infinite number of them in Cologne, where on St Peter's day they saw all the relics there which I have described. And though they have a longer overland journey to get to Aix-la-Chapelle than they would to Rome, they come here in greater numbers. From Aix-la-Chapelle we went to spend the night at Maastricht, which is four miles away.

Maastricht is a sizeable walled town, and though the house fronts are all wood they are large and well built and make a fine sight. Inside they are most comfortable. The streets are very wide and well paved; the squares very beautiful. A river called the Maas passes through the middle of the town, of a good width and navigable for twenty-five German miles towards Burgundy, where it has its source. It ends in Holland, where it joins the Rhine. There is a fine stone bridge over it, and though the town belongs to the Catholic King as ruler of Flanders, beyond the bridge the civil and spiritual authority belongs to the bishop of Liège, and the town as a whole is in the diocese of Liège. The main church, which is built in a fine square on the other side of the bridge, is dedicated to St Gervase[4] and is large and very beautiful. It has a steeply raised choir beneath which is a beautiful vaulted crypt with columns made of local stone. The body of the aforesaid St Gervase lies there. In the choir is an enormous paschal candle made with the highest possible skill in so varied a way that I have never seen one like it, or more beautiful.

---

[1] Salome was the dancer, asking for the Baptist's head as a reward at Herodias's instance.
[2] The sons of St Felicitas, martyred together in the mid-second century.
[3] Alexander Borgia, Pope 1492–1503.
[4] An error; it was dedicated to St Servatius, the first bishop of Maastricht. But phonetically, 'Servaas' would suggest 'Gervasii'.

July 3. From Maastricht we went to lunch and dine to Diest, seven leagues away. It is a fine, large and strong walled town and the women are mostly very lovely.

July 4. From Diest we went to lunch and dine at Louvain, a sizeable walled town containing numerous canals which rise and fall with the tides of the ocean. It has fine streets and squares. A large and very fine church[1] which has a beautiful organ. In the main square we saw a town hall as fine as any seen in the rest of our travels, pleasingly constructed in stone carved on the exterior from top to bottom with very delicate and most ingeniously contrived foliage, one band of carving above another as the manner is in those parts. There is a university with all faculties and the townspeople say that it has about six thousand students. We also saw a fine brass tomb being made for the bishop of Cambrai who is still alive.[2] At a bowshot outside the gate Monsignor de Chièvres[3] has a fine palace as well as another inside the town where his nephew the Cardinal de Croy (or of Cambrai as he is called, being the coadjutor of the bishop there) was then staying.[4]

July 5. From Louvain we went to lunch at Malines, four leagues away. It is a very large walled town, very strong and fine, with the broadest and most beautiful streets we had yet seen, paved with small stones placed upright and sloping towards the sides so that they retain no water or mud. The chief church[5] is very beautiful, with a square in front of it longer and much wider than the Campo dei Fiori in Rome; this too is paved in the same way as the streets. Inside the town are many canals with tidal waters, for they eventually reach the sea. Margaret, daughter of the Emperor and aunt to the Catholic King has a residence there;[6] she spends most of her time there or in Brussels. From Malines we went to dine in Antwerp, four leagues away. And an Italian mile away from Malines

---

[1] Probably St Peter's, which faces the town hall.

[2] The bishop, Jacques de Croy, had died in 1516; perhaps de Beatis means that he ordered the tomb (cf. Maximilian) while still alive.

[3] Guillaume de Croy, Sieur de Chièvres, had played a key role in the early political education of Charles as Archduke of Burgundy both before 1515, when he came of age, and subsequently. In 1517 he was High Chamberlain of Charles's household.

[4] Also named Guillaume, he was the nephew of the High Chamberlain. De Beatis describes how he was given his cardinal's hat, below, p. 89.

[5] Saint-Rombaut, the cathedral.

[6] After the death of her husband, the Duke of Savoy, she became Regent of the Netherlands during Charles's minority, 1507–15. Later in this July, on the eve of Charles's departure for Spain, her constitutional position with relation to the governing council was left vague, but she was reconfirmed as regent in 1519 and died in that office in 1530.

we had to take a boat to cross a river which flows into a branch of the sea; it is tidal and flows past the walls of Antwerp.[1]

Antwerp is a large and very populous town and according to the account of the Italian merchants who reside there, of whom there are not a few, it is no smaller than our Italian Bologna. Fine streets, squares and houses, for the most part of stone, and a most beautiful church with a tower which will be almost a match for that of Strasbourg when it is finished.[2] Running through it are a number of very wide canals. There is a fair which starts on the day of Pentecost and lasts for a month and a half and as much longer as they want to keep it going. It is without doubt the foremost in Christendom for all kinds of merchandise, and there is another one like it in September. We arrived towards the end of the Pentecost one, and though the Hollanders had left because the Duke of Guelders had invaded and burnt a considerable town,[3] we found such a crowd of people and such a quantity, variety and richness of goods that we were struck with astonishment. An arm of the sea comes past Antwerp, as I said. It is an Italian mile across and is joined by a large river[4] which separates Brabant, which begins at Cologne or, as many say, at Aix-la-Chapelle, from Flanders. There is a fine harbour with an infinite number of ships in it and a fine semi-circular quay built out into water which is so deep that ships no matter how big can moor alongside it; and it is well paved for ease in loading and discharging merchandise from them. In the fish market one morning apart from great quantities of sea fish and salmon there were forty-six sturgeon, some of them so big that one of their carts, which are by no means small, would not have been able to carry more than two.

July 10. From Antwerp, where we stayed four days, we left after lunch to spend the night at Bergen op Zoom, six leagues away. A very fine walled town, it belongs to the prince of Bergen and is in the diocese of Cambrai.

July 11. After Bergen op Zoom, where we left our horses, we embarked at a harbour almost an Italian mile away where there

---

[1] The Scheldt. The higher rise and fall of oceanic tides was commonly remarked on by Mediterranean travellers.

[2] The north tower of Notre-Dame, the cathedral, was not completed until 1530.

[3] Charles of Egmond's resentment at Habsburg domination in the Netherlands had already led him in 1511 to send an army to raid in Holland. De Beatis refers to an incursion that plundered its way from Medemblik to Asperen before being checked. The attitude of Egmond was one of the chief factors that had delayed Charles's sailing for Spain.

[4] The Scheldt.

were many boats and other craft; the arm of the sea is nearly three Italian miles across there, and a number of channels flow from it into the town. We took only two cobs with us for my lord's use and embarked between 13 and 14 o'clock, having waited for the tide, as one must when sailing in these channels and inlets neighbouring the ocean. And because the wind was contrary we only just managed to reach the island called Zeeland where the Catholic King was staying: we had to land with difficulty on the dikes and all ride along them in carriages for two Italian miles to the end of a certain tongue of land opposite a walled town called Veere or Campveere which is sited at the very tip of this island of Zeeland. We got there later than three o'clock at night in a boat from a Biscayan ship. The bishop of Cordoba,[1] chaplain-major to His Highness came with us.

July 12. From Veere we went by carriage early in the morning to Middelburg, a town in the island where the Catholic King was waiting for an opportunity to embark for Spain. Because of the presence of the Catholic King we stayed ten days in this town, which is large, fine and strong; a wide channel enters deep into it. And on the day Monsignor arrived, which was a Sunday, he [the Cardinal] went to call on His Majesty accompanied by the prior of Castile, the Marquis of Pescara and the bishops of Cordoba and Badajoz together with many other Spanish and Italian knights and lords, notably the Neapolitan ambassadors who were then at the court.[2] The Cardinal was received with the greatest honour and favour by His Majesty and we accompanied him to sung mass in the Benedictine monastery which is attached to the palace where he was staying. This palace, which has many very comfortable rooms and a spacious courtyard planted with carefully spaced lime trees, belongs to the monastery. After a mass of the Holy Spirit, sung by the prior or abbot of the monastery, mitred and holding his cross, and with music provided by the Catholic King's singers, His Majesty and our most illustrious

[1] Michel Pavye.

[2] Born in Naples of Spanish parents, Ferdinand, Marquis of Pescara (1489-1525), though spending his life as a *condottiere* in Italy, was one of those many born in southern Italy who thought of themselves as Spaniards and who, from Charles's accession to the crown of Aragon in 1516, looked on him as their natural sovereign. Together with the envoys from Naples (six, accompanied by about one hundred prominent Neapolitans) his presence gave a pronouncedly Italian flavour to the ceremony surrounding Charles's departure. The Bishop of Badajoz was Alonso de Manrique. Both he and the Bishop of Cordoba, though Spaniards, had long been at Charles's court in the Netherlands.

Monsignor (who had been in the same little 'chapel', the usual silk curtained enclosure, with him though on a neighbouring bench) rose and went in front of the high altar where the Count of San Bonifacio,[1] a Paduan, apostolic treasurer and nuncio, delivered a Latin address and presented the papal brief to the bishop of Badajoz. Having read this aloud the bishop administered the formal oath and handed the red hat to the Lord of Chièvre's nephew who was thus to be known as Cardinal of Croy or Cambrai. He was seventeen or eighteen years old and a Benedictine. He made a fine Latin oration expressing his gratitude first to the Divine Majesty and the Apostolic See, then to the Catholic King and his uncle with great sincerity and tenderness and with tears. After this function, His Majesty, accompanied not only by the Flemish and Spanish lords but by the Margrave of Brandenburg and the Count Palatine (that is, not the Imperial Electors themselves, but their brothers who are promising young German lords), and together with our illustrious Monsignor and the newly created Cardinal returned to his lodging and the two Cardinals dined with him.[2] His Majesty was accompanied by a Flemish halbardier, of twenty years and quite beardless, who was the tallest and best proportioned man who could ever be seen. Next day the Cardinal called upon Milady Margaret,[3] his Imperial Majesty's daughter, a person of about thirty five, I would say, not ugly at all, and of a great and truly imperial presence; she has a certain most pleasing way of laughing. She spoke a good while with the Cardinal, in excellent Spanish. And on the same day he called upon Milady Eleanora, the Catholic King's sister, who is about nineteen or twenty years old and very pleasant.[4] I thought the Catholic King seemed very young, seventeen or eighteen,[5] and although he has a long, cadaverous face and a lopsided mouth (which drops open when he is not on his guard) with a drooping lower lip, his aspect nonetheless has decorum, grace and great majesty in it. As

[1] Lodovico da S. Bonifacio, referred to by Castiglione in *The Courtier* as a student of the Neoplatonist philosopher Beroaldo, an active papal diplomatist, especially under Leo X, canon of Padua since 1514.

[2] With the new cardinal. For a fuller description of this ceremony, with references to the Cardinal of Aragon. see Vital, op. cit., 33–6.

[3] See note on p. 86.

[4] She was eighteen. Later married first Emanuel of Portugal and then Francis I. For her this stay at Middelburg was a temporary tragedy; in love with her passionate suitor, Frederick, Count Palatine, the liaison was detected and broken off by Charles, who needed her for a more important dynastic match.

[5] Born 24 February 1500, Charles was seventeen.

for his physique he is tall and splendidly built, with a neat, straight leg, the finest you ever saw in one of his rank, and in our master's opinion – he is a judge of these matters – he is no mean horseman. Each day he usually attends two masses, said and then sung. He eats very sparingly and always – I saw this on many occasions – alone, although in public. I do not know what he does nowadays, but he did not then dine with great ceremony; immediately after lunch or dinner His Majesty graciously gave audience to anyone where he sat at the head of the table, though the bishop of Badajoz, a Catalan, who attended him as his interpreter in all tongues, emphasized that now His Majesty did not speak or give an answer to everyone who petitioned him. On the 17th the Cardinal paid another visit to His Majesty and spent an hour with him in private, and on the 21st he took his leave of him and the two aforementioned ladies.

July 22. Early in the morning the Cardinal and the others left Middelburg in carriages[1] to embark at a port a league away called Flushing, whence the Catholic King later[2] left for Spain. This port is a sizeable town and what with Biscayan, English, Portuguese, Flemish and Breton vessels there were about 300 sail, not to mention a few smaller ships and certain covered boats – of which there were an infinite number – called sloops. We heard mass there, and having lunched embarked for Holland and went to stay the night at a town called Dordrecht which is walled, very fine and has 3,000 hearths; it is at the tip of the island of Holland on that side. I call it an island because it has the sea on one side and for the rest it is cut off by two narrow canals, crossed by two bridges. The waters from the Rhine and Maas flow into them, mingling and passing out into the arms of the sea which lead to the ocean.

July 23. From Dordrecht we crossed the Rhine, which flows past the walls, by boat. The extent or width of the river is about half an Italian mile. There we got into carriages. A league away is a town called Rotterdam, the native city of Erasmus, a man deeply versed in Greek and Latin, who has produced many volumes of writing in every branch of learning.[3] The city is very fine and has 1,800 hearths, and we lunched there. After eating we climbed into

---

[1] 'Carrecte': the word is used for a passenger vehicle of any design.
[2] On 8 September.
[3] In this month Erasmus moved to make Louvain his base for a number of years.

our carriages again and after another two leagues we came to another very fine town called Delft, which has about 5,000 hearths, and in the main parish church there we saw the arm of the Magdalen. The town contains many deep and broad canals. At three o'clock German time, which is nineteen hours Italian time,[1] we got again into our carriages and left there and after a league came to an unwalled town called The Hague, as fine as any in the world and worthy of comparison with any other city, no matter how large and fine. And though Holland as a whole contains the best looking women in Flanders, here they are particularly beautiful. It contains about 6,000 hearths. In this town we saw a very fine palace belonging to the Catholic King with a lake in front of it; also a fine church. And we spent the night there. That day we covered six leagues.

July 24. From there we returned to hear mass in Rotterdam, passing through Delft. We went the whole way by carriage and lunched in Rotterdam. Three leagues further on we came to a very fine town called Gouda, with about 4,000 hearths. An extremely large canal passes through it where there are always an infinite number of boats of all sizes. And three leagues from there, still by carriage, we reached and passed through another very fine town called Schoonhoven, and after another three leagues we reached a fine town of some 3,000 hearths called Gorinchem. This part of Holland ends at this point, and we took to boats to travel a league on the waters of the Rhine and the Maas, which, as I have said, come together here. On the left hand of the rivers lies the country of Guelders and on the right is Brabant. And after this league, which we travelled by water from fear of the Duke of Guelders who was in the neighbourhood with his troops, we came to a town called Workum on the riverside. It is neither large nor fine and belongs to the Count of Orna. An arrow's flight away is a strong castle[2] of the Catholic King's which stands on the border of this country of Guelders. In the aforesaid town of Rotterdam there are more than 300 ships and far more than 1,000 in the rest of the island. On the day we spent the night in Workum we travelled thirteen leagues.

---

[1] There was no standard way of counting the hours. In this case 'Italian' time is what has become the modern 24-hour cycle from midnight, 'German' time is based on 12-hour cycles based on midsummer nightfall – 10 p.m. (modern time), the hour at which town gates were shut. [2] Loevestein.

July 25. After hearing mass, we left Workum in carriages and went for lunch to a place called Loon op Zand[1] four leagues away. After lunch we continued another three leagues by carriage to a very fine town belonging to the Count of Nassau[2] called Breda and spent the night there. This town has 2,000 hearths. There we looked at the chief parish church, which is fine, and spaced around it are thirteen very tall, bare and many-branched trees, each branch containing five or six herons'[3] nests with great numbers of young birds. The old ones behaved in a very parental way to them and it made a very pleasing sight. And there are also herons' nests on top of the roofs of the neighbouring houses. When the young birds grow up they leave, but then each year they come back and make their nests in the same spot, and no one does anything to disturb them, so one can say that there are more herons in that one place than in ten other places where they gather in large numbers. We spent the whole of the 26th there waiting for the horses we had left in Bergen when we embarked for Zeeland. Bergen is eight leagues from Breda, where we saw a castle belonging to the aforesaid count of Nassau, extremely fine with a very large garden, three quarters of it planted with many fruit trees of the sort that grow in this country, so well laid out that it could have been in Italy.

July 27. From Breda we rode to lunch and dinner in Antwerp [Anversa], in Flemish called Antiverpia according to its Latin name, Amverpia.

July 29. We spent a day in Antwerp and then went for lunch and dinner to Malines, four leagues away. And to make up for the first time, when we simply stayed for a meal and then went straight on, we examined practically the whole town, which is superior to all the other towns of Brabant and Flanders from the points of view of site, buildings, streets and everything else belonging to a town. Three or four canals flow through it, deep and all navigable. There is also a fine large church with a very large square in front of it as I noted before when we passed through. We saw Princess Margaret's residence which is very fine and well appointed though not particularly imposing. It has a rich and

---

[1] A detour presumably caused by the presence of troops across the main Gorinchem–Breda road.

[2] Henry III, b. 1483, Stadthouder from 1515 of Holland, Zeeland and Friesland.

[3] Sic, but perhaps storks.

highly decorated library for women. The books are all written in French and bound in velvet with silver-gilt clasps. There are also fine panel paintings and other pictures by different artists, all of them good masters. There are marble heads of the late Duke of Savoy, her husband, of happy memory, which shows that he was an extremely handsome youth, as he is said to have been, and of her highness when a young girl, made with the greatest skill and giving, they say, an excellent likeness. In this town they make all sorts of crossbows extremely well, stocks and bows as well as bindings, sheaths, cranequins and all necessary equipment. The Cardinal had already ordered a large number[1] which reached him later in Rome. The Cardinal with a few others went to dine and spend the night at a place belonging to the Catholic King's grand falconer, two Italian miles away. This is a very roomy and fine palace situated in a country area, an excellent place for partridges. It is surrounded by water and you enter over a drawbridge. The Cardinal dined excellently and the grand falconer, who is called Johan Aa,[2] is a most pleasant man of some sixty years.

July 30. Leaving Malines, we joined the Cardinal and the others who had been with him at the aforesaid palace and went on with him to lunch and dinner in Brussels, four leagues away. Two leagues out of Malines we came to a rather sparsely inhabited village called Vilvorde where there is a fine castle.

Brussels is a very large town and a fine one. Part of it lies in the plain and part on a hill and it is the capital of Brabant. We saw the town hall with its massive tall tower facing a spacious square paved, as is the general custom in these parts, with certain small stones which create a very pleasing effect. This palace is so commodious that you could easily ride all over it on horseback. It contains thirty-six fountains, some of which rise to half the height of the tower. There is an especially fine fountain in the square and according to the burgomaster, the principal official in all walled towns in both Upper and Lower Germany (the office changes hands each year), there are 350 of them in the town as a whole. We also saw the Catholic King's palace where his father King Philip[3] was born. It contains a large and very lofty hall where

---

[1] Finely made and embellished crossbows were much prized among wealthy huntsmen.
[2] Perhaps Jean Vander Aa, of Louvain, father of the scholar Pierre Vander Aa.
[3] Duke (not King) of Burgundy from 1482 to 1506. The palace was destroyed by fire in 1731 and the remains later cleared to make the Place Royale.

they joust without saddles when the weather is too bad for jousting outside in the great square in front of the palace. Beside it lies a great park with stags and goats and other animals, and a garden made in the form of a huge maze with many rooms and paths over two paces wide and walls twelve spans high closely plaited and woven from certain shoots which are found in the depths of woods; they bear leaves like those of the hazel but smoother and shinier and the effect is most beautiful. There is also a fine tennis court surrounded by sloping half-roofs and beneath these and over the walls (for the game is played in a sunken area) large numbers of spectators can look at the game. They use rackets and play very well. We also saw the Count of Nassau's palace which is on rising ground, though he himself lives in the level part near the square with the Catholic King's. The palace is very large and fine in the German style, such as we saw and is known to exist throughout the two Germanies. It has a spacious courtyard, a large number of rooms and a fine façade. It is panelled throughout and small rooms and as many extremely large ones are panelled up to the vaults with oak planks carved in wavy lines to look like camlet, as I shall say later on. In the palace are very beautiful paintings, among others a Hercules and Deianeira, naked figures of considerable size, and the story of Paris with the three goddesses most perfectly done. Then there are some panel paintings of various bizarre themes where seas, skies, woods, the countryside are simulated, together with figures who emerge from a mussel shell, others who defecate cranes; and men and women, white and black, with different postures and expressions, birds, animals of all kinds rendered with great naturalness, things so pleasing and so fantastic that they could not be properly described in any way to those who do not know them.[1] There are some rooms where we noticed a most ingenious secret device: a niche in a corner, carefully decorated and constructed in the same wood I have mentioned, which also serves to conceal a door leading into another room in such a way that if it were not pointed out you would never have guessed that there was a door there at all. There is also a large room

---

[1] Gombrich, in the article cited in the note on p. 10, suggests that the Hercules and Deianeira 'is very probably the painting by Mabuse now in the Barber Institute in Birmingham. Dated 1517, it was probably one of the latest acquisitions then on view'. He identifies the panels de Beatis goes on to describe with Bosch's Garden of Delight in the Prado, and notes that the value of this description is that it 'confirms once more Bosch's popularity among noble collectors'.

containing a bed 34 spans *di canna*[1] broad and 26 spans long with
bolsters at the head and the foot, sheets and a white quilt, and we
gathered that the Count had it made because he liked to hold
frequent banquets and to see his guests get drunk, and when they
could no longer stand on their feet, he had them thrown on to
this bed. We also saw a splendid kitchen there in the middle of
which was a vast fireplace, divided by a wall two rods high, in
such a way that a fire could be made against either side and thus
two fires could readily be used at the same time. Here in Brussels,
Pope Leo is having 16 tapestries made, chiefly in silk and gold.
They are said to be for the chapel of Sixtus in the apostolic palace
in Rome. Each piece costs 2,000 gold ducats. We went to the place
where they were being made and saw a completed piece showing
Christ's delivery of the keys to St Peter, which is very beautiful.
Judging from this one, the Cardinal gave it as his opinion that they
will be among the finest in Christendom.[2] This town contains
more than 8,000 hearths and the former archdukes used to stay
there with pleasure because the game is abundant, the water
excellent and the air fresh because, as I said, it lies on a hill.

July 31. From Brussels we went to lunch and dinner in Ghent,
a journey of ten leagues, and three leagues from Brussels we came
to a place called Asse, belonging to the Count of Nassau, and two
leagues further on to a very fine town called Aalst which belongs
to the Catholic King and is in Brabant.

August 1. We stayed in Ghent, the capital of Flanders. The town
is very fine and larger than all the others, containing about 20,000
hearths, and is more than three times as large around as Naples,
as we could easily see from the tower, where there is a very fine
clock. It is climbed by a spiral staircase of more than 300 steps.
The Cardinal and all the rest of us went up. It is not all inhabited,
however, for it contains meadows and many gardens, and though
it is not walled it is surrounded and protected on all sides by three
rivers which render it extremely strong; there is a fourth but this
joins one of the others a little way outside the town. They are called
the Lys, the Scheldt, the Lieve and the Moere. The Catholic King

[1] The Roman *canna* contained either eight spans (for measuring cloth) or ten (for
building measurements). De Beatis perhaps uses the phrase to mean that it was measured
in his presence with a measuring staff; the bed was an object of intense interest to visitors.
[2] The first set of tapestries has been transferred from the Sistine Chapel to the Vatican
art gallery; the cartoons from which they were woven are in the Victoria and Albert
Museum, London.

was born and brought up there and there is a university. In the very fine chief parish church, called St John's,[1] is a raised and very extensive chancel with a graceful crypt of the same size beneath containing many chapels. On the right side of this is a chapel with a panel painting whose two outer sides have two nude figures of almost life size, Adam on the right and Eve on the left, done in oils with such perfection and truth to life both as to the proportions and colouring of the parts of the body and to the use of light and shade that one has no hesitation in saying that this is the finest painting in Christendom. According to the canons there they were done a hundred years ago by a High German master called Robert and they look today as though they were fresh from the master's hand. The subject of this work is the Ascension of the Madonna. As the master's death prevented him from finishing it, it was completed by his brother who was also a great painter.[2] The town contains many parishes and has two large abbeys; part of it lies in the diocese of Cambrai and part in that of Tournai. As I have said, the town is very strong and impregnable, for when they want they can flood and cover the country for a league around. And the river Lys, which is very large, runs through the middle and there are a number of fine stone bridges over it. We saw the Catholic King's palace there.[3] It is surrounded by water and approached by a bridge where there are several lions, one of which, a male lion, is of a very great size, larger in the opinion of the Cardinal and all the others than any of those to be found in Florence.[4]

August 2. From Ghent to lunch and dinner at Bruges, a distance of eight leagues. We came through many other places on the way but none of much account.

Though not among the largest, Bruges is one of the finest towns in Flanders. It is in the diocese of Tournai. Certainly its streets, squares and every other feature make it extremely magnificent. There are many wide navigable canals with very fine stone bridges. The war it was involved in with the Emperor because they

---

[1] Re-dedicated to St Bavon in 1540.

[2] De Beatis shows that the altarpiece was then in the crypt, under the chapel in the raised chancel where it is now. The canons appear to have misread 'Hubert' for Robert in the inscription of 1432 which said that the work had been completed on his death [in 1426] by his brother Jan van Eyck. He has also mistaken the main subject, which is The Adoration of the Lamb; the Virgin merely appears beside Christ the King in the upper row of panels.

[3] The Château des Comtes.

[4] Where lions were had long been, and still were, kept as civic emblems and curiosities.

held his son (the present Emperor, then lord of Flanders through his wife's dowry) prisoner, lasted many years and brought considerable ruin. It also lost it the trade fair, which was transferred to Antwerp,[1] which is why that town has become so rich and important; nevertheless there are many merchants and there is a great deal of craft and industrial activity, cloths, the finest hats, either shaggy or clipped, that can be found anywhere in the world, and wool which bears comparison with silk. It is three leagues from the sea, and though there is a channel leading from the sea used by a large number of boats, as nothing has been spent on it during the many years since the fair was transferred, large ships cannot get through it. We were there for so short a time, leaving early in the morning, that we did not see more than a few things with any care, but we did visit the church of Our Lady where there is the tomb of the Empress Maria, mother of King Philip and wife of the Emperor Maximilian; it is of gilt brass and is finely worked.

August 3. From Bruges we went for lunch and dinner to Nieuwpoort, seven leagues away, passing many villages and farms at intervals on the way: four leagues from Bruges is a walled town called Imbruch.[2] Nieuwpoort is on the ocean sea and belongs to the Catholic King. It has some thousand hearths and is large in circuit though a great deal of it is not built up.

August 4. From Nieuwpoort to lunch and dinner at Gravelines, a walled town belonging to Madame de Vendôme,[3] eight leagues away; this lady is French, but it is within the jurisdiction of the Catholic King as lord of Flanders. It is small and unpleasing but has a fine church. A league out of Nieuwpoort we rode along the beach, half an Italian mile down the sand as it was low tide, which

---

[1] Maximilian gained Flanders though his marriage – arranged by the Emperor Frederick III – to Mary of Burgundy. On Mary's death in 1482 a reaction against Habsburg rule brought Maximilian to reassert his authority in Flanders against the rival claim of France, supported by local separatist passions. Years of confusion and local warfare followed and in 1488 the citizens of Bruges, mainly to protect themselves from a German army raised by Frederick, shut their gates with Maximilian inside, virtually imprisoning him. When released, Maximilian's reaction was to favour Bruges' rival, Antwerp, especially by encouraging German firms, like Fugger and Welser, to operate there, but there was no compulsory closing of the fair; the natural geographical advantage of Antwerp, and the burgeoning economic vitality of its hinterland, in association with the gradual silting of the upper Scheldt, accounted for the shift of importance de Beatis (naturally enough at the time) explained in terms of one political decision.

[2] Thus in text. I cannot locate this place.

[3] Marie, daughter of Peter II of Luxemburg, widow of the Comte de Vendôme who had been enfeoffed with Gravelines by Charles VIII in 1493.

seemed a strange and marvellous thing. We rode five leagues in this way to a town called Dunkirk, also belonging to Madame de Vendôme. Between there and Gravelines we travelled at a little distance from the shore.

August 5. From Gravelines to Calais for lunch and dinner. A bowshot out of Gravelines and not far from the sea you cross a medium sized river by boat; it is only fordable at low tide. It divides Flanders from Picardy, which is under the King of England as far as Calais, and in addition his jurisdiction extends as far as Tournai, for His Majesty, campaigning with his Imperial Majesty, took it from the French in the first year of Leo's pontificate.[1]

Now we have reached Picardy and, as I have said, left Flanders, I think it appropriate that in the same way that I spoke in general terms about the characteristics and customs of Upper Germany earlier on I should not pass over the same topics with regard to Flanders,[2] especially as this is the homeland of our lord the Catholic King.

Flanders is all flat land and apart from Brussels – which as I said is partly hilly – I do not think there are fountains in any of the towns, though there are a number of rivers. The people commonly use wells and in those near the sea and on the island of Zeeland and in Holland the water is soft and half salt. They use the same sort of carts as in Upper Germany. The towns are very clean and for the most part of a pleasing appearance with their streets, squares and churches. Many of the houses have gardens planted with roses, pinks and quantities of lavender or spikenard; lacking the vine they use gooseberries a great deal. Though there are many vines which have been trained to form arbours in gardens and beside the street doors of houses they either produce no fruit, or, if they do, it comes very late and even then has no natural flavour, being good only for verjuice; they have no grapes which will ripen. Most of the house facades are of wood with the other walls of brick, as in Upper Germany, though in Antwerp, Malines, Brussels, Ghent, Bruges and a few other substantial towns there are many houses built throughout of stone and well designed. Those of wood are so skilfully constructed that they do not merely not offend the eye but positively delight it. They use oak for panelling and mouldings in rooms, for doors and windows and

---

[1] See note, p. 63.　　　　[2] Rather, the Netherlands as a whole.

whatever else is made of wood. It is tawny coloured and modelled in folds, like camlet; it is hard and lends itself well to carving. The beds are made of down but are not as large as those in Upper Germany, and they have decorated pieces around and over them made of the same wood, well carved and pierced. And indeed in Flanders, as in Upper Germany they carve stone and wood most skilfully. But there is no oak in Upper Germany[1] and though Italy does have some it is not to be compared with the oak of Flanders which, though it is brought by sea from the direction of Russia and from the mountains,[2] is not worked anywhere else so well as it is in Flanders, especially in certain cupboards which are in all the rooms and are very fine. The whole coast, as we have seen, as well as the rivers and channels running into it, is subject to the rise and fall of the sea, which they call the tide. The roofs are covered with small slabs of black stone[3] which comes from the bank of the Rhine; they make a really beautiful and delicate looking covering, the colour of fine lead. As in Germany the Flemish churches are usually vaulted with the most complex vaults and ribbing that can be imagined. Everywhere there are tall and very narrow bell towers, with fine bells. Their clocks go by twelve hours and twelve, starting from noon, and before they sound the hour certain small bells play three part and well harmonized motets by way of warning; in many places these bells also signal the half-hour. In Germany and Flanders as in all northern regions we found night in summer to be an hour shorter than in Italy. In all the Flemish churches there are chandeliers in the choir and finely made lecterns and other altar furnishings, and there are large numbers of brass tabernacles. Cauldrons, scrapers, pots and other kitchen implements are made of the same metal which comes from England where it is extracted in great quantity and it is the subject of a copious and competitive trade. They have large numbers of cows and sheep but few goats; the pastures are very fine. The cows are much larger than the German ones. Few are red, most having patches of black and white, though some are completely black and others are marked with dark patches so handsomely that they are all that such animals could be desired to be. The sheep's wool looks like silk. And they make good cheese, one of which is like *ravigiolo*

---

[1] Pastor understandably inserts (!). But de Beatis may have seen none on his route.
[2] ? from the Baltic countries, shown as heavily mountainous on contemporary maps.
[3] Slate.

though when it is not fresh but a few days old. There is another very popular green one made, as far as we could find out, with the juices of a number of scented herbs as they do in Upper Germany; it has a very sharp taste. The horses and mules are very large, especially in Holland.

Apart from keeping their bodies and clothes clean, they are so meticulous about not dirtying the floors in their houses that in every room, before you go in, there is a cloth to clean your feet with, and the floors have a dusting of sand. When women have given birth to a male child they let it be known by tying a kerchief to the door knocker (which all the doors have). And any wrong-doer or criminal, even if he had killed a thousand men, who then takes refuge there before the woman goes to be churched forty days after her delivery (as is the custom also in Italy) is quite safe there and cannot be apprehended under any circumstances.[1] Large numbers of brassicas are found throughout Flanders, especially sprouts, and it is said that in Holland some are so large that a single one is enough to stay a man's appetite; in Flanders, as in Germany, they lay in great stores of them, preserved with salt, and in winter when the whole country is covered in snow they eat them with various kinds of seasoning.

The women generally wear a very thin veil of Holland or Cambrai samite on their heads. The panels of their gowns are narrow, so that you see the whole shape of the body, and are mostly of black serge worn over an extra petticoat, and when they are out shopping they lift up the hems in front and behind and secure them to fastenings attached to the belt for this purpose. They are commonly tall and very genial, with a high complexion, pink and white quite without cosmetics, fucus or any artificial aids to beauty at all. They wear well-fitting stockings and slippers two fingers high, a short mantle that just covers the shoulders and some of the old women wear long mantles pleated over the head and with a lappet on the forehead very much like the ones worn by our women in the region of Bari. And married women and gentlewomen also wear long cloaks of black serge gathered across the back like the Italian tertiaries; it is a fine and decorous garment. It has to be admitted, however, that throughout both Flanders and

---

[1] The anonymous Milanese, who also describes the custom of decorating door knockers (ring-shaped, according to him, the kerchief tied to the top if a boy child, to the bottom if a girl) says that the privilege is only good for 24 hours. Op. cit. in bibl., f. 36v.

Germany nearly all the women have bad teeth, caused by butter or the beer they consume (their breath, however, is good because they are healthy and have good digestions) and if any of their beauties does have good teeth her precedence among the others can be attributed to that. In Flanders, as in Germany, the amount of butter and dairy products that are eaten causes many to be lepers who live outside the centres of population, as in Italy.

There is a great quantity of a sort of earth which they use instead of coal and it burns very well.[1] Though wines are more expensive than in Germany every inn has both red and white. Good meat, poultry and rabbits are all common, but there are fewer partridges and pheasants. Having no oil, except nut oil, they always flavour their food with butter instead. My Lord had two cooks, one of whom always went ahead with the steward or harbinger, to make things ready, so neither His Lordship nor his retinue used the local seasonings, though we twice sampled them, on meat and fish, in Germany and Flanders and liked them less than those of France, which comprise a thousand stocks and flavours to improve the preparation of food.

The houses in many villages and towns, made from stone and brick, resemble, as to chimneys, windows and doors, those of Italy more than German ones do. However, to save space the stairs, well built as they are, are all curved or spiral. And in Flanders, as in Germany, there is no hamlet of peasant houses, however humble, that does not have a timepiece to show the time without the sun, with wheels and counterweights like a clock, though they do not strike the hour. And each has a decent church.

Their linen, which, whether of Holland or of Cambrai, is equally fine, is for the most part made in nunneries, which are numerous. Their hempen cloth is not like that made in Italy, being almost as fine as our linen, and they make of it another material called half-holland, which is coarser and not so broad, for household use. This is made all over Flanders though most, and that of the best quality, comes from Holland whence it takes its name. And note that were flax and hemp not imported from Russia. Prussia and foreign lands their own would not suffice for a small part of what they produce. It is made so white with clean

---

[1] Peat. Cf. Querini's definition of 'turba' (peat): 'una certa sorte di terra piena di radicette, che essendo in pezzi si abruccia come fa il carbone'. Albèri, cit. above, p. 37, Ser. I, i, 12.

water; they hang it on stretchers open to the air by night and in the sun by day, soaking it over and over again whenever it gets dry with clear, cold water. They ripen the flax and hemp in stagnant, filthy water having harvested it while still quite green. When the women cut them, crowds of them run about the streets holding up travellers by tying up their legs and stirrups to the leathers with flax and will only release them in return for a gift of money, for with the money they collect, when the harvest and the dressing of the flax is done, they celebrate and hold festival among themselves.

The native speech and idiom of the Flemings, though almost all can speak French,[1] is much softer than the Germans' and differs in many words so that they cannot readily understand one another. The beers of these parts are better than those of Germany and are made in great quantities. There are innumerable windmills. They have wild cherries in great number, plums, pears, walnuts and hazelnuts. Good fish of every kind abound, mussels and the tenderest of oysters, though they are not very large; river fish too are abundant, especially sturgeon and salmon. Wheat, rye and oats: all copious, as are various sorts of vegetables, except chick peas. By August the tenth the grain and oats were still unripe.

Since we entered Flanders there was hardly a day when it did not rain, with most cruel winds, so that the Flemish July and August were like a Roman November. Indeed, though we had five or six days of heat in Speyer, three before and three after St John's Day, so excessive that it was insupportable both by day and night and worse than we have ever experienced in Italy, we otherwise did not suffer from the heat at all.

The people are as pleasant and amiable in Lower as in Upper Germany. Above all, they are so honest that if you left all the gold in the world lying about their house they would not think of touching it. The inns claim to be the best, and women are so highly esteemed that they are in charge of them, managing everything and making out the bills. And in the same way, whether shopping in the squares, or selling merchandise or working at every trade, women are as active as men. Churchgoing is so constant that there is never a day, even a working day, when the churches are not full at service-time, and in the naves, aisles

[1] The anonymous Milanese says that while this is true of gentlemen, innkeepers, merchants and many craftsmen, it is not of plebeians and country people. Op. cit. f. 16v.

and chapels are many benches boxed in like those in public schools, many of them private, so that only their patrons can sit there. No-one walks about in the churches or makes merry there as in Italy. And there are numerous women who have the charge of altars and the custodianship of holy relics, which, if not to be praised, can be attributed to the great devoutness of the female sex and to the trusting nature of these people. In every parish church there are two sung masses a day at least, one for the dead and another for that day's saint, and the Salve is sung each evening. There is not a church without a great number of servers of from ten to twelve years old. The priests take a long time over the mass, in which, as in other ways, they are different from and to be contrasted with those of Italy. And they celebrate in such low voices that no-one can make them out, nor do they make the servers or others say the responses. At the end of every mass they give holy water to everyone standing nearby.

In Calais, which for all its great strength is not a very fine town, we stayed until the 8th of the month. It lies on flat ground, with the harbour to the north, where the sea washes close to its moats, and when the tide is not at the ebb (which involves here a distance of almost an Italian mile) the water is very deep. The walls are extremely thick and the broad ditches full of water; on the east, south and west the walls and ditches are uniform and there is also a very wide counter-ditch containing a very large body of water. And what makes it untakeable is this: three or four channels, sunken like sewers, run in from the sea and are controlled by sluices which can be opened at will to let in so much water that in half an hour the country around is flooded to an extent of four Italian miles. All the same, the King of England keeps a garrison of 500 men, including many horse, and all are armed with bows and axes. In addition there are three forts which are all defended, with many Englishmen in them. There is only one gate, which is opened at that time of year at two in the morning and closed in the evening at dinnertime, that is at the twenty-second hour.[1] Nor would it be opened were the King to arrive in person until the next day at the hour mentioned. In the same way it is closed in the morning till the people have eaten their mid-day meal.[2] The

---

[1] 2 a.m. = 2 hours after dawn. Normally de Beatis uses the Italian 24 hour cycle commencing at sunset.
[2] Cf. Andreas Franciscus in 1497, quo. above, p. 51.

Englishmen in the town, beginning with the governor Mr Richard Wingfield[1] and the troops there, are as tall, fine looking and splendid men as you ever saw, and from this you can readily imagine what the majority of Englishmen are like. And all delight in shooting with bows, which are of yew, as tall as themselves. And though all of them shoot at the target strongly, according to the governor aforementioned (a very courteous man, acquainted with Italy and to one of whose sons one of my reverend master's retinue stood as sponsor in his confirmation), the King of England has an archer of his guard so powerful that every time he shoots he can pierce a barrel containing three *some*[2] of wine from base to crown so that the dart or arrow comes out, which, though it seems very difficult, is not impossible. And it is said that the King shows this to all the important men who come to his court.

All the merchandise from England is discharged there, and all who want to go to that island embark there. Being of the highest importance to the King, as his only port on the mainland, he guards it, as we have seen, with great fondness and jealousy, and for this reason its governors are forbidden, on pain of death, to pass the gate for whatever cause during their term of office.

We waited there to cross to England from the fifth to the eighth, and had already arranged for a ship to take us across and were prepared to go aboard in the morning when this Mr Richard, the governor, told Monsignor that large numbers in that island were dying of a disease they call the sweating sickness because it kills by making men sweat, within 24 hours at the most, and is highly contagious, and that in London, the capital of that kingdom, 500 had died of it in a day.[3] So his reverence cancelled his journey, and decided to visit the Most Christian King,[4] who was at Rouen.

August 8. From Calais we went to lunch and dinner at the port of Boulogne in Picardy, seven leagues away, passing an infinite number of hamlets. The town is independent, though within the

---

[1] Sir Richard Wingfield (*c.* 1469–1525) was not the governor but the deputy of Calais, a role which enabled him to be seconded frequently for diplomatic missions in France and the Netherlands. At this moment he was acting as special commissioner to settle disputes between English and French merchants.

[2] As a measure of liquid capacity, the *soma* (with regional variations) represented about 155 litres.

[3] No false alarm; Cardinal Wolsey nearly died this month in this influenza epidemic. See above, p. 10.

[4] Francis I, King of France 1515–47. The title 'Most Christian' was a papal concession to kings of France, cf. 'The Catholic' for kings of Spain.

jurisdiction of the King of France; its governor is M. de la Follette. It is large, sited on a low hill and with a sizeable population. Below it is a suburb[1] of considerable extent. It is in the diocese of Thérouanne. As it faces Calais the King keeps it well fortified, with redoubtable bastions at the gates. It also has an inconsiderable castle and a very fine church called Notre Dame de Boulogne which is held in great devotion not only by the local population but people from elsewhere and even from distant parts. It is completely vaulted in a very graceful manner. The Madonna, a very moving figure, in black, is made in some sort of wood, in relief; around her altar, which is near the entrance to the choir on the right-hand side, are four marble columns topped by a very beautiful ornament of brass. And there is a chandelier also of brass in the choir which is finer than any we have seen since Speyer. We looked at many silver gilt tabernacles in the treasury, with numerous relics: hairs of the Madonna, and some of her milk and of Jesus Christ's blood, a thorn from his crown, a piece of the cross more than a span and a half in size, a quarter of Christ's first shirt and many relics of saints, a quite large cross entirely of gold, a number of votive hearts of solid gold and one weighing twelve marks given by King Louis, father of the King Charles who was in Naples;[2] other offerings, gifts from dukes of Burgundy, show them on horseback and are most skilfully made in solid gold, though the biggest is hardly larger than one hands-breadth. Also in the treasury was a large bible which they say belonged to the Madonna. In the middle of the church hangs a great claw of a griffin. And the church came to be built in this manner: nine hundred years ago a boat that miraculously brought the image previously mentioned and all the aforesaid relics was stranded in the harbour, and until the church was built (where the image is now placed) every morning a certain amount of money was found with which the greater part of it was constructed.

Though we had seen the island of England from a tower in Calais, whence the passage in good weather generally takes six hours, from Boulogne, being as I said on a hill, we saw it more clearly: it looked very white and long.

August 9. From Boulogne we went to lunch and dine at

---

[1] 'Borgo': built up area outside the walls of a town.
[2] Charles VIII (1483–98) conquered Naples in 1495; his father was Louis XI (1461–83). The church was pillaged in 1567 and again in 1793, when the statue was burnt.

Montreuil, a town belonging to the French crown, fine as to streets and squares; three fine churches are being rebuilt. Though the people, men and women, of both these towns speak French they are like Flemings in dress and all other ways.

August 10. From Montreuil to lunch and dinner at Abbeville, a royal town in the diocese of Amiens. The houses are not impressive but it is large, with nearly 4,000 hearths, and a river called the Somme runs through the middle; it is five leagues from the sea and it rises and falls with the tides and is navigable from many leagues upstream and down to the sea. Here all the women wear priests' hats over their veils which suit them very ill as they are generally extremely ugly. And when the sister of the King of England passed through the town on her way to marry King Louis[1] and was called on by them, she slyly said that they were all the lovers and mistresses of priests and wore the hats for love of them.

August 11. From Abbeville we went for lunch and dinner to Blangy, an unwalled village in a valley. It belongs to the crown and a small river runs through it which on this side divides Picardy from Normandy, so that the place is part Picard, part Norman, part in the Picard diocese of Amiens and part in the Norman diocese of Rouen. The bishop of Bayeux[2] came here to meet Monsignor. The women are ugly and do not wear priests' hats but a bastard form of the Flemish white veils.

In this part of Picardy you travel through level and lovely and fertile country with some fine woods; there are many cows resembling those of Upper Germany rather than those of Flanders, though it is so near. There are also pink pigs and many sheep. They use carts pulled by horses. The inn rooms are generally well appointed, with two beds in each, one for the master and one for his servant, not a truckle bed, however, but a low bedstead with its members made in the Flemish style, and in oak, but not so well. And though because it is so cold vines do not grow, good red wine is found in all the inns, though it is dear. The women are ugly,

[1] Mary of France, sister of Henry VIII, married Louis XII in Abbeville in September 1514.
[2] Lodovico Canossa (1476–1532). Sent to Frances I by Leo X in 1515 he made such a good impression on the new monarch that he persuaded the Pope the make him Nuncio and Bishop of Bayeux in 1516. He was a friend of Raphael's and one of the speakers in Castiglione's *The Courtier*. And see below, p. 122.

though I cannot speak for elsewhere in Picardy, which is a large and important province.

August 12. From Blangy we went to lunch and dinner at Neufchâtel, which means 'new castle'[1] in Italian. It is a walled town, not much to look at, and belongs to the crown.

August 13. From Neufchâtel we went after breakfast to dinner in Rouen and entered late so that the French lords would not have to come to meet his Reverence. At the command of His Most Christian Majesty we were given comfortable lodgings.

On the 14th, which was the day before the Assumption of the Madonna, at 18 hours Monsignor, accompanied by Monseigneur de Lautrec,[2] the Master of the Horse,[3] Monseigneur de Laval[4] (a relation of His Reverence) and many French lords and Italian gentlemen went to visit the Most Christian King who was staying in the archbishop's palace.[5] And he was greeted with much honour and graciousness by His Majesty, and after talking to him in his private room for about an hour, His Reverence took his leave and went to visit the Queen, who was staying in another apartment in the palace with the King's mother and her sister who was wife to the deceased Duke of Nemours, Giuliano de'Medici.[6] The Queen is young, and though small in stature, plain and badly lame in both hips, is said to be very cultivated, generous and pious. And though the King her husband is a great womaniser and readily breaks into others' gardens and drinks at many sources, there it is a matter of common report that he holds his wife the Queen in such honour and respect that when in France and with her he has never failed to sleep with her each night. And whenever Her Majesty says that she intends to visit her duchy of Britanny, a place of great importance whose inhabitants are formidable men and natural enemies of the French, the King trembles and fears it. His mother is an unusually tall woman, still finely complexioned, very rubicund and lively and seems to me to be about forty years old

---

[1] *Castello nuovo.*

[2] Odette de Foix, Viscount of Lautrec, Marshal of France (1485–1528). Governor of Milan after Francis I's victory at Marignano.

[3] See below, p. 181, note 1.

[4] Guy XVI de Montmorency, Count of Laval. Governor of Brittany. He died in 1531.

[5] The archbishop was Georges d'Amboise the Younger, who followed his uncle in this office on his death in 1510.

[6] Francis married Louis XII's daughter Claude, Duchess of Brittany, in 1514. His mother was Louise of Savoy and his sister, Philiberta of Savoy, was briefly married to Pope Leo X's brother Giuliano before he died in 1516.

but more than good, one could say, for at least another ten. She always accompanies her son and the Queen and plays the governess without restraint.

The King is very tall, well featured and has a pleasant disposition, cheerful and most engaging, though he has a large nose and in the opinion of many, including Monsignor, his legs are too thin for so big a body. He is very fond of the chase, especially of hunting stag with the spear. On the feast of the Madonna the King confessed and took communion as he does on several feast days in the year, exerting the power he has to cure poor men who have scrofula, a gift, it is said, conceded to all kings of France; and the scrofula gradually dries up simply because the King touches it and makes the sign of the cross over the sufferer.

On the 16th His Reverence went again to call upon the Most Christian King, the Queen and his mother, staying with them quite informally from after lunch until 22 hours when the King rode with him to a game of tennis where the King and many other young lords played. And at the end of the day the King took His Reverence to dinner in the archbishop's palace where he was staying. And there was good cheer and much dancing, the Most Christian King being among the dancers.

On the following day Monsignor called on the Cardinal of Bourges[1] who had been to call on him as soon as he arrived in Rouen. This Cardinal was staying in the monastery of St Ouen which now, thanks to an exchange made for the bishopric of Bourges, belongs to Monsignor di Cibo[2] but formerly to the Cardinal himself; he [Cibo] has made it into a very fine church, though it is not altogether finished. The rooms are magnificent and very agreeable, the garden fine; there are large courtyards and an extensive square in front of the monastery. There are many relics set in silver and gold in the sacresty, among other things a gold casket containing a holy martyr's bones made for the Cardinal before he gave it up, on which ten thousand francs were spent. Many monks serve the monastery and excluding the cost of their food and clothing the annual income, I was told, is some five thousand écus.

The city lies in a valley and is very large and populous. There is much trading activity and various crafts, especially the making

---

[1] Antoine Bohier du Prat, archbishop of Bourges and cardinal since April 1517.
[2] Innocent Cibo, abbot from 1515.

of cloths which are very delicate in colour as well as in weave, almost all are closely finished and are measured by the ell, two of which make a rod and a span of our measure. The houses are of wood frames filled with masonry in the German style and are large and very comfortable. The squares are fine, though the streets are somewhat muddy and not very wide. There are many fountains and a number of canals run through the town. On the left side, coming from Paris, a river passes a long stretch of the walls: this is called the Seine, from the Latin *Secana*, and is very wide. It is navigable from Paris, through which it runs, and divides into various branches before reaching the sea; this is eighteen leagues from Rouen, where the river is still tidal. Along the banks there were many merchant ships and other vessels, and in the town a stock of wood for fuel as large as any I have seen was assembled. You cross the river by a very fine stone bridge with eighteen arches, eight very large ones in the middle, the others sized to accord with the slope. On the opposite bank is a fine and extensive suburb. The city is well provided with fruits of various kinds, though not melons, figs or grapes; there are none of these because it is a very cold region. Fish are very abundant, both river fish, like trout, salmon and sturgeon, and all sorts of sea food, especially shellfish, oysters and black and white mussels. The cathedral is large and has a fine carved facade with sculptured figures; it has two very tall bell towers, one not yet finished, and though the stone is soft these are similarly carved with great skill. And there is a bell as large as any we saw. In the middle of the cathedral lies the late lamented Cardinal of Rouen,[1] in a marble tomb six spans high with his life size figure resting on the top in relief surrounded by an iron grille. The accommodation in the archbishop's palace, which was built by his Reverence, is extremely fine, all built in stone and very luxurious, with reception rooms and smaller chambers richly ceilinged, and many well planned suites. There is also a fine square garden, without trees, however, as is the custom in those parts; in the middle is a highly decorated marble fountain, throwing up a very high jet. The city contains many well served parish churches. The inns are excellent and their red wines are good, though it is not a wine-growing area.

On the 18th his Most Christian Majesty rode out four leagues

---

[1] Georges d'Amboise (1460–1510).

from Rouen to drive stags and follow other forms of the chase, and in the course of this sport, to visit the valleys towards Moulineaux, a town belonging to Monseigneur de Bourbon,[1] on account of the christening of a son recently born to that lord. Monsignor did not accompany His Majesty as he had wished, having been invited, because during the night he had been attacked by gout in both feet and had to stay for over a fortnight in greater pain and discomfort than he had ever experienced.[2]

On a low hill opposite the city, a short distance away, is a village where a monastery has been built, dedicated to St Catherine. There are many buildings, and it is occupied by twenty-five monks of the order of St Bernard. In the church they show the saint's finger and oil from the lamp at Mount Sinai where her body was taken by angels. The monastery is worth about 10,000 francs a year. The abbot is elected by the monks and confirmed by the King, as the monastery is within his gift. There is a very deep well in the middle of the courtyard. The water is drawn by means of a very large wheel which works two small ones carrying the ropes connected to the buckets, which are very large, containing perhaps a *soma* each, one descending as the other rises. The big wheel is turned by dogs trained for the task and which respond almost like human beings to their master's voice with such understanding that as soon as the full bucket comes up they stop and jump out of the wheel. They are very large animals, and as few as three or four of them can turn it with great effort; but there can be as many as eight of them, and they make a fine sight. You approach the monastery by 770 stone steps, which have a level area some ten spans broad every twenty steps for taking breath, as the ascent is exhausting. It is not very broad, but fine; parts of the steps and the sides are already in disrepair.

On the third of September Monsignor left Rouen after lunch in a litter accompanied by the former duke of Milan, 'Il Moro' Massimiliano Sforza, by the Count of Caiazzo[3] and by many other French and Italian gentlemen, notwithstanding that the majority

---

[1] Charles de Montpensier, Duke of Bourbon, Constable of France, served Louis XII in his Italian campaigns, becoming briefly governor of the Milanese in 1515. He was killed during the storming of Rome in 1527. His mother was a Gonzaga.

[2] As reported to Venice by the ambassador: 'The Cardinal of Aragon is here in Rouen ill with gout and keeps his bed.' Dispatch of 20 August. Sanuto, *Diarii*, XXIV, col. 630.

[3] Roberto Sanseverino. His father had at first fought for Lodovico Sforza (to whom the nickname Il Moro was usually reserved) in 1499 and then, resentful of being passed over in the command, deserted to France. Count of Caiazzo since his father's death in 1501.

were in attendance on the Most Christian King. He went to stay the night at a town three leagues away called Pont-de-l'Arche from its being sited on the Seine. At the head of the very fine stone bridge is a castle; a branch flows into its moat from the river which throughout its course contains a vast number of small islands which are a great pleasure and delight to look at. A league and a half from Rouen we had to cross the river by boat, because on leaving the town we had crossed it by the bridge referred to. And here we found Don Alvaro Osorio's servant, Alonso, and the young French page and letters from Don Alvaro; not until then having had news of him since we left Innsbruck three months before, where he had stayed on ill with that page, it had been assumed by everyone that he had been killed in some forest with all his companions.[1]

September 4. From Pont-de-l'Arche Monsignor left after lunch, still in his litter, to call on the King at Gaillon, four leagues away, and take leave of His Majesty. And entering the park where His Majesty was expected to hunt stag with the spear, he got down from his litter and mounted a horse and on His Majesty's coming they rode after a number of stags but because the hour was late they killed none. Then, accompanied by Cardinal de Boisy the brother of Monseigneur the Grand Master of France[2] and by Monseigneur de Lautrec, he crossed the park into the garden of the palace and thence passed on to the village where he was to stay with part of his entourage, because he could not stay in the palace for the great number of lords and ladies who were there with the Queen and the King's mother, notwithstanding the many rooms it has. The rest of our party with most of the horses went to lodge in Tournebut, a village on the left bank of the Seine a league and a half away. I have a vivid memory of that day and those places, for all of a sudden (I being lodged in the village with Monsignor) at about one hour of the night, my bag, containing various personal belongings, writings,[3] and cash amounting to tens of ducats was stolen from my saddle. And, as I have written

[1] The first of only two references in the Journal itself to the names of the Cardinal's companions. See pp. 11, 135 and 187, however. Henry IV of Castle granted the marquisate of Astorga to an Alvaro Pérez Osorio, but that was as long ago as 1465.

[2] Adrian Gouffier, Cardinal since 1515 and Arthur Gouffier, Seigneur de Boisy, formerly tutor to Francis I.

[3] As the Journal is as detailed and accurate up to this point as hereafter there is no suggestion that his notes for it were among the writings lost. Most likely those were duplicates of the Cardinal's correspondence.

warmly of the Germans and Flemings who, several times when we left a piece of silver in acknowledgement of their services courteously returned it, being an impressively honest and faithful people, even (and this is especially praiseworthy) the poorest and most wretched of them, so I am obliged not to conceal the truth about the French, having suffered at their hands this sorry trick, which at the time upset me greatly. And it is true that in all those provinces of France, leaving aside the aristocracy who live more openly, splendidly and liberally than anywhere else in Christendom, as I shall explain, the common people are as contemptible, idle and vicious as can be imagined.

The aforesaid castle or palace was built by Monsignor de Rouen on a hill from which, looking eastwards, is the finest view of meadows, stretches of water and hills that could be wished for. It has a park two leagues around surrounded by a stout high wall which also encloses the palace garden. So as to be seen from below, the wall runs across the hillside. The park contains a number of dense and beautiful small woods and open spaces for hunting. There are also many hunting lodges, and fine stags, wild goats, common and white deer, and innumerable hares and rabbits. The garden is a large square divided very attractively into smaller squares by paths with well-made wooden railings painted green. Each ends in a decorative gateway. On one side, against the park wall, is a very fine aviary full of many sorts of birds, especially pheasants and partridges; they have a channel of water from a fountain running through the middle, and along the garden front where it is open to the air, though protected by iron netting, are trees with grass beneath them for the enjoyment of the birds. From two other sides, leading towards the main gate which opens on to a large lawn, whence you pass into the court of the palace, are very long and well paved wide paths protected with a lined roof panelled section by section in oak so smoothly finished as to look like silver. The roofs are protected from the rain by slabs of a dark stone that looks just like lead. The walls are covered with paintings of various imaginary subjects, very well executed. The garden sides are open with rows of wooden pillars rising from bases, also coloured green. In France these covered ways are called galleries, in Italy cloisters or loggias. There is no such gallery from the main gate to the gate which leads into the park at the point where the aviary begins, though the design envisages one.

In the middle of the garden is a very beautiful fountain with marble urns chased with figures and a *putto* on top; water is thrown very high from a number of sources. It is enclosed in a large pavilion of carved wood, very richly decorated in pure azure and gold. It has eight sides, each terminating in a half-dome, and is very spacious and magnificent. Inside the garden, opposite the park entrance, is a building, also octagonal, of wood filled in with bricks. It is skilfully painted and decorated in azure and gold with eight windows, one in each facade, which are filled with very lovely glass. It is roofed like the pavilion and as, indeed, the palace is. The lodge is used for sleeping in the middle of the day in summer. In each quarter of the garden are a few trees, but mostly shrubs, rosemary and box. These are worked into a thousand whimsical shapes: men and horses, ships and a variety of birds and animals; in one quarter the royal arms and some antique lettering is laid out most cunningly in a number of varieties of small plants.

From the garden you pass on to the lawn and thence (via a drawbridge), as I have said, into the courtyard in the middle of the palace. This forms a large square, and the courtyard in the middle is also spacious; all that shows, both inside and out, is of excellently worked stone. And the stone mouldings of windows and doors all have heads modelled after ancient marbles, and these are over the doors and on the facades facing the courtyard which has in the middle a sumptuous marble fountain with huge pillars, each made of one piece and carved with many beautiful figures; its jet throws very high.

In the palace itself, which is made into a fortress by a wide moat that surrounds it, are a vast number of rooms, and two most elegant loggias, one above the other, on the same side as the perspective described above, which are tall and airy, with their lofty marble columns. In one of them are effigies from the life of King Charles, King Louis and his queen, Monsignor de Rouen, Monsignor the Cardinal of Sanseverino,[1] a very true to life one of the Princess of Bisignano,[2] and of a number of other French lords and ladies, all in coloured relief, though whether of wood or stone I do not know. There is also a beautiful chapel, suited in size to the palace, containing stone sculptures round its inner walls, made as in the life, of all the lords of the house of Amboise,

---

[1] Federigo, died August 1516.
[2] Eleanora, widow of Bernardo Sanseverino, Prince of Bisignano who died in 1511.

to which the aforesaid Monsignor de Rouen belonged. The ceilings of the public apartments and the bedrooms and dressing rooms are, in their different ways, carried out very richly and with a high degree of craftsmanship. One, where my Lord stayed for a night on the invitation of the Archbishop of Rouen (nephew of the aforesaid cardinal) after the King had left, was of oak carved in arrow-head vaults and the whole of the walls were panelled in the same wood so elaborately that though the room was not large it cost 12,000 francs. To complete their furnishings every single one of the public rooms is hung with the finest tapestries and the bedrooms with velvet, cut velvet, damask or brocade, with bed hangings to match. The windows are so numerous and so beautifully figured that they cost 12,000 écus. We saw, too, quite a fine library with books bearing the arms of Aragon that had belonged to the late King Ferdinand the First, sold in France in her extreme need by the most unfortunate queen, wife of King Frederick of sainted memory.[1]

The palace is as fine and beautiful as any I have seen, especially from without with its carved stone, brass ornamentation and series of roofs, and being built, as I have said, on a hill, much of which had to be cut away, cost 700,000 francs according to the opinion of authoritative Frenchmen; to anyone who has seen it this will not seem impossible. All the same, it cannot be denied that both the rooms and the facades looking on to the courtyard have been poorly designed. The palace was built by Monsignor de Rouen to rival that of Le Verger, which I shall describe later on.[2] And though he left it on his death to the archiepiscopate of Rouen yet it weighed on his conscience, and having spent so much out of vanity, he showed a deep repentance, saying: 'Would to God that I had given to the poor the money I have spent on Gaillon.'[3]

September 7. His Reverence rode out from Gaillon after lunch, and we arrived for the night at Mantes, a journey of eight leagues. Three leagues away from Gaillon we came to a village called

---

[1] Isabella del Balzo married Frederick in 1487 after the death of his first wife, Anna of Savoy. Frederick, King of Naples from 1496 was expelled by the Franco-Spanish campaign against Naples in 1501, accepted a French safe-conduct and died at Tours in 1504. His father, Ferdinand I, was King of Naples from 1458 to 1494, and was the grandfather of the Cardinal of Aragon. See Family Tree, p. viii.

[2] On p. 130.

[3] De Beatis quotes this as: 'places a Dio che l'argento che ge dispesi in Gaglion l'haves bagliat ad povera gent', a phonetic approximation of the French he heard and might be presumed to have understood.

Vernon-sur-Seine where France proper begins; on other sides Normandy, which is extensive, stretches further towards Paris. Mantes is a very agreeable and orderly place, though with houses of the in-filled wooden frames that are used all over France. Though there is a fine church adequate for such a place, another very fine one is being built there.

September 8. From Mantes we went to lunch at Poissy, six leagues away. As we left the town we crossed the Seine by a large stone bridge. Three leagues from Mantes is a hamlet half on one and half on the other side of the river, and there, too, one crosses by a fine stone bridge. It is called Meulan. Poissy is another very pleasing village with excellent lodgings. It is on the other side of the river which is crossed by a very large and wide stone bridge, a very fine one with five big mills on the right-hand side facing the current. In the village there is a convent of nuns of the Dominican order, over a hundred of them, whom we saw singing nones all together in the choir, which is closed off by stout iron gates. The church is very fine and the monastery very large; both were built by King Louis, who was sanctified as Saint Louis.[1] In the inn where we lunched I met Fra Janno, a knight and prior of Rhodes, a man of great wealth who has been a famous sea captain and corsair. He was passing through. He is a fine looking man, thin of face and figure and for a man of his age (he is over seventy), very hale and robust.[2]

After Poissy we went on to dinner in Paris, six leagues further on, crossing the river Seine five times by boat, as it splits into several branches. Two leagues out you pass over the first branch close to a cut-down wood of oak and other trees which have never grown again. It is called the Wood of Treachery, because it was in that wood that Ganelon of Mayence betrayed Charlemagne;[3] it still retains the name and bears impressive witness to it. For a branch taken from that wood, whether large or small, as soon as

[1] Louis IX, King of France from 1226 to 1270.
[2] Unidentified.
[3] De Beatis has 'Gayno de Maganza', the form used in *Il viaggio di Carlo Magno in Ispagna*, ed. A. Ceruti, 2 vols. (Bologna, 1871). This is an example of one of the Italian prose conflations of the Charlemagne legend which transposed the trial of Ganelon for betraying Roland from Spain to the outskirts of Paris. There, in the countryside, Charlemagne orders the trial. Ganelon flees, is caught and bound. His champion, offering trial by single combat on his behalf, is defeated by the champion of Roland's family and Ganelon is torn in quarters by four horses. 'Next morning Charles and his men entered into Paris.'

it is thrown into water sinks to the bottom, which many of our party who threw branches in the Seine found to be true. And lest it be thought that this could be caused by the nature of the water, every other sort of wood, except those from this wood, which is thrown into it readily floats.

Paris is a city which, as can be seen from the bell tower of the cathedral church, Notre Dame, which commands the whole of it, is no less populous than Rome, and I would say more so, were I not afraid to make a rash error of judgement, for it cannot be so easily estimated after only one survey. It is set in level ground in beautiful countryside where for a league or two around are a large number of fine large villages and many vineyards which produce the best and pleasantest wines I have ever drunk. The river Seine, divided into several branches, all navigable, runs through it, crossed by five very broad bridges, three of stone and two of wood. These have houses on either side which continue the line of the streets in such a way that you would not distinguish them, were they not all made in an identical style and size. Among them, I think that of the goldsmiths is about 100 *passi* long; and they work gold and silver in as much quantity and with as much skill as anywhere else in the world. The revenues from the bridges, which are not small, belong to the King. The cathedral church, built on the river, is a broad and large church but not very beautiful. By the first pillar on the right of the central nave as you enter is an imitation hill of marble supporting a St Christopher of stone almost the size of Marforio.[1] The city's houses are mostly of wood though they are big and comfortable and well designed. Most of the streets are somewhat narrow and very muddy and so crowded with carts that riding through them is more hazardous than navigating the banks off the Barbary coast. These streets and squares are all paved with large black stones very well set together. And throughout the town such a variety of crafts are pursued in the open both by men and women that I do not think that any other place in the world has half as many crafts as has this city. Having been there only for a few – and not unoccupied – days, I was not able to see the whole or even the greater part of it, so I cannot describe its features in great detail; for many of

---

[1] After Pasquino, the most important of the 'talking statues' of Rome, a large antique torso to which pasquinades were attached. The statue of St Christopher was destroyed in 1786.

them I have had to rely on what I was told. The city is said to have thirteen gates. Every subject is taught there except black magic, which is forbidden. Including those in grammar schools, there are about 30,000 students, which I find impressive, and yet this was confirmed to me by many priests and friars, French and Italian, who were studying there.

In the public palace is a Great Hall[1] (this is what they call it) with rows of columns in the middle; round it reliefs of all the kings of France up to King Louis are placed. They have swords in hand; the bellicose hold them aloft, the peaceloving and unwarlike with the point downwards. The room contains many benches where lawsuits are heard and also goods of all sorts are sold, beginning at the foot of the stairs where there are a great number of booths. Then comes another room, very long, but not so wide, surrounded by stalls where they sell all the gold and enamel objects made in Paris: a wealth of novel and ingenious things especially of wire, also an infinite number of jewels and every other sort of luxury ware. Also there is the magnificent room where Parliament is held. Though this is not easy to see, My Lord got in, together with the Neapolitan ambassadors returning from the Catholic King and with all the rest of us, at a time when the Parliament was sitting, thanks to the orders given by the Most Christian King to one of his gentlemen whom he had charged to accompany My Lord from Gaillon, and who had orders to show him whatever there was to be seen. The first Parliament was in that magnificent room, which has a ceiling in deep relief, skilfully carved and completely gilt. Many prelates and ecclesiastics who are members were present, and a large number of councillors, who were seated with decorum and the utmost gravity. However, many of these councillors came out to meet My Lord as far as the Great Hall. Then there were three other parliamentary meetings, of much smaller numbers, each sitting by itself, in other rooms, also highly decorated. In the courtyard of this palace is the Sainte Chapelle which is not very big and comprises two churches, one above the other, both very well served by honourable and wealthy canons. In the upper one is an altar heavily decorated in gold on which is a tabernacle, which one can reach from either side by two brass spiral staircases behind the altar, each with hardly room to

---

[1] 'Gran sala'. I.e. de Beatis notes that French 'salle' is like the Italian 'sala'. Now Palais de Justice.

spare for one person. And up there on the level of the tabernacle is a small landing where My Lord and all of us saw the following relics: the crown of our Lord Jesus Christ in a tabernacle of crystal decorated with gold and a carbuncle the size of an egg and shining like the sun which, if it is as pure as they say, is worth a king's ransom. The crown is intact save for the thorns, which, however, can be seen to have been removed, and forms a very broad and thick circle of some sort of thin withies which we could not identify though My Lord and all of us saw them very clearly. There was also a piece of the wood of the holy cross over a span and a half long set in a golden cross, and in another tabernacle, also of gold, they show another lance of Christ. We also saw a golden cross with many very large pearls, rubies and other valuable jewels, and other relics which, too, were set in gold. And in the middle of this chapel which, though not large is highly decorated especially through its windows which are some of the largest and most beautiful that I have yet seen, hangs a griffin's claw, each talon of which is a span and a half; if real this can be said to be a marvel, if artificial, a work of great skill. These two chapels were built by Saint Louis, King of France, on his return from the Holy Sepulchre and in the upper one which, as I have said, is called the Sainte Chapelle, he placed those most glorious relics, brought by His Majesty from Jerusalem.

In Paris there is a monastery called the Penitents' built by King Louis in his late lamented majesty's own palace, where there are about eighty women robed in white who have all been public prostitutes; the abbess is a relation of this king. They live on charity and on what they make with their own hands. They are enclosed and no-one can enter without difficulty and without a permit; no woman who has not been a public prostitute is accepted there. Almost all the young girls in the town go there to learn to read. In the city are the following distinguished men: Jacobus Faber,[1] most learned in every branch of Latin and Greek scholarship; Guillaume Budé,[2] a royal councillor who as well as being a lawyer has written on other subjects; Cop,[3] physician to

---

[1] Jacque Lefèvre d'Étaples (c. 1455–1536).

[2] (1465–1540). Both scholars had studied in Italy.

[3] Guillaume Cop, a Swiss, had settled in Paris in 1495. Earlier in 1517 both he and Budé had written at Francis I's instance, to invite Erasmus to reside in Paris.

the Most Christian King and learned in both one and the other tongue. There is also the bookseller Assensus, very learned and of austere life.[1]

September 10. We went to St Denis, a village two leagues away from Paris where stands the abbey of St Denis; a very fine church, and in addition to its devotional standing I believe it to be the richest in Christendom for gold, silver and jewels. The houses are large and comfortable; there are also many peasants' houses. Here all the dead kings and queens of France are buried, even though their hearts are buried in different churches according to their devotional preference. These tombs are set on the floor, mostly within the choir, and are of marble standing to a height of some seven spans, by no means magnificent. On top of the lids are their recumbent life-size figures in half relief, though the last King Charles is shown kneeling upon his. Some are surrounded by wooden railings, and locked, and others are not, so that after their deaths these French kings manifest a great humility. The main altar is approached by steps, and within a cavity gilt and ornamented with many jewels is the body of St Denis the martyr. It lies in a golden chest, and whenever the kings of France intend to go in person on some enterprise they lift out this chest with their own hands and place it on the altar, where it remains until His Majesty returns from the enterprise and puts it back in its place with his own hands. There is also a silver baton said to have been given to Charlemagne by the angel. It is called 'gloria magna' or, colloquially, 'gloria fiamma'.[2] This may only be borne by kings of France when they war against the infidel. On the right side of the altar, behind a barred aperture, is the head of St Denis set in solid gold, and on the left a gold tabernacle with a nail and a thorn from Christ's crown. There is also a gold cross more than eight spans high, not of solid gold, however, but of gold plate, bearing a crucified Christ of about four spans, and another cross under the first one (which is raised up on high and secured with a thick iron chain); this, too, is of gold and measures almost seven spans. We

---

[1] Probably, as Pastor suggests, Henri Estienne the Elder, who had settled in Paris in 1502 and in the next year set up what became one of the most important scholarly presses in France; he was a friend of Cop and printed most of Lefèvre's works.

[2] The words appear to refer to the 'oriflamme', but this was a standard, derived from the banner of the abbey but popularly identified with Charlemagne. It seems that de Beatis has skipped, rather than misread, one of his notes here.

also saw a piece of unicorn's horn[1] nine spans long. Then we went upstairs to where the treasury is and saw, above all, a very large pluvial all embroidered 'alla moresca'[2] with gold and most valuable pearls. In a great cupboard were a large number of relics all set in gold decorated with every kind of jewel and most beautiful great pearls, the costliest of kings' and queens' crowns, most beautiful vases of chalcedony and agate, a large piece of wood from the holy cross, thorns from Christ's crown, the crown of St Benedict's head, the two fingers St Thomas placed in Christ's wound, and many other relics. King Pepin's sword, Archbishop Turpin's and other arms of the paladins, together with the habiliments and sceptre used when the kings of France are crowned are kept in a chest contained inside another chest reinforced with iron. The monastery belongs to the monks of St Benedict, and the abbot is a brother of the Grand Master of France.

On the invitation of the monks My Lord and all the rest of us lunched there. And a little while after lunch My Lord mounted and returned to Paris, making four leagues journey all told.

September 12. We set out from Paris and went to lunch at Villepreux, a distance of six leagues. Two leagues out of Paris we heard mass at a church called Notre-Dame-de-Boulogne,[3] which is greatly venerated. Then we immediately crossed a fine stone bridge spanning an arm of the Seine. This is called St-Cloud bridge because there is a village on the other side named after that saint. It is said that no King of France has ever attempted to cross it either on foot or horseback because they find it prophesied that when a King of France does cross it will surely collapse. And when kings of France pass this way, they have taken to crossing the river by boat in order to avoid the bridge. After lunch we left Villepreux, which is a small town, and went on to dinner at Montfort, a distance of five leagues. This too is of little account and has indifferent lodgings.

September 13. From Montfort we went to lunch at Dreux, quite a small village seven leagues away, and for dinner continued as far as Rueil, another fairly small village six leagues further on.

September 14. From Rueil to lunch at Rugles seven leagues away,

---

[1] Other visitors pronounced (or were told) that it was a rhinocerus horn. E.g. Münzer's 'vidimus in choro inferiori patrum in alto pendere cornu rinocerontis, quod vocant unicornu, et etat magnum et longum pedum sex cum dimidio'. Op. cit., 220.

[2] In the Moorish style.

[3] Now Notre-Dame-des-Menus.

and to dinner at Chambrais six leagues beyond that. Both are small villages.

September 15. From Chambrais to lunch and dinner at Lisieux, at a palace outside the city belonging to the local bishop,[1] where we found Cardinal de Boisy staying with the bishop. Here we halted for two days and received excellent hospitality. And on the sixteenth, which was the fourth vigil of the Holy Cross, we went to lunch in the city in the bishop's apartments. Afterwards we were shown two cellars where there were many large casks (among them one eleven spans in diameter and twenty-one long) in which they keep cider, which is made from apple and pear juice (the two kinds separately, however). The city is of no great account, nor attractive, but has a very fine situation and is well supplied with corn, wines, water and many other things, especially game animals. It has fine churches (a new one, indeed, is being built at the bishop's palace where we stayed, outside the city walls) and also good, well-maintained houses. There is a great square garden, which is very well laid out, but only with plants and shrubs, for trees cannot be grown there because of the extreme cold. In the middle of the garden is a marble fountain: large and well wrought with putti which spray the water to a great height.

September 17. From Lisieux, after lunch, we went to dinner at the abbey of St Barbara,[2] which belongs to canons regular of the order of St Augustine. In the church, which is very beautiful, is the head of St Barbara, an object of great veneration throughout France. The abbey is large and has good accommodation. In certain basements or cellars we again saw casks used to keep cider and among them one which we found to measure seventeen spans in diameter and twenty-seven in length.

September 18. From St Barbara's we went to lunch and dinner at Caen at the abbey of St Stephen,[3] which lies outside but close to the town walls, on the Bayeux side, and belongs to the order of St Benedict. The abbot is the bishop of Castres, who is a monk, his bishopric (which is in Languedoc) being a monastic foundation, and is a Gascon himself. The abbey has a very fine situation. It has large, fine rooms, including two great halls which are very

[1] Jean le Veneur, 1505–39.
[2] Ste.-Barbe-en-Auge, on the R. Dive. Transferred to the Jesuits of Caen in 1606.
[3] St-Etienne, or Abbaye aux Hommes. The abbot was Pierre III de Martigny. When de Beatis goes on to speak of it as 'newly restored' he may be confusing it with St Pierre.

lofty and entirely vaulted. The church is large and newly restored, and as well designed as any we have seen in France. There are many relics, the most noteworthy being the skull of St Stephen the First Martyr. A silver casket of great weight, well gilded and cunningly wrought, contains countless relics, according to the list. The town is large; there are many guilds and fine churches, and the largest of these, which is called St Peter's, is roofed with lead. There is also a university with about four thousand students, and books are printed here in quantity.[1] Spiritual authority belongs to the bishop of Bayeux, who also holds the bishopric of Tricarico. He obtained the bishopric of Bayeux from King Francis after being the apostolic nuncio of His Holiness Pope Leo to His Most Christian Majesty for a few months. As a layman he was called Count Ludovico di Canossa of Verona. He is without doubt a highly accomplished person: a refined courtier and a man of intellect and learning. Being so beloved of our master, he came out to meet him some leagues before we reached the town of Caen.

September 19. From Caen to lunch and dinner at Bayeux, which is seven leagues distant. The city is neither large nor very attractive, yet it has a fine situation in a very fertile area lacking only wines. It has the cathedral, which is really large and beautiful. Here there are many relics mounted in silver and gold, and two gilded silver chests which each cost twelve thousand francs. There is a great piece of the wood of the blessed cross and two pieces of unicorn horn which both measure between nine and ten spans.

September 20. We left Bayeux after lunch in the company of the Bishop and came to a castle appertaining to his bishopric, called Neuilly, seven leagues distant. This castle is a very secure stronghold lying a league and a half from the ocean, and when there are floodtides the water spreads over all the surrounding fields. Nearby, along the road from Bayeux, there are many peasant cottages. The castle, which has good apartments, is entered by a succession of bridges all spanning wet moats. In one of these are two fine water-mills that can be worked only when the tide is ebbing with the current of the river, which is very deep and surrounds the castle. We halted here for one day and ate heartily from a plentiful supply of chickens, water-birds, thrushes, rabbits, capons and peacocks.

[1] See Léopold Delisle, *Catalogue des livres imprimés ou publiés à Caen avant le milieu du XVIe siècle*, 2 vols. (Caen, 1903–4).

September 22. From Neuilly we went to a place two leagues away belonging to the bishopric of Bayeux and lying on a peninsula between two stretches of water. Here we had a great fox-hunt, but although the place was renowned for, and abundant in, this species of animal, fortunately for them we only caught one. After lunch the Bishop took leave of our master and departed, and we, with the Cardinal, set out and rode to St-Lô, which is a town belonging to Cardinal de Boisy, situated on a hill. It has a fine church, and although the fortified area is not great, the encircling suburbs are extensive and make it a very considerable town. It is six leagues from Bayeux.

September 23. We left St-Lô after lunch and went on to dinner at Villedieu. This is just a small place with inferior inns, being situated not on a highroad but on a route frequented only by pilgrims travelling to Mont-St-Michel. It lies seven leagues from St-Lô.

September 24. Setting out from Villedieu after lunch we went to dinner on Mont-St-Michel, a distance of seven leagues. Five leagues past Villedieu is Avranches, a small, fortified cathedral town, which is well laid out on a hill and which we passed through. And on reaching the plain we immediately came upon a great expanse of sand which stretches almost to the base of the Mount. Over this section of the route we rode with a guide at low tide: to Mont-St-Michel a distance of two leagues, making a total of seven leagues from Villedieu.

Mont-St-Michel is a round hillock of rock rising from the sand, quite modest in circumference but tapering upwards from its base to a great height in the form of a pyramid or diamond. Many commodious buildings cluster in pine-cone fashion up its sides, and from afar present a splendid sight. It is fortified with walls which are mainly of solid construction and with squat towers which are well designed.[1] Construction work still continues, moreover, so that short of being starved into submission, given adequate defending forces within it is impregnable to all the armies of the world, chiefly because of the tide which comes up every six hours. At full moon the sea surrounds it completely for a distance of two leagues. Entry is by a single gate which is extremely strong, and because of the importance of the place the Most Christian King

---

[1] I.e. well adapted for the use of artillery.

keeps many archers there. The church of St Michael is built at the summit, where there is a belfry so high that the local people say that from the top one can see England and the frontiers of Spain. This, given sufficiently powerful eyesight, I would readily believe possible in view of the altitude, for it is an extremely high place with an unobstructed view. The church itself is not very big, but a large new choir being built on to it at the present time will be a considerable extension. Benedictine monks live there. They have fine, spacious quarters, including a cloister which affords the most distant and delightful prospect that anyone could imagine.

The church is fortified like a castle, and entry is by two or three gates guarded by the royal archers. This shrine is greatly venerated by all Westerners and originated (as far as we could gather from its history which is there in writing) in the manner we shall hereafter describe. People flock to the Mount in vast numbers, and they go there solely out of devotion to St Michael. Good inns are provided for them. The local occupation, in which both men and women commonly engage, consists merely in colouring the sea shells they find on the neighbouring sands in various hues, sticking them to strips of cloth dyed red, yellow or black, and selling them to the pilgrims, who wear them across their shoulders like stoles. They likewise manufacture St Michaels of various kinds from silver and tin. They also make an enormous number of horns in copper, painted earthenware and glass: not, however, as large as the trumpets made in Milan but much smaller. Such articles are sold in great quantities, for there is not a pilgrim who does not buy some and, decked out with shells and St Michaels, go winding a horn all the way home.

The church was founded in the following manner.[1] In the reign of Childebert, King of France, who ruled not only the west and the north but also part of the south, in the year of Our Lord   ,[2] when Aubert was bishop of Avranches, the Mount was called Mons Tumbae, being formed in the shape of an ancient tomb, about it lay a great forest and the sea did not approach to within a great distance of it. Some hermits went to live there, judging it a secluded place well suited to the service of God, and built two

[1] See sources in *Acta Sanctorum* (58 vols., Antwerp, 1643 seq.), Septembris, tomus octavus, 74 seq. especially para. 336.

[2] The bishop's vision is traditionally dated 707. The dates are blank in all mss; perhaps de Beatis could not read it in the transcription from the Latin he made on the spot and subsequently translated.

little churches, traces of which are apparent to this day. A priest of the neighbourhood sent them regular supplies of food on the back of a donkey, which would always go and return by secret ways, so that no-one ever set eyes on it, and the rumour arose that angels dwelt on the Mount. And since it pleased God that this should come to pass, it came to the bishop in a vision that he should build at the top of the Mount a church in honour of St Michael which would be as famous and frequented in western as the church of Mt Gargano[1] is in eastern parts. The bishop did not believe this first vision, nor a second which he received, and so in a third vision he was given a sign: hidden away in a cave at the place where the church was to be built he would find a bull-calf which had been stolen by a thief. Finding this to be so, the pious bishop believed that it was truly the will of God and not an aberration inspired by demons, and he prayed God that it should please Him to reveal how great an area he should take for the construction of the church. And hearing a voice ring forth from the cave that he should build over the area he would see unwetted by dew, he acted as instructed. The bishop then wished to have for this church some relic translated from Mt Gargano, and it came to him in a vision that he should send two canons thither. Canons were duly sent, and by grace of the then governor of the church of Mt Gargano they brought back a piece of the stone where the angel alighted in the church and a piece of red cloth from the altar which Michael built in that place with his own hands, as may be found related in more orderly fashion in the aforementioned Latin history, which I copied out.

September 25. From Mont-St-Michel after lunch we went on to dinner at Bazouges, which is seven leagues away. Two leagues from the Mount we came to a town called Pontorson with a river before its walls which is not very broad and is spanned by a wooden bridge. Beyond this river begins Brittany, or rather Upper Brittany, for Lower Brittany, where Breton speakers live, has other frontiers. The village of Bazouges consists of just one street of poor lodging-houses and still poorer dwelling-houses.

September 26. From Bazouges after lunch we went to dinner at Rennes, a distance of seven leagues. The Cardinal was met outside the town by Monseigneur de Laval and his son, and by many other

---

[1] The promontory reaching out from the northern Apulian coast and cradling the Gulf of Manfredonia. The church is the Santuario di S. Michele Arcangelo.

noblemen who happened to be assembled there for the parliament, then in session. Monseigneur de Laval is his kinsman by marriage, having married the daughter begot in France by the late lamented King Frederick by his first, French, wife, and while in Rennes we were shown great honour and kindness by this gentleman.[1]

The town of Rennes is as large as any other in Brittany: densely inhabited, very populous, rich in industry and strong. It is surrounded by large suburbs, and two sizeable rivers flow within the walls. The streets are rather narrow and muddy. Given the character of the town, the churches are not very beautiful. It is a city and lies on level ground. More than half of it belongs to Monseigneur de Laval, the rest of whose estates are in the vicinity. These yield about twenty-five thousand ducats a year, and the salary he earns as governor of Brittany brings his income up to more than thirty thousand. He is tall and lean, and between forty-five and fifty. He has remarried, though by the daughter of the late-lamented King Frederick he had a son, now sixteen or seventeen years old, and most courteous and refined, and two daughters, one now fourteen, the other twelve, who are at Tours with the daughter of the Most Christian King, staying at Plessis, a palace which will be described later. We halted at Rennes for two days; and while there we ate a fish they catch in the ocean which is like a pig and has the fat, flavour and name of a pig.[2]

While at table with our master, together with the Bishop of Nantes,[3] who had come with many more noblemen to meet the Cardinal, Monseigneur de Laval told us about the duck and ducklings of St-Nicolas, a locality of his four leagues distant from Rennes. He assured us that every year on the feast of St Nicholas, a duck, followed by her offspring, appears at vespers and mounts the altar. After staying there for a while, she walks round it once and then takes herself off home at her own good pleasure, leaving one of the ducklings behind. No-one sees where this goes or who takes it, though the people watch attentively every year. Prodigious miracles have occurred to all who, in contempt of St Nicholas, have tried to harm the ducks.

After this he told of a wood he owns, where there is not a single living creature, and all attempts to introduce one, by whatever

---

[1] Count Guy de Laval in 1500 married Carlotta, daughter of King Frederick of Naples by his first wife, Anna of Savoy.   [2] Cochon de mer, or porpoise.
[3] François Hamon (1512–32).

means, led to their instant death on entering the wood. He also said that at a certain place on the edge of his estates, where a great stone is fixed to mark the boundary, there is a great spring of water, and whenever, after confession and communion, he scoops some up in his hands and throws it over the stone, rain immediately falls, even if the sky is perfectly clear. For this is a grace which God has vouchsafed to the first-born of his house: one he saw performed by his father several times and which has never failed in his own case from the time he first attempted it. He also said that Monseigneur de Rohan[1] (who vies with him for precedence, their two houses being the leading families of Brittany) has a wood with a lake, and in all trees of this wood, of whatever species, which you cut into you will find his escutcheon; and similarly, in the bones of the fish caught in the lake, and in all the stones in the wood, breaking them according to the size of the piece, you find the arms of the House of Rohan. You find them, again, in the plumage of all birds of prey born in the wood. And in another wood belonging to Monseigneur de Rohan, a saintly member of his family was once at prayer, and being disturbed by the chirping and singing of the nightingales he cursed them. As a result, not one nightingale has ever been found there since, nor indeed any bird singing there at all. These ancient traditions, privileges and favours of God and nature have been cited and alleged before the parliament of Paris in defence of their prerogatives by the two illustrious houses in their dispute over precedence. However, the two houses alternately enjoy precedence according to the favour shown them by the kings, their superiors.

September 28. The Cardinal set out from Rennes after lunch, accompanied by the Bishop of Nantes and by Monseigneur de Montfort, the son of Monseigneur de Laval, and we went to stay the night at Bain, a village seven leagues away consisting of a single street.

September 29. From Bain, when we had lunched, we went to Nozay, a village of the same importance and again seven leagues' journey away.

September 30. From Nozay we went on to lunch at a hamlet four leagues away called Héric, and then to dinner at Nantes, where the governor and many noblemen rode out to meet the Cardinal.

---

[1] Head of the family was then Charles de Rohan, Count of Guise, married since 1512 to Giovanna di Sanseverino of Bisignano.

Nantes, if not a very large city, is not a small one either, and is certainly the finest and strongest in Brittany. Its strength lies in its being largely surrounded by a very big, broad river called the Loire, Ligeris in Latin, which passes within twelve leagues of Lyons and has its source only a little further away. It lies two leagues from the ocean, and the river is tidal, with large fish in it of every sort. It is situated on level ground, but within valleys. The walls are extremely thick, of recent construction and well designed, and the moats very wide and deep. A smaller river, the Erdre, flows within the city and on the side nearer the valleys forms a marsh in which it would be impossible to camp. A fine, large castle stands on the bank of the Loire, with very strong ramparts and moats; within, it has comfortable living quarters and more than adequate artillery, which includes some fine pieces in addition to those said to have been removed by the King of France. In a church belonging to the Carmelites is the monument of the Duke and Duchess of Brittany,[1] the grandparents of the present queen of France, comprising two well-proportioned rectangular tombs set in the centre of the choir. The tombs themselves are of black marble, but the figures are entirely of alabaster, with swages or corded mouldings about them which are also of finest alabaster. At the four corners are figures of the four virtues, fortitude, temperance, justice and prudence, in full relief about seven spans high and of good workmanship. Effigies of the Duke and Duchess, also of alabaster and in full relief, rest on the tombs: on the right the husband with a lion at his feet, on the left his wife with a dog under her feet. Both (according to the friars at the church) are from life. For a modern work, it is a very fine thing indeed.[2] The friars keep it solemnly locked away behind wooden railings and covered with black curtains.

We stayed here at Nantes for two days, the first and second of October, lodging at the Bishop's residence beside the cathedral, which is a very fine church. The Bishop is a most noble person: learned, virtuous and very generous. From him we received a most

---

[1] Francis II and his second wife, Marguerite de Foix; their daughter Anne of Brittany inherited the Duchy from them in 1488 and brought it to the crown of France through her marriages with first Charles VIII in 1491 and then Louis XII in 1499. Though the crown thereby gained certain rights over Brittany (e.g. the removal of artillery for national purposes), the duchy was not formally incorporated until 1532. The tomb was transferred in 1817 to the cathedral of St Peter. Anne died in 1514 and Brittany remained with the crown through her daughter Claude's marriage to Francis I.

[2] Finished in 1507 by Michel Colombe, working to the design by Jean Perréal.

affectionate welcome and many favours, including an offer of coins bearing his image to each of us servants. Though some of us needed money, we all refused out of regard of our master. But when we had been commanded by him, we finally had no alternative but to force ourselves and put it in our purses, with all the politeness and courtesy imaginable. He gave our master a saddle-horse and two curtals, and showed the utmost concern to be of service to him.

October 3. Leaving Nantes after lunch, the Cardinal was escorted for a league by the Bishop, the governor and Monseigneur de Montfort, and for dinner he reached Ancenis, seven leagues away. En route we came upon only a few poor inns. For most of the way we rode along the bank of the Loire.

October 4. From Ancenis we went to lunch at a village called St-Georges six leagues away. Four leagues from Ancenis is a village on the Loire called Ingrandes, where a great rock marks the boundary between Brittany and France. For dinner we continued to Angers, Angioya in Italian, whence our term Angioyni [Angevins]. This was another four leagues' journey.

Angers (the bishop of which is the brother of Monseigneur de Guise,[1] son-in-law of the late Prince of Bisignano, and is also bishop of Lyons) is very large and strong, and entirely surrounded by suburbs. It is divided by the river Loire,[2] which splits into several branches all spanned by wooden bridges with houses upon them, in the manner of the Paris bridges I have described. The city passed to the French crown by the inheritance which the Duke of Lorraine[3] (who was of the house of Anjou and died heirless) left to King Louis, and the present King has presented it to his mother. In the cathedral of St Maurice (which is of great size but no beauty, being in the form of a long, narrow chapel without aisles) on the left-hand side is the tomb of King René, who was at Naples at the time of King Alfonso I; this also contains the King's wife. In his epitaph he is given the title of King of Naples. The tomb itself is in black stone, but the figures resting upon it – of the King and Queen, together with other full-relief carvings

---

[1] François de Rohan (*c.* 1479–1536). He was also *arch*bishop of Lyons.

[2] In fact, the Maine.

[3] René (1409–80) of Anjou, Duke of Lorraine, Count of Provence and from 1435 titular King of Naples (where he resided only from 1438 to 1441) until his death, though the crown passed in practice to his rival Alfonso I of Aragon in 1442. He agreed, under pressure from Louis XI, to cede Anjou on his death to the French crown.

– are of a marble so fine as to look like alabaster. There is also the tomb of a bishop of the city called Jean-Michel of Sorrento,[1] who is considered to be a saint. And in the same church there is a huge organ, quite the equal of any we have yet seen excluding the one at Constance, which, as I said, was not finished. This sounded really grand when the Cardinal and the rest of us heard it played. The canons told us that the large pipe was twenty-six spans long. There was also a smaller organ which sounded extremely well, though less so than the one at Innsbruck, which, as I have said, is quite outstanding among those we saw.

October 5. From Angers we went to lunch and dinner at Le Verger, four leagues away. This is a fortified palace, lying on level ground but surrounded by deep wet moats. It was built by Maréchal de Gié,[2] the father of Monseigneur de Guise, son-in-law (as I have said) of the late Prince of Bisignano. Though it cost less than Gaillon, built by the late lamented Cardinal of Rouen, and is less imposing, being situated on the plain, whereas the latter is on a hill, it is much better designed and has more comfortable apartments. It has a fine park surrounded by great walls, and a garden, though neither is as fine as the ones at Gaillon. Here we found the aforementioned wife of Monseigneur de Guise, who is most charming and beautiful. She is known as the Lady Jeanne, and was married so young that although Italian she does not speak a word of Italian, but dresses and speaks wholly in the French manner, as if she had really been born there. We halted here at Le Verger for one day, relaxing and enjoying a very courteous welcome by the Lady Jeanne who, as well as being (as I have said) beautiful, is also most kind. Her husband was in Paris at that time, attending to certain important lawsuits.

October 6. Leaving Le Verger after lunch, we went to dinner at La Flèche, six leagues away. After four leagues is a village called Durtal, and there are also a number of hamlets consisting of just a few houses and poor inns.

October 7. From La Flèche we went to hear mass at Le Lude, a village four leagues away; and from there we continued to lunch at Château, four leagues further on, and to supper at a village called Sonzay, which is another two leagues beyond that.

---

[1] Bishop, 1439–48.
[2] Pierre de Rohan, known (from his branch of this large clan) as de Gié, Grand Marshall of France, died in 1513.

quale morse lli in uno oratorio sopra a cto leclo
di paglia cō una pietra per capizale che habbia
mo uista: sono gia x anni, in la nocte del vene
di sancto, et di eta de circa nonanta anni: e mol
to piccola. ¶ Ad quel tempo anchora che la regu
la del p.to fusse stata approbata et confirmata
fin dal Pontificato di Papa Iulio ij di s.ta et immor
tal gloria: no pero era canonizato et posto nel cata
logo de ghialtri Sancti. In una tabella si e
anchi uisto il retracto del Buono huomo de na

Morte del p.to

R·cordo del buō hō

turale che
gra barba
Scorno et
graue et
Sanctita
tra in par
dere da
fu et alti

tonea una
bianche:
una faccia
prioia di
del n si po
et copren
la qui appo
cata Stipa

Beatus Franciscus de paula.

Plate 1. François de Paule (N. 1, f. 75ᵛ)

rs

e said, is
a little
nded
f

...zay we went to lunch and dinner at Tours,
...; and near the town we had to ferry across
...chosen not to take the bridge in order tø
...he Blessed François de Paule of Calabria,[1]
...nd deeply revered by all Frenchmen. He
...called after him, which is near the park of the
...istian King. This church, which is very small, was built
by Brother François himself, and it was here, in an oratory, ten years ago on the night of Good Friday, that he died aged about ninety, lying on a pallet and with a stone for a pillow. At the time of our visit he had not yet been canonized and included in the catalogue of Saints, though his rule had been approved and confirmed during the pontificate of Pope Julius II, of most holy and immortal glory.[2] We saw the pallet and stone on which he died, and also, on a panel, the Good Man's portrait from life. He had a great white beard, was very thin and had a grave and most pious countenance, as may be partially appreciated from the print [3] [Plate 1] placed and fastened here.

In the left-hand wall above the high altar is set the urn of the late-lamented King Frederick of Aragon,[4] covered with a brocaded black silk cloth. From there we proceeded to lunch in the town. Our master went to Plessis, a short way outside the town, in order to see or, rather, call upon the daughter of the Most Christian King, wife (if indeed wife she ever really becomes)[5] of the Catholic King, and the two daughters of Monseigneur de Laval. The King's daughter is about three years old and full of promise. Of the other two, the elder is a very young fourteen-year-old and the younger a rather plain twelve-year-old. Plessis is a royal palace of great renown, but in reality does not seem deserving of such high praise. The town of Tours is hardly inferior in size to Rouen in Normandy. It has a fine situation, lying on level ground. The

---

[1] Francesco (1416–1507) of the village of Paola in Calabria, founder of the Order of Minims (the 'least', i.e. the humblest, of monks). He was imported in 1482 by the highly superstitious Louis XI, whose time was then spent as much as possible at Plessis-les-Tours, as a sort of talisman to quiet his fears of sickness and assassination. After Louis's death in 1483, Francesco was protected by Charles VIII (who furnished the church referred to in the next lines) and by Louis XII.

[2] He was, in fact, canonized by Leo X in 1519.

[3] Only in N. 1.

[4] Died in Tours, 9 November 1504. His bastard brother, Cesare, died there also, and within a few days: on 14 November. From the point of view of family piety, the visit to Tours was doubly poignant for the Cardinal.

[5] Louise. The match was adumbrated in 1516 but fell through.

Loire runs most of the way round it, and this, as I ha⸱
a very broad, deep river. Two smaller rivers pass the tow⸱
further away. Like all other French towns, Tours is surro⸱
by suburbs. Sword blades of great perfection are made here.

October 10. Leaving Tours, where we had spent the whole ⸱
the ninth, we set out after lunch for Amboise, seven leagues away.
This, though but a small town, is cheerful and well-situated. The
town itself lies in the plain, but it has a castle on a knoll which,
if not a fortress, has comfortable apartments and a delightful
prospect. Here King Charles, who was at Naples, loved to reside,
as his father, King Louis, loved Tours, and King Louis, his
successor, Blois.[1] Our master went with the rest of us to one of
the suburbs to see Messer Leonardo Vinci of Florence, an old man
of more than seventy, the most outstanding painter of our day.
He showed the Cardinal three pictures, one of a certain Florentine
woman portrayed from life at the request of the late Magnificent
Giuliano de'Medici, another of the young St John the Baptist as
a young man, and one of the Madonna and Child set in the lap
of St Anne. All three works are quite perfect, though nothing good
can now be expected from his brush as he suffers from paralysis
in the right hand. He has successfully trained a Milanese pupil, who
works extremely well.[2] And although Messer Leonardo cannot
colour with his former softness, yet he can still draw and teach.
This gentleman has written on anatomy in a manner never yet
attempted by anyone else: quite exhaustively, with painted
illustrations not only of the limbs but of the muscles, tendons,
veins, joints, intestines, and every other feature of the human body,
both male and female. We saw this with our own eyes, and indeed
he informed us that he has dissected more than thirty corpses,
including males and females of all ages. He has also written (or
so he said) innumerable volumes, all in the vernacular, on

1 Charles VIII (conqueror of the Kingdom of Naples in 1495), Louis XI and Louis XII.
2 Leonardo, who had settled in France in 1516 at the invitation of Francis I, was in fact
64 years old. The St John and the St Anne are now in the Louvre. Much speculation
surrounds the identity of the portrait. Francis I owned the Mona Lisa, but being a portrait
of Lisa, wife of the Florentine Pierfrancesco del Gioconda, it cannot have been commissioned
by Giuliano. Giuliano could, however, as part of the negotiations with Francis I which
led to his marriage with Philberte of Savoy and his being made Duke of Nemours, have
been the intermediary responsible for transferring the picture (unfinished, according to
Vasari, and not handed over to Pierfrancesco) to France; de Beatis may have misheard what
he was told at this meeting. Leonardo's cherished assistant was Francesco Melzi, to whom
on his death in 1519 he left all his artistic and literary possessions. Not knowing Leonardo
to be left-handed, de Beatis probably assumed that the restricted freedom of arm movement
that had followed a stroke had affected his right arm.

hydraulics, on various machines and on other subjects, which, if published, will be useful and most delightful books.

October 11. From Amboise we went to lunch and dinner at Blois, a distance of ten leagues, riding along the bank of the Loire nearly all the way. En route we came upon many villages, but none was of much account.

The town of Blois is larger than Amboise, though not as big as Tours. It is situated (and notably the castle) on a hillside above the Loire. It is in some degree ennobled by having once been the favourite residence of King Louis, who was not only born at Blois but chose to die there. The castle is not a fortress, but there are some very fine apartments and some delightful façades, internal and external, carved in soft stone. In the courtyard is a collegiate church which, for a church of this kind, is very fine and where the services too are excellent. The canons enjoy an annual stipend of four hundred francs, and the patron is the King.[1] In the castle, or rather palace, we saw a library consisting of a sizeable room not only furnished with shelves from end to end but also lined with book-cases from floor to ceiling, and literally packed with books – to say nothing of those put away in chests in an inner room. These books are all of parchment, handwritten in beautiful lettering and bound in silk of various colours, with elaborate locks and clasps of silver gilt. We were shown the *Trionfi* of Petrarch illustrated by a Flemish artist with quite excellent illumination, the *Remedium contra adversam fortunam* also by Messer Francesco [Petrarch], a large-format historiated Book of Hours, the *Mysteries of the Passion* containing Greek painting of great beauty and antiquity, a lavishly-illustrated *Metamorphoses* in both Latin and French, and many other very fine books which we did not have time to look at. One of those which we did see was bossed at its corners and in the middle with ten large oval cameos of most subtle workmanship. Among these books are many which the arms on the clasps show to have formerly belonged to King Ferdinand I or to Duke Ludovico Sforza: the former bought in France from that most unhappy lady, Queen Isabella, after the death of King Frederick, the latter won during the invasion of the Duchy of Milan.[2] There was also an oil painting from life of a certain lady

[1] The chapelle St-Hubert was founded by Charles VIII. The franc was a gold coin of high value (*c.* 1⅖ écus), not in common use.
[2] After Frederick's death in exile in France, 1504; taken from Milan after the defeat of Lodovico Il Moro in 1500.

of Lombardy[1]: a beautiful woman indeed, but less so, in my opinion, than Signora Gualanda.[2] We were also shown a very fine, large astrolabe, with the whole universe painted on it, and in one of the two inner rooms there is a most ingenious clock showing many astrological phenomena, signs of the Zodiac and the like.

The palace overlooks three gardens full of fruit-trees and foliage, access to which is by a gallery adorned on either side with real stag's antlers set on imitation stags carved from wood and coloured quite realistically. However, they are built into the wall at a height of about ten spans, one opposite the other, with only the neck, breast and forelegs showing. There are also many wooden dogs – hounds and greyhounds – set in facing pairs on projecting stones, which are lifelike not only in size and form but also in their coats, and some falcons set in similar fashion on hands which are also built into the wall, dogs and falcons having been favourites of King Louis. There is also an imitation reindeer with real antlers which extend in branches each over a hand wide; the rest of the animal has all the features of a stag, except that it is longer and has a great beard under its muzzle. In the garden, to the left of the entrance, is an imitation of a hind with a great pair of horns that came from a real hind which, according to the inscription, was killed by the Marquis de Bau[3] and given by him to the Duke of Lorraine, who in turn presented them to King Louis.

The great garden is completely surrounded by galleries, which are wide and long enough to ride horses down at full gallop. They have fine pergolas resting on wooden trellises, but according to the Cardinal these would be somewhat low for the full manège and high jumping on powerful chargers. In the middle is a domed pavilion over a beautiful fountain which supplies the water for

[1] Possibly the Leonardesque 'Portrait d'une dame de la cour de Milan' in the Louvre. The comparison would be a very natural one to make.

[2] In the margin of N. 1 at this point (mentioned only among Pastor's notes on textual variants and thus, perhaps missed by writers on Leonardo) de Beatis added the Christian name: 'sra Isabella Gualanda'. N. 2 simply has 'la Sra Gualanda'. It is not known who she was: the Gualandi, hitherto an important Pisan family, were banished when the Florentines conquered the city in 1406, and settled in various parts of northern Italy. Neither is the unnamed Lombard lady identifiable. It does seem likely that de Beatis is comparing the portrait at Blois with the sitter whose portrait he had just seen at Amboise. That the painting in the Louvre known as the Mona Lisa really is the portrait of Pierfrancesco del Giocondo's wife rests on unsure evidence (see Cecil Gould, *Leonardo, the artist and the non-artist*, London, 1975, 110 seq.). Thus it *may* be a portrait of Isabella Gualanda (or Gualandi) and, in this case, the possibility that it was actually commissioned by Giuliano becomes open.   [3] Untraced

those in the other gardens. The latter are situated possibly over six rods below the main garden. All these gardens have been created from barren hillside by a certain Don Pacello,[1] a Neapolitan priest who, because he was such a dedicated gardener, was brought back to France by King Charles when he went to Naples. They contain almost all kinds of fruit to be found in Terra di Lavoro[2] except figs, for although there are a few fig-trees they produce tiny fruit that hardly ever ripens. I saw many bitter-orange-trees and other large citrus trees, which produce very decent fruit, but they are planted in wooden boxes full of earth and in winter are pulled in under a roomy loggia in the garden, safe from snow and harmful winds. Above this loggia are the quarters of the gardener-priest, who has become very rich with benefices in comparison with his former situation. There are many plants and herbs for salads – endives and long-stalked cabbages as fine as in Rome.

Here at Blois (which is in the diocese of Chartres) our master saw a stable belonging to King Francis where there are thirty-nine horses, including about sixteen chargers. The Master of the Horse, Galeazzo Sanseverino,[3] who has charge of them by virtue of his office, had one of his French stable-lads show their paces. The boy, who was thirteen, rode with all the grace and skill possible in a youth of that age. Some of the wholly French-bred animals jumped and galloped with great mettle. The others included one of the breed belonging to my most illustrious lady, the Duchess of Milan,[4] which had been presented to the King by the Duke of Ferrara, one bearing the brand of the Duke of Termine[5] (both of these performed extraordinarily well), and the dapple-grey of the breed belonging to Signor Vincenzo Monsolino,[6] which our master's major-domo Fra Annibale Monsorio[7] sold in Rome for

---

[1] Pacello (or Pacillo) de Mercoliano.   [2] I.e., Campania.

[3] Son of Galeazzo Sanseverino, Count of Caiazzo. One of Ludovico Il Moro's leading captains, married to his bastard daughter Bianca. A famous horseman, he passed after Ludovico's defeat into French service, being appointed Master of the Horse by Louis XII in 1505, an office in which he was continued by Francis I, under whom he was killed fighting at the battle of Pavia in 1525.

[4] Isabella of Aragon (1470–1524), daughter of Alfonso, Duke of Calabria (who became King of Naples briefly in 1494–5) was married in 1488 to Gian Galeazzo Sforza, Duke of Milan, succeeded on his death in 1494 by his uncle, Ludovico Il Moro. She retired to her duchy of Bari and ruled there from 1500, retaining the courtesy title Duchess of Milan. It is not clear whether de Beatis's use of 'my' implies that he had served her court in some way or is acknowledging her authority; Molfetta is only a small distance north of Bari.

[5] Ferrante di Capua, a distant member of the Aragonese royal house.

[6] The Monsolino were Neapolitan feudatories based on Faicchio, near Benevento.

[7] Abbot of Santa Maria d'Avanzo in Apulia.

a hundred ducats to Lorenzo il Magnifico,[1] who presented it to the Most Christian King: though not a great charger, but rather like a curtal in build, the King is very fond of it, and that day it performed really well and jumped with great spirit. In addition there was an exceptionally large bay colt which our master judged to be as big as the dapple-grey belonging to Messer Bartolommeo della Valle[2] and which was said to have been born at a certain town in the Duchy of Lorraine. There were also certain horses from the Grisons which were extremely fast and nimble-footed, a number of fine hacks and a dozen Sardinian horses which had only lately reached His Majesty, who had sent off specially for them: the finest, best-tempered and most responsive to have come out of that island for many a year. We saw them being handled like jennets, manoeuvred like chargers and ambling more steadily and smoothly than hobbies. They had been presented to His Most Christian Majesty at the express command of the Catholic King.

October 13. From Blois, where we had spent two days, we went after lunch to dinner at Romorantin, eight leagues away. Half way there is a village with good lodgings called Fontaines.

October 14. From Romorantin, which is a town of middling size, we went to lunch at Vierzon, seven leagues away, and then continued to a town called Mehun, four leagues further on; but finding no overnight accommodation, because the mother of Monseigneur de Bourbon happened to be lodging there that night, we had to go on to supper at Bourges, which was another four leagues' journey.

In Bourges, which is very large, with streets and squares as fine as any town in France, our master stayed at the bishop's palace by the grace of the Cardinal of Bourges, to whom it belongs as archbishop;[3] and though the latter was absent we were given a very kind and hospitable reception by his representatives. Bourges manufactures large quantities of woollen cloth of every colour, and there are many guilds. We could not explore or walk about very much because of the plague that was abroad. However, we did see a church which, though not cruciform like most modern churches, is large and very beautiful.[4] A fine brass chandelier hangs

---

[1] 'Magnificent' was simply a title of honour. This is Lorenzo Duke of Urbino (1492–1519), grandson of Lorenzo the Magnificent who had died in 1492.
[2] Untraced.
[3] Antoine Bohier, Archbishop of Bourges and cardinal from April 1517.
[4] The cathedral.

in the choir. In the treasury are a solid gold cross of most cunning workmanship and a magnificent crozier with much gold about it, both commissioned by the aforementioned Cardinal, who presented them to the church. They had been received, in fact, only a few months before our visit. The relics here include (clad in silver gilt) the head of St William, the head of St Lucy, part of the head of St Stephen the First Martyr, the hand of St Andrew (entirely preserved) and some wood from the Holy Cross. There are also two enamelled gold osculatories of really delicate workmanship: on one is the crucified Christ with the two Marys, on the other the Virgin clasping her dead son to her breast. Then there are some large crosses and many other items of silver. In the Sainte-Chapelle, which is not far from the cathedral, there are the following relics: the head of St Cosmas, the two fingers of St John the Baptist ('Ecce agnus Dei'), three thorns from the crown of Christ, set in a finely-wrought gold crown rather like a *camauro*[1] in form but flatter, some wood from the Cross, a piece of the seamless coat of Christ, and various other relics adorned with gold and silver. This Sainte-Chapelle[2] is larger (albeit less lavishly decorated) than the one in Paris and is served by more canons and clerks. It was built and endowed by the Duke of Bourges (the second son of a King Charles), who is entombed in a great marble monument seven spans high set in the middle of the choir. It should be noted that in neither Upper nor Lower Germany, nor in France, did we see tombs in the Italian manner: elaborate, sumptuous ones raised up in arched tabernacles against the walls, but only the elongated type which, whether high-standing or low, always rest on the ground. At the same chapel the canons showed us a great chalice made of a material they call chalcedony, with gold ornamentation. Our master, however, thought that it looked like crystal, but so finely wrought (with a noble paten engraved with flowerlets and other delicate devices) that I doubt if its equal could be made at the present time. We also saw some gold rings with most subtly-wrought cameos and other precious stones set in them, and a pair of gloves covered with pearls, for when pontifical mass is celebrated in the chapel.

October 15. From Bourges after lunch to dinner at Dun-le-Roi,

---

[1] Papal bonnet (usually with ear flaps) made of satin or velvet.
[2] Demolished in 1757. The tomb (of Duke Jean de Berry – not Bourges – (1340–1416), son not of a Charles, but of King John II of France), was transferred to the cathedral.

which is seven leagues away and quite a fine town. A river passes through the middle of it. It is called 'Don du Roi' because, after belonging to the House of Bourbon from ancient times, it gave itself to the King of its own accord. It has many suburbs round about. The route crosses a flat, barren district, and there is only one village consisting of a few poor cottages.

October 16. From Dun-le-Roi we went to lunch at Le Brethon, a small village with rather squalid inns, eight leagues away. About five leagues beyond Dun-le-Roi we rode for two leagues through a great wood thick with huge oaks and extremely clear of undergrowth.[1] One tree near the road, enclosed with palings, is exceptionally thick and tall, and the French deservedly call it 'queen of oaks'. We went on to dinner at Cosne, which again is a village with mediocre lodgings, another three leagues' journey away.

October 17. From Cosne we went to lunch at Verneuil, a distance of eight long leagues, and from there continued to dinner at Varennes, making a total distance of eleven leagues.

October 18. From Varennes to lunch at St-Martin, a distance of eight leagues. Two leagues from St-Martin is Droiturier, a village; two leagues further on, La Palisse, which is only a small town but has good lodgings. It lies by a river and is entered by a bridge when the river, normally a mere stream, is swollen. It is from here that Monseigneur de la Palisse takes his name.[2] Three leagues beyond is La Pacaudière, and one league further, St-Martin.[3] From there to supper at St-Germain, which is a well-laid-out little town with excellent inns, another three leagues' journey away.

October 19. From St-Germain to lunch at St-Symphorien, a distance of five leagues. We heard mass at Roanne, which is a sizeable town with good inns, where the Loire begins to be navigable as far as the ocean. We went on to dinner at Tarare, three miserable leagues' ride up and down mountains. After one league of this mountain is the inn of La Fontaine, and a league beyond that, at the end of the descent, is another inn – new, large and very comfortable – called La Chapelle.[4] At that time of the year we found two spans' depth of snow.

[1] Forêt de Tronçais.
[2] Jacques de Chabannes, Seigneur de la Palisse (Palice), *c.* 1470–1525, Marshal of France, fought in Italian Wars 1494–1515.
[3] The route is confusing: from Varennes he passed successively through Lapalisse, Droiturier, St-Martin d'Estréaux, La Pacaudière on the way to St-Germain l'Espinasse.
[4] Near Le Pin Bouchain.

October 20. From Tarare to lunch at Lyons, a journey of six leagues. Half way is L'Arbresle, a village with not many houses. Lyons is a city lying in a well-situated valley. On the right-hand side as you come from France it is set close up against the hillside, and the walls that start at the gate by which you enter the city, once past the suburb on the bank of the river Saône, run across this hill and enclose a good part of it before reaching another gate by which you leave when bound for Italy; a few houses are scattered here and there over the hillside without any regular street-system. On the left-hand side, the town is bounded by the Rhône, which joins the Saône at this point. The latter river runs through the middle of the town and is spanned by a fine stone bridge. At an abbey called Ainay,[1] which is at the lower end of the town, where the Saône loses its name and from there on is called simply the Rhône...[2] The Rhône flows out of Lake Geneva, and in addition to the Saône, which comes down from beyond Burgundy and is a big river, it receives the waters of the Sorgue, the Valence[3] and two other rivers which will be named later. This city or town (bishop of which is the brother of Monseigneur de Guise, as I said when speaking about the city of Angers) has a large suburb both at the gate by which you enter when coming from France and at the one you leave by to set out for Italy. At the point where Saône meets Rhône there is a fine, long stone bridge leading to the suburb, which, being on the far side of the river, marks the beginning of Dauphiny. The town is not very large, nor yet small. The streets are well laid out, the houses generally of stone. The women of Lyons are some of the most beautiful in France. Merchants of every nation live here, but especially Italians, and because of all the trade the men, the women and the very earth have something of fair Italy about them. And so, such as it is, I judge Lyons to be the fairest town in France.

October 26. After lunch we left Lyons, where we had spent five days, and went to dinner at Bourgoin, six leagues away. Half way there is a village called St-Laurent.

October 27. We left Bourgoin after lunch and went to dinner at Aiguebelette, seven leagues away. This is a village of few houses but good inns, being a place necessarily frequented by everyone

---

1 Destroyed; all that remains is the church of St-Martin-d'Ainay.
2 The sentence is incomplete.
3 'Valenza'. Perhaps the Isère which de Beatis might have associated with Valence.

passing to and from France. Three leagues from Bourgoin is La Tour, a very small town which you pass through. Two leagues further on is a more substantial town, Le Pont, so called because of a bridge you cross there, spanning a smallish river which marks the frontier with Savoy. The last two leagues as far as Aiguebelette are cursedly bad going, since you are riding the whole way over rocks and stones, which are an unspeakable nuisance.

October 28. Leaving Aiguebelette after lunch we went to dinner at Chambéry, a distance of two leagues. The first consists in climbing, then descending from, a mountain which, relatively speaking, is very high and steep; the second is over level terrain. To climb the mountain most of our party hired cobs, mules or donkeys from the village because these local animals are used to climbing.

Chambéry is a town lying in a level valley-bottom. It has fine houses, streets and squares, beautiful women, many guilds, and men of integrity. Here, by grace of the Duke of Savoy,[1] who was at Geneva (whence, having been besought by the Cardinal from Lyons through a specially despatched messenger, he sent two protonotaries with his own key and an order concerning the other two keys that are kept by the town officials), in the evening at twenty-two o'clock we saw the Holy Sindon or Shroud in which the Lord Jesus Christ was wrapped when he was taken down from the cross.[2] This is kept at a church built, for greater security, within the courtyard of the castle and is shown (according to what we were told by the canons of the church, which is collegiate) only on Good Friday and on the three days of May when the Invention of the Cross is celebrated – and then only from the walls of the castle in the direction of a certain meadow outside the town walls which is set aside for pilgrims. At these times vast numbers of people flock from near and far to see it. Indeed, it can be said to be the most venerable and wonderful relic in Christendom. As far as we could judge, in appearance it is like the drawing below[3]

---

[1] Charles III, Duke 1504–36.

[2] This famous and much investigated relic is in Turin cathedral, whither it was transferred in 1578. It was damaged by fire in 1532 and in the wars of the 1540s was sent for safe keeping to Vercelli and then Nice.

[3] No drawing in Pastor's ms. On N. 1, f. 85r one is placed 'below' this phrase, but is barely visible; its size shows that N. 2 was copied from it. A prayer is added in N. 2: 'Deus qui nobis in sancta sindone, in qua corpus tuum sacratissimum de cruce depositum a Ioseph involutum fuit, passionis tuae vestigia reliquisti, concede propitius ut per mortem et sepulturam tuam ad resurrectionis gloriam perducamur. Qui vivis et regnas cum Deo Patre in unitate Spiritus Sancti, Deus per etc.'

173.

E' questo Linteo, è alto da cinq palmi et mezo incirca, et longo poco più de la statura di chr°: pero duplicata dà la parte dauantiet de' dietro: quali statur' del gloriosißimo corpo sono impresse, et umbrate del preciosißimo sangue di chr°: doue efficacißimen apparено li segni de le battitur' de le corde de le manj, de la corona del fronte, de le ferir' de mano, et piedi, et specialm.te di quella del s.mo Lato. со cert'e gocce di sangue sparse fora del sacratiss°: disegno talmete et a Turchi donare bono diuotione, & Terror', no ch a christianj detto Linteo ne fu mostrato da sopra lo altar' magior.

Deus, qui nobis in sancta Sindone, in qua Corpus tuum sacratissimum de Cruce depositum à IOSEPH inuolutum fuit, Passionis tuæ uestigia reliquisti Concede propitius ut per Mortem & Sepulturam tuam ad Resurrectionis gloriã perducamur Qui uiuis & regnas cum Deo Patre, in Vnitate Spiritus Sancti Deus per &c.

Plate 2. The Holy Shroud (N. 2, p. 173)

[Plate 2]. We were told that a dispute once arose between two brothers of the most illustrious House of Savoy as to which of them should guard the Sindon, and so they agreed to divide it down the middle. But when a tailor put his scissors to it to cut it, he was struck blind instantly. They therefore left it whole; whereupon, to enhance the miracle, by the mercy of Christ crucified the tailor's sight was restored.

This winding-sheet, sindon or sudarium is about five and a half spans high and only a little longer than the imprint of Christ, which is double – a front and a rear impression. These images of the most glorious body are impressed and shaded in the most precious blood of Jesus Christ and show most distinctly the marks of the scourging, of the cords about the hands, of the crown on the head, of the wounds to the hands and feet, and especially of the wound in the most holy side, as well as various drops of blood spilled outside the most sacred image – all in a manner that would strike terror and reverence into Turks, let alone Christians. The sheet was shown to us completely uncovered, without any other veil in front of it and well spread out on the high altar, its usual location. Our master kissed and touched it, but could not tell what kind of material it was made of; yet he assured us that it did not seem to him to be either silk or linen. They say that the dimensions of these divine imprints are found to be different every time they are taken, and that they are as clearly visible from a distance as from close range. This most holy relic (so we were told) was acquired by the most illustrious lords of the House of Savoy at the time of the Holy Enterprise, on which one of them accompanied the Norman brothers Godfrey of Bouillon and Baldwin. [1] Some say it was bought by a Savoyard soldier who came by a prisoner without the means to pay his ransom and was offered the Sindon by the man's wife in return for his freedom. Others claim that it was the lord of Savoy himself who obtained it from the woman in the same manner. At one time the Dukes of Savoy used to carry the relic about with them (albeit with the utmost veneration) wherever they rode. The predecessor of the present duke, yielding to the entreaties of his wife, the Lady Margaret, the daughter of His Imperial Majesty,[2] enshrined it in this chapel

---

[1] Baldwin, first king of Jerusalem (1100–18) and his brother Godfrey (d. 1100), sons of Count Eustace II of Boulogne, leaders of the First Crusade.

[2] The predecessor of Duke Charles III referred to here was Philip II, who married Margherita (but of Bourbon) in 1472. But there is further confusion with Marguerite de Charney, who was supposed to have given it to Duke Lewis (duke 1440–65) in 1452.

of the castle, and from that time Chambéry has hardly ever been affected by plague as it used to be, when outbreaks occurred annually; and knowing from experience that as soon as the Sindon is removed from the town, which is the capital of the Duchy of Savoy, the plague assails them, they would in no wise allow it to be carried away; and for safety they secure it with two locks and keys.

October 29. Leaving Chambéry after lunch we went to the Grande Chartreuse, five leagues distant over mountainous terrain the whole way. The mountains are not particularly rocky, but are so steep that I reckon it to be the longest and most unpleasant journey that was ever made.

The monastery called the Grande Chartreuse (founded by St Bruno, the head of the Carthusian order, by the miracle we read of in his life, which has been printed) is situated in a valley between two exceedingly high mountains, bristling with crags, where there is never any scarcity of snow. A league before reaching the monastery you enter the valley through a pass barred by a gate; on the far side there is no exit at all. As founded by St Bruno, the monastery was situated on a hill and built close up against the bare rock of the mountain to the right. Here the saint lived with his companions until he returned to Calabria to build S. Stefano del Bosco, his second monastery, where he died and his body still lies.[1] But an avalanche demolished this original monastery a long time ago, killing many of the monks, and it was subsequently rebuilt in the valley-bottom. Eight years ago, when it stood on its present site but was built mainly of timber, it was almost completely destroyed by fire owing to the negligence of a barber; but already, thanks to the zeal and diligence of the prior (who is the general of the Carthusians but lives permanently at the monastery), it has been entirely restored with stone vaulting and with so many buildings and fine living quarters that there would be room enough for an army. Forty-five monks live here, along with over a hundred and fifty minor clerks, lay brothers, oblates, and other lay and secular servants. And in addition to the cloisters, where there is room for seventy monks, there are the quarters for all the nations with Carthusian monasteries, which, according to a table we were shown, are more than two hundred in number.

[1] St Bruno (*c.* 1030–1101), founder of the Carthusian Order, withdrew late in life to Calabria, where he founded the Certosa di Santo Stefano, near Catanzaro.

And again, half an Italian mile below the monastery, they have stables, with room for three hundred horses in all, which are set aside for these nations and used at the time of the general chapter held here every year. We were told by the monks that the Grande Chartreuse has an income of less than four thousand ducats a year. But as a place for repentance and the service of God it is quite ideal: lonelier than can be imagined, subject continuously to snow and extreme cold for three quarters of the year and approached by no-one who is not going there expressly to visit the monastery. It is called Chartreuse after a nearby village, and also after a little river flowing down the valley, which has the name Chartreuse.

October 30. Leaving the Chartreuse, where we dined badly and lunched still worse (for no meat is eaten there) and slept very ill on pallets with no sheets but only heavy sheepskin blankets, we went to stay the night at Grenoble, a journey of five leagues, and again up and down all the way. But it was not nearly as steep as the ride from Chambéry to the Grande Chartreuse, though here we did encounter a good deal of snow en route.

Grenoble is a fortified town in Dauphiny, where a parliament is held as in Paris. It lies in a level valley-bottom between very high mountains. This is beautiful and over a league wide; it is covered with vines, as are also the lower slopes of the mountains, and there are many fruit-trees. Down the middle flows a river called the Drac, which, as is pointed out as one comes over the mountain from the Chartreuse, seems to form a Greek δ. This river, which is of a good width and depth, passes through one part of the town and is spanned by a stone bridge with some very fine shops on it. A short way from the town flows another river called the Isère, which meets the Drac not far away and thereafter continues to be called the Isère.[1] Their combined waters flow into the Rhône. Grenoble has fine houses, streets and squares, and a large population, and belongs to the King. Here we saw the tomb of the noble and most handsome body (for undoubtedly his soul is already in heaven) of the most illustrious Lord Infante Don Alfonso of Aragon,[2] the second son of the late-lamented King Frederick and of the most unhappy Queen Isabella. The tomb is in the convent of St Clare, within the walls, which is run by nuns of the order of St Clare who are strictly observant and live

[1] De Beatis has confused the Isère (which flows through Grenoble) with the Drac in this passage.   [2] Born 1498. Died in exile.

exemplary lives: at no time do they eat meat, they fast daily and they always sleep on straw without undressing. The tomb is in a small chapel to the left of the high altar: raised up and set in an arched tabernacle built on to the wall, covered with brocade, and surrounded by a curtain of black velvet. In two chapels of the same church of St Clare (which is nothing special), there are two alabaster images carved with many figures and lovely intaglio-work.

October 31. From Grenoble we went to eat at St-Marcellin, abstaining from meat as it was the eve of All Saints. This was a journey of seven long leagues. St-Marcellin is quite a fine town and has good lodgings. On the way, two leagues from Grenoble, there is a small walled town, and after that three more small towns. At one of these, a league from St-Marcellin, called Larbe, one passes down a long street lined on either side with makers of box-wood combs and of other, lathe-made, goods.

November 1. From St-Marcellin we went to hear mass and take lunch at St-Antoine-de-Vienne, two leagues away. The church dedicated to this saint is built on an eminence and is very large and handsome. On the left-hand side of the nave as you enter, near the choir, there is a fine, big organ with many stops and rich decoration, including a painting of the Annunciation and many other lovely things. Here we saw and kissed the arm of glorious St Antony, which is clad in silver. We also saw the bones of his body, which are kept in a casket fitted with an iron grille. This is housed in a shrine consisting of a silver-gilt structure resting on two wooden pillars behind the high altar. The casket was placed on the altar for the Cardinal to look at and the bones inspected one by one. We were able to infer from them that the Saint was very tall. In the same casket there is also the cloak of St Paul the First Hermit, which has almost entirely rotted away.[1] At this church there are many monks, who wear black-hooded capes over their habits, and many altar-boys, also dressed in habits, who are educated there. The services are very fine indeed. And there is a hospital where the sick are tended with great care and much good is done.

This place is called St-Antoine-de-Vienne because it is in the diocese of Vienne, but the city of that name is actually about seven

---

[1] It was supposedly made of palm leaves.

leagues distant. Beyond the church, lying partly in the valley and partly on the hillside, is quite a sizeable town with good lodgings, called St-Antoine after St Anthony, as indeed many French towns are named after saints. Here large quantities of silver Saint Anthonies, bells, *tau*-shaped crosses,[1] arms and little pigs[2] are sold both by clerics and laymen; and they are mostly made of low quality, thoroughly debased silver.

We lunched at St-Antoine and went on to dinner at Valence, six leagues away. Three leagues from this city there is a substantial town called Romans, which is skirted on the Valence side by the river Isère and has a stone bridge.

Valence is a fine city. A school of canon and civil law is maintained there, but that is the only faculty. Built at intervals for half an Italian mile from the town in the Montélimar direction are six little chapels in which the mysteries of the passion of Our Lord Jesus Christ are illustrated in the most beautiful wall paintings: the work of a Flemish artist, we were told. The last has a Mount Calvary with the crucifixion, and a fine church is being built there. These shrines are indeed an object of great veneration, for not a day goes by without their being visited by men and women without number, who kneel and pray in each chapel, beginning with the one nearest the city gate. A large area round Valence, including some sizeable towns is named after the city and called the Valentinois. Beyond Valence, apart from certain narrows formed by low hills, a fine broad plain stretches all the way to Avignon. Over to the right, towards the mountains, flows the Rhône. There are many vineyards – the wines are excellent – and a few almond trees and olives as well. Duke Valentino, the son of Pope Alexander VI, took his title from Valence, and he had an income of eleven thousand ducats a year from the city and the rest of the duchy; but since his downfall and death,[3] Valence has been an appurtenance of the French Crown.

[1] The Tau (T-shaped) cross was worn as a badge by the monks of his Order as the first letter of the Greek word for God the Father, Theos.
[2] Symbol of the sensuality and gluttony St Anthony Abbot was tempted by and rejected during his hermit life. A common attribute of the saint in art. For other religious souvenirs see the silver madonnas sold at Notre-Dame-de-Bollène and the 'Magdalen' cords at La Sainte-Baume.
[3] Cesare Borgia (b. 1475) was created Duke of Valence by Louis XII in 1498. On the Pope's death in 1503 Il Valentino (so nicknamed partly because of his duchy but also because when in orders he had been Cardinal of Valentia) lost the power he had acquired in the Romagna, was sent in 1504 to Spain as a prisoner, escaped to Navarre and was killed in a skirmish near Viana in 1507.

November 2. We heard mass for All Souls and had lunch at Valence before going on to dinner at Montélimar, seven leagues away. The town is large, with rather ordinary houses and streets, and there are good lodgings. Three leagues from Montélimar is a substantial town called Livron and half a league further on another one called Loriol.

November 3. After lunching at Montélimar we went on to dinner at Notre-Dame-de-Bollène, a distance of five leagues. Two leagues beyond Montélimar is a town called Chateauneuf-du-Rhône, and a league beyond that another one called Donzère. The territory of the Church[1] begins at a little chapel half a league past Donzère, and after another half league there is a town almost in ruins belonging to the Church, called Lapalud. We then went one Italian mile out of our way in order to see Pont-St-Esprit, which spans the Rhône. This has twenty tall, wide arches, is finely built in a pleasing stone and is still better paved. According to the measurement taken by one of our grooms with a piece of cord, it is four hundred paces, with arms spread,[2] long. It is broader and straighter than the bridge of Avignon, though not so long. At that time of year, however, the water did not extend beneath all the arches, but we were told that in springtime the river is so full because of the snow melting that it spreads outside the bridge. At the end of the bridge is the town of Pont-St-Esprit, which is very pleasant and belongs to the King of France along with all the rest of the area beyond the Rhône.

Notre-Dame-de-Bollène is a tiny church with only seven cloistered nuns, who are of exemplary life and say the office daily, and four chaplains. The Madonna there came to be venerated forty years ago in the following way. Two hundred years ago the village was sacked and burned by a wicked captain along with several other places in the area. Afterwards, some of his men, fearing divine punishment, hid away this image, which is a relief three spans high, together with certain other relics, in an aperture where the altar of the church is now situated. And there it lay, buried by the debris, until it was rediscovered, thanks to a divine revelation granted to a man of holy life, and most reverently

---

[1] Avignon and its surrounding territory was bought for the papacy from its overlord the Countess of Provence, in 1348.

[2] 'Ad braze spase'. Presumably he went along the string stretching it with arms extended and counting as 'paces' the number of times he did this.

removed to its present location; since when it has worked many miracles and is said in those parts to do so continually. For, as I have said, it is greatly venerated and attracts many visitors. Close to the church there are a number of houses offering board and accommodation, and many silver madonnas are sold there for devotional purposes.

November 4. From Notre-Dame-de-Bollène, where we heard mass very early, we went to lunch and dinner at Sorgues, a distance of five leagues. One league beyond Notre-Dame there is a village called Mondragon, and two leagues further on a village consisting of one long street at the foot of a very high hill, surmounted by an extremely strong fortress called Mornas, which dominates the bank of the Rhône and belongs to the Pope. A league beyond that there are two strong castles built on rocky islets formed by the Rhône. These belong to one of the sisters of the Cardinal Archbishop of Auch, Legate in Avignon.[1] Just opposite on the left bank, situated on an eminence is a delightful town called Châteauneuf, also belonging to the Church. Beyond Montélimar almost all the way to Avignon there are many box trees and an abundance of lavender. Lavender and lavender-water are much used in Germany and Flanders, and in all the provinces of France as well.

November 7. From Sorgues, where we stayed for three most enjoyable days with the aforementioned Cardinal Archbishop of Auch's two sisters, waiting for the Cardinal who was on his way from Auch, we went on to lunch at Avignon, a distance of two short leagues. The two Cardinals were met outside the city by all the nobility and clergy and by officials and troops of the Cardinal Legate in large numbers.

Avignon, as everyone knows, is a city of the Church, and from it the Comtat (containing Carpentras,[2] a city, and many other towns) takes its name. It lies in the plain except for the palace and the cathedral, which are built on a rocky eminence. It is a very round city, encircled by high, thick stone walls, which are well constructed and adorned with massive towers. And in all those, and they are many, which serve as gates into the city there are bells. Between one tower and the next, as the interval is

---

[1] François Guillaume de Castelnau, appointed Legate in Avignon by Julius II in 1513; Cardinal of Narbonne.

[2] Carpentras was actually in the comtat or county of Venaissin.

considerable, two proportionately spaced half-towers project outwards about six spans, with arched slits let into their outer face. A row of tooth-like corbels support the battlements, and this is most decorative. The moats are broad and, although not very deep, can be filled at will to a depth of twelve spans.

Within the ramparts, although the ground is not fully occupied, there are many houses, all finely built in stone, and streets that would be fine were they not so ill paved as to make riding difficult and walking extremely so, cobbled as they are with a kind of round pebble that ruins your feet. The women are very attractive, and although they dress in the French style most of them do not wear the French chaperon but a special head-dress of their own which is far prettier. There are many court ladies of the utmost grace and refinement. We also saw many parish churches and religious houses – Dominican, Augustinian, Franciscan (both Conventual and Observant), Carmelite and Celestine. At the church of the Celestines are the body of Blessed Peter of Luxemburg and the tomb of Pope Clement III, who built the church.

On the western side, the city is skirted by the river Rhône, which rushes past the walls with extreme violence. It is spanned by a great stone bridge consisting of twenty-three arches, though at the end adjoining the far bank, which is in Languedoc and belongs to the King of France, seven of them stand on dry ground. It is said, however, that when the river is swollen there is water under them all. This bridge is not as broad as Pont-St-Esprit. Nor is it as straight: indeed it has numerous bends in it so as to withstand, I believe, the force of the current. And it is so well paved and slippery that it is extremely unpleasant to ride across, as is evident merely from the fact that seldom, if ever, does anyone ride over it. According to the measurement which I had taken in my presence, it is four hundred and sixty-six rods long;[1] yet the distance from the city gate leading on to the bridge to the limit to which the Church's jurisdiction extends is less than forty rods, and I have not been able to discover any reason why it should not extend right to the middle, as seems fitting, except that the Most Christian Kings usurped it in former times. Jews may go as far as this limit, but if they as much as set foot on the French side they

[1] The *canna* was as subject to regional variations as the *palmo* or span was; it also differed according to use; thus in Rome the *canna* as a measure of cloth was just under two metres, as a building measurement, 2·2 metres. Cf. note on p. 95.

may be killed with impunity. The river forms many islands; and there is no doubt that if it were to flow for many leagues in the same way as it flows for a few (for it is but a short distance from Lake Geneva or 'Gebenna',[1] whence it issues, to Marseilles, which is close to its mouth), instead of being just large, as it now is, it would be extremely large, as large as any great river in Europe. As it is, it is so swift-flowing that, except for the Tigris which, as the historians[2] tell us, is called Tigris, meaning 'arrow' in Latin, by reason of its rapid flow, there is no swifter river in the world; as may readily be observed in the city of Lyons at the place where it joins the Saône, for it thrusts apart the waters of that river with the ease of a great dolphin or an expert swimmer gliding through a calm sea.

On the other side of the city, half a mile to the east, is the Durance, a treacherous river, but this immediately flows into the Rhône. Three streams flow through the city and one through the moats. These are all produced by the Sorgue spring, which rises at a village called Vaucluse about six leagues distant, gushing out from a cliff with such abundance that if it flowed as a single stream instead of splitting into six or seven (one of which forms the river Sorgue) it would be a very big river. To the north, four leagues away, is Mount Ventoux, celebrated by Messer Francesco Petrarca[3], though in fact the whole of Avignon can be called *ventoso* [windy], for a savage wind blows there most of the time.

The city has a university comprising all faculties, and large numbers of merchants and nobles. The cathedral, which stands alongside the great palace and was built (so they say) by St Martha and dedicated to Our Lady, is squat and unimpressive, for it cannot be built to any great height because of the wind or extended outwards because of the nature of the site. It has twenty canons as well as the dignitaries, and when they take part in services they wear the *cappa* and *rochet*, like the canons of St Peter's in Rome. Several popes who died at Avignon while the Apostolic See was there are buried in its chapels. In the porch outside the door by which one enters the building there is a painting of St George on the right-hand wall, which Messer Francesco Petrarca is said to

---

[1] The Latin name for Geneva.

[2] Both Strabo (*Geography*, 11, 14, 8–9) and Pliny (*Natural History*, vi, 127) explain that Tigris is the Median (or Persian) word for arrow.

[3] See Petrarch, *The ascent of Mont Ventoux*, in *The Renaissance philosophy of man*, ed. E. Cassirer et al. (Chicago, 1948).

have commissioned while he was at the Papal Court in Avignon; and the maiden who, according to the story, was about to be devoured by the dragon is held by many to be Madonna Laura painted from life, on her knees with her hands raised heavenwards. Whoever she is, she has a graceful, country-girl's air, and on her head she is not wearing a chaperon according to the modern custom of France, but a kind of fillet with a tail in the Neapolitan manner. And on the wall are written or painted the following lines by the poet, which are addressed to St George, entreating him to quench the hidden firebrands of war. Some interpret them as being love poetry. Others familiar with the history of those times say that the lines were written à propos a certain war which the King of England was secretly planning to wage on the French.

Lines by Petrarch

Miles in arma ferox, bello captare triunphum
Et solitus vastas pilo transfigere fauces
Serpentis, tetrem spirantis pectore fumum,
Occultas extingue faces in bello Georgi.[1]

Near the cathedral, on a great square stretching before the Palace of the Popes, is a very handsome and well-designed little palace in the modern style with towers. This was built by Pope Julius of most happy and immortal memory[2] while as a cardinal he held the archbishopric and legation of Avignon, and presented by him to the archbishopric. The great palace, where the Popes resided for so many years,[3] is a remarkable structure: built of huge blocks of stone, vaulted throughout, containing rooms without number, and fortified, for it has six great external towers (one of them just like the Borgia tower in the Vatican Palace in Rome) as well as a number of small internal ones. It rises to an immense height, with so many staircases (many en caracole or spiral) and so many doorways, all of stone, that it is like a labyrinth; and although it has fallen badly into disrepair through never being fully occupied

---

[1] 'O St. George, warrior keen to do battle, accustomed to pursue victory in war and drive thy spear through the huge throat of the dragon breathing foul smoke from his breast, put out the hidden firebrands of war.' These four hexameters do not appear to be attributed to Petrarch by modern scholars.

[2] Giuliano della Rovere, Pope as Julius II from 1503–13; the Cardinal of Aragon had been a close supporter and associate, hence the interest expressed here. He only rebuilt the façade of the Petit Palais.

[3] The papal court and administration was centred on Avignon 1305–78.

since the return of the Apostolic See to Rome, there are still some
fine halls, some in sound condition and others in need of repair.
The one where conclaves were held, which is very large and long,
and the Consistory Court are intact. The one that has seriously
deteriorated is the largest of all, but I do not know what purpose
it served, unless perhaps it was reserved for public audiences. There
is also a chapel which is larger and loftier than the Sistine in the
Vatican palace and has underneath it a very fine hall where the
Rota[1] used to sit. The ground is hollowed out beneath the entire
palace, which is thus extremely well-provided with cellars and
other underground appurtenances. It also encloses a square courtyard of very harmonious proportions. Nor is there a window,
large or small (and there are windows without number), which
is not fitted with a grille so thick and massive that, including the
iron chains built into the vaults and walls and other ironwork
holding the blocks of stone together, the palace is estimated to
contain 300,000 hundredweights of iron. The reason for this is that
formerly Avignon and the rest of the Comtat were pledged to the
Church by a prince of the House of Anjou who was then lord
of the city, on the understanding that he would reimburse the cost
of any improvements, and the Pope of the day incurred this
excessive expenditure in building the palace so that the prince
should never be able to meet it and the city, with the whole
Comtat, thus remain in the hands of the Church, as in fact
occurred. The Cardinal Archbishop of Auch has carried out a good
deal of restoration work and continues to do so at the present time.
The whole city can be made secure with chains.[2]

We spent a fortnight at Avignon held up by the return of
Gascon troops from the Urbino campaign.[3] On our last evening
the Cardinal Legate gave a public banquet at the palace at which
many beautiful ladies were present, and after dinner there was
dancing until midnight with unconstrained merrymaking and
diversions.

November 20. We left Avignon after lunch and went on to spend
the night at Arles, seven leagues away. After one league we had
to send a party ahead to break the ice, so that the boat could draw

---

[1] The court of final appeal for cases arising from canon law; so called from the circular
bench on which the judges sat.   [2] i.e. across the streets.
[3] Francis I lent French troops to the Medici Pope Leo X in his war to oust Duke
Francesco Maria della Rovere from Urbino and replace him by his nephew Lorenzo
de'Medici. The campaign had ended in September 1517.

in to the bank of the Durance. Four leagues from Avignon there is a town called Tarascon, which is in Provence and belongs to the King. The principal church there is dedicated to St Martha, and on our way through we saw her head which is covered with silver. The town is not very large, but has a castle similar to the new castle at Naples, albeit on a smaller scale. This was built by the father of King René.[1] Though not a very broad river, the Durance is very swift-flowing, and on the day when, as I said, we crossed it by boat an Italian mile from Avignon, it was bringing down many huge pieces of ice. This is where Provence and the jurisdiction of his Most Christian Majesty begin.

Arles lies in the plain, a large well-constructed city, with houses entirely built in stone, and graced by many fine noblemen and women. It has the Rhône within a stone's throw to the right (as one travels towards Marseilles), and when we were passing through, both banks were ice-bound for much of their length. Here, in the church of St Anthony, where there are brothers of the same order as the ones at St-Antoine-de-Vienne, we saw the head of St Anthony, which is set in silver. This is exhibited complete with the jaw, and the bone is unmistakably real. The missing parts, including the beard, are supplied in silverwork. And the flesh of the saint is presented to be kissed inside a cross, also made of silver. The church itself is small. Arles cathedral, on the other hand, is a very fine church with a great organ, and there we saw the head of St Stephen the First Martyr. This has a stone wound over the right eye and was brought (so they say) by St Trophimus, the first archbishop of the city, who came from Jerusalem in the company of Mary Magdalen and converted the people of Arles to the Christian faith. The head of St Trophimus too, covered with silver, is in the same cathedral.

Here the state of confusion that exists in the matter of Christian relics becomes all too apparent, for we visited a body of St Anthony, as I have said, in the diocese of Vienne, yet another was to be seen at Arles. A few words on this subject therefore seem called for at the present juncture.

In the course of this journey we have seen or heard tell of a great

---

[1] René of Anjou (d. 1480) was the son of Louis II, King of Provence and Naples. The 'new castle' (Castel Nuovo) at Naples was founded in the thirteenth century and re-modelled by Alfonso I from the 1450s.

number of these prodigious relics, these many-headed hydras and many-bodied geryons.[1] For besides the body of St Anthony, there is the spear of Christ shown at the Sainte-Chapelle in Paris and the head of St John the Baptist on display at Amiens in Picardy, regardless of the fact that both of these relics are in Rome. There is the skull of St Stephen the First Martyr in the church of Saint-Etienne at Caen in Normandy, the piece shown at Bourges and the complete skull to be found at Arles. One finds many arms and feet – and any number of hands and fingers – all belonging to one and the same saint. Half of all the nails of Christ's crucifixion on show would supply a hundred crosses. And one could mention so many other cases of this kind, where important relics are duplicated or triplicated: though one must exclude relics like the wood of the cross or thorns from the crown, for many pieces of the wood are to be seen, but the cross was very large, and thorns are to be found in many places, yet the crown too, as we saw at the Sainte-Chapelle, is quite large, furnished with bare withies and quite thornless. Consequently, one cannot arrive at any firm conclusions in these cases, as one can with other relics, where precise numbers are involved.

However, I would not pretend to determine which of the duplicated relics are genuine and which false, since that is not my affair, but simply state that so much confusion and uncertainty does not cast the slightest discredit on the Divine Being or the Holy Trinity, or in any way invalidate the Ten Commandments of the Law, which command us to believe in one God, or the Twelve Articles of the Faith. For God is the creator, and all His saints are His creatures and have reached that rank by His grace. To believe is godly, and relics may be venerated, with due caution as to their authenticity. The errors in question have come about through the remissness of ministers, who have taken little trouble to avoid them yet ought on no account to have approved any relic before its authenticity had been properly investigated, or allowed duplicated relics to exist anywhere in Christendom from the very beginning. For now that the abuse is old and ingrained, it must needs be tolerated, since there are so many cities, lands and peoples, each with their ancient sanctuaries and relics, which rather than

---

[1] One of the Labours of Hercules was to carry off the cattle belonging to the three-headed monster Geryon. This is the only passage in which de Beatis refers to classical mythology.

forgo them would submit to being destroyed and burnt a thousand times over.

November 21. We left Arles after lunch and went to dinner at Salon, seven leagues distant. The Archbishop of Arles, a Spaniard,[1] was there. He is the spiritual and temporal lord of the town, and in the castle, where he has fitted out a fine apartment, we were received most hospitably. The town itself is of little account. Between Arles and Salon one rides the whole way across a rough, stony plain, all strewn with pebbles.

November 22. From Salon we went to dinner at Marseilles, a distance of seven leagues, riding the whole time through rosemary, which grows everywhere on the hills in that area. Half way is the Etang de Berre, which looks like a great lake. Salt is extracted from it. It is said to be quite shallow, with a mouth only two bowshots wide. The name Etang de Berre comes from a certain town called Berre, which is built at the tip of a low foreland on the lagoon and looks very attractive from a distance. Three leagues from Marseilles there is a village situated in a hilly, stony locality (indeed, this day's journey was just one long succession of ups and downs) and called Les Pennes,[2] and I believe that it is so named because life certainly cannot be very gay for those who live there, given the unfavourable situation of the place. Near Marseilles we found olives in abundance, but the trees were small.

Marseilles lies on level ground and stretches out between not very steep hills. The city itself is narrow and elongated, and so too is the harbour, which enters it from the side and is completely shut in and secure, surrounded as it is by hills, as I said, and narrowing to a mouth only a stone's throw wide, which is guarded by two forts and can be closed with chains. As you enter the harbour, which is not very large, especially widthways, but extremely deep, you have to your left the city, and to your right an arsenal[3] that can take nine galleys at a time and near to it another one, under construction for the king, which when finished will hold twenty. This has been built up to the level of the vaults, some of which have already been erected in stout masonry, and is surrounded by moats full of water. There are also towers at the corners and

---

[1] Juan Ferrer, Archbishop since 1499.

[2] French *peines*, sorrows or afflections. This is characteristic of de Beatis's taste (and that of his contemporaries) for folk etymologies. Cf. his previous observation about 'Ventoux' and his later one about 'Nizza' and 'Genua'.

[3] 'Arcenao'; cf. the dockyard or Arsenal of Venice.

embrasures to protect the flanks, so that it has considerable defensive strength – as is necessary, indeed, since it stands separate from the city and could easily be attacked and burnt were it not fortified and garrisoned. There were thirteen French galleys in the harbour, including three big ones which were all laid up, and many foreign ships and galleons, the most notable being an extremely fine galleon belonging to Fra Bernardino, known as the Great Corsair, who is a Knight of Rhodes and a native of Provence.[1] At the time of our visit (when he came to dine with the Cardinal) he was staying in Marseilles, where he has a house, but he also has a castle nearby which was a gift from the King of France. He had several conversations with the Cardinal and important matters were discussed. His galleon is massively timbered, new and extremely well fitted out, especially in point of artillery, carrying as it does twelve cannon, twelve falconets and a hundred arquebuses. He also had a large ship in the harbour, likewise well armed, and a galley which was laid up.

The city is not particularly beautiful in itself. In the cathedral is the tomb of St Lazarus.[2] Ladies' mantles of every colour and of finest quality are an important manufacture. On the right-hand side, a short way past the arsenals in the direction of the hills, is the abbey of St-Victor, which was formerly a benefice of the late-lamented Cardinal Sanseverino and is now Cardinal de'Medici's.[3] Here there is a fine though not very large church, vaulted throughout on two levels. This is fortified on account of the Moors, who raid it repeatedly. The abbey houses about fifty Benedictine monks who are each maintained by a separate endowment. In the upper church are the heads of St Victor and St Martin, some of the flesh of the Innocents, and a rib of St Lazarus, which is very thick and over two spans long, thus clearly indicating that this saint and his sisters were giants of a sort. And there are countless other relics, including a tooth of St Peter, all

[1] Fra Bernardino (so styled both by Sanuto, *Diarii*, xxv, cols 465, 584, and the anonymous Milanese f. 77v) operated against Turkish vessels as a free lance and also in association with papal galleys.

[2] In Provence Lazarus, an early fifth century bishop of Aix was often confused with the biblical Lazarus (after whom the knights of the Order of St Lazarus, active in France from the thirteenth century, were named) who was reputed to have come after the resurrection with the Magdalen to Marseilles, of which he became the first bishop. Though one of the earliest (1475–81) and finest examples of Italian sculpture in France (by Francesco Laurana) it is consistent with de Beatis's attitude to the arts that he does not comment on it.

[3] Giulio de'Medici, later Pope Clement VII. Federico Sanseverino died in 1516.

mounted and kept in silver shrines. To the left of the altar is the tomb of Pope Honorius V,[1] who was elected to the Papacy after being abbot here and who died at Avignon. In the lower church, I saw the cross of St Andrew, which is very large and plated all over with iron except for a patch that can be uncovered for the devout to kiss; this, however, is normally kept locked, so that one cannot tell what sort of wood the cross is made from. Saints without number are also buried there, but of especial interest are the corpses of four of the Seven Sleepers,[2] and the oratory where the glorious Magdalen stayed before she went to do penance on the mountain of the Sainte-Baume.[3] Here we also saw the seat, hollowed out in the stone, on which she would rest her blessed body, and from its length, and from other facts shortly to be mentioned, it may be inferred that she was, as I have said, a woman of great stature. At all events, she was a great and glorious saint.

November 24. From Marseilles we went to lunch at Auriol, five leagues away. Three leagues from Marseilles is a small town called Aubagne, belonging to the bishop of the city. Half a league before Auriol is a castle called Roquevaire, built on a rocky eminence, with a village below. And both Roquevaire and Auriol, which also has a castle on a hill, and its few houses lying partly on the hillside and partly on flat ground, belong to the monastery of St-Victor, which has many more castles round Marseilles and bestows a vast number of livings scattered as far afield as Spain. I believe that these livings bring the commendator, Cardinal de'Medici, revenues of about two thousand ducats.

November 25. From Auriol we went to mass and lunch at the Sainte-Baume [Bauna] (or according to some, 'Balna'), a distance of two long leagues, riding through snow-covered hills the whole way. The snow was not deep, however, nor was it a bad road. As we approached our destination, with the mountain ridge to our right, we rode through a fine forest. The Saint-Baume is the highest mountain to be found anywhere in those parts, dominating the whole of Provence and particularly the coastal region. It rises

---

[1] In fact, Urban V, Pope, 1362–70.

[2] The Seven Sleepers of Ephesus, whose waking in the mid-fifth century from two centuries of sleep was revered as an analogue of the Resurrection.

[3] While lacking the *cachet* of Compostela, the region Marseilles–Saint-Baume–St-Maximin was the nearest to a 'Holy Land' Europe afforded, thanks to the legend that the Magdalen had been set adrift from Palestine in an open boat which had miraculously brought her to Marseilles.

to cliffs of bare rock which soar sheer to a great height, and in the rock face is a great cave where unbeknown to anyone and unseen by human eyes St Mary Magdalen lived as a penitent for thirty years. Here, various rooms have been let into the walls of the grotto and a door added, so as to form a chapel with living quarters and amenities for the friars – Observant Dominicans only five in number – who administer this great shrine. Inside the church one is shown a small cave, now enclosed behind an iron door, where the glorious saint slept for so many years on the bare rock. All who visit the sanctuary as pilgrims are given pieces of the rock to quench the heat of fever, and cords measured against the saint for women in childbirth. The length of these cords is taken from a recumbent wooden statue said to have been commissioned by St Maximin to life-size dimensions. Rain falls everywhere in this cavern-church (although set deep in the rock) except in the cave where the saint used to sleep. There is also a spring of purest water, the state of which never varies, yet the friars and visitors drink from it and use it for washing and all other necessities. The water does not gush out from the rock but wells up in a hollow. The Cardinal and all the rest of us drank some as an act of devotion. At the top of the mountain is a chapel at the place to which the glorious saint was conveyed by the angels seven times a day, where she would stay in prayer and angelic conversation: as is attested by the verses of Messer Francesco Petrarca,[1] who came here on a pilgrimage and stayed for three days and three nights. These are the lines.[2]

Versus Petrarche quos condidit existens in spelunca beate Marie Magdalene:

Dulcis amica Dei, lachrymis inflectere nostris
Atque humiles attende preces, nostreque saluti
Consule (namque potes), nec enim tibi tangere frustra
Permissum gemituque pedes perfundere sacros
Et nitidis siccare comis, ferre oscula plantis

[1] That Münzer copied these same verses suggests that de Beatis at the Sainte-Baume is copying a printed hand-out for pilgrims. Op. cit., 64–5.

[2] The thirty-six Latin hexameters on the Saint's life as a penitent at the Sainte-Baume which Petrarch composed while there in the autumn of 1337 were long afterwards sent to an old friend, Philippe de Cabassole, Cardinal Bishop of Sabina, at his request, together with a letter describing the visit in some detail (*Epistolae seniles*, XIV, 17). Both the letter and the verses are to be found, with translations, in *Francisci Petrarchae poëmata minora quae exstant omnia*, ed. D. Rossetti, Milan, 1834, Vol. III, Appendix II, pp. 18–25. (J.M.L.).

Inque caput Domini preciosos spargere odores.
Nec tibi congressus primos a morte resurgens
Et voces audire suas, et membra videre
Immortale decus lumenque habitura per evum
Ne quicquam dedit etherei Regnator Olimpi.
Viderat ille cruci herentem nec dira paventem
Judaice tormenta manus, turbeque furentis
Jurgia et insultus equantes verbera linguas,
Sed mestam intrepidamque simul digitisque cruentis
Tractantem clavos, implentem vulnera fletu,
Pectora tundentem violentis candida pugnis,
Vellentem flavos manibus sine more capillos.
Viderat hec, inquam, dum pectora fida suorum
Diffugerent, pellente metu; memor ergo revisit
Te primam ante alios: tibi se prius obtulit uni.
Te quoque digressus terris et ad astra reversus
Bis tria lustra cibi numquam mortalis egentem
Rupe sub hac aluit, tam longo in tempore solis
Divinis contentam epulis et rore salubri.
Hec domus atra tibi stillantibus humida saxis
Horrifico tenebrosa situ tecta aurea regum
Delitiasque omnes ac ditia vicerat arva.
Hic inclusa libens, longis vestita capillis,
Veste carens alia, ter denos passa decembres
Diceris, hic non fracta gelu, nec victa pavore,
Namque fames, frigus, durum quoque saxa cubile
Dulcia fecit amor spesque alto pectore fixa.
Hic hominum non visa oculis, stipata catervis
Angelicis septemque die subvecta per horas
Celestes audire choros alterna canentes
Carmina corporeo de carcere digna fuisti.

After thirty years the saint was taken thence by angels to
St-Maximin, and on Easter Day, after receiving communion from
the hand of St Maximin, she lay down on a certain stone which
is in the church of St-Maximin and forthwith gave up the ghost.

From the Sainte-Baume we went on to St-Maximin, after
lunching partly from food provided by the friars, who do not eat
meat, and partly from the supply we had brought from Auriol.
After half a league of steep descent from the Sainte-Baume there

is a village situated on a rocky eminence, called Nans, and this too belongs to the monastery of St Victor.

St-Maximin is a modern town of medium size on the site of the former Urbs Aquensis,[1] which was converted to the Christian faith by the preaching of the Magdalen and had St Maximin as its first bishop. It lies on level ground and belongs to the King. The church of St Maximin is there, and it is of great size and beauty, although not entirely finished. It is served by more than seventy friars of the same order as the ones at the Sainte-Baume. I was informed that they are not subject to the General of the Dominicans and do not acknowledge any superior except their own prior. In an underground chapel, or rather grotto, beneath the church, the head of the glorious Magdalen is enshrined in a silver casket on the altar, with a silver mask which can be raised showing the head behind a glass cover. Through this one can clearly see that it is quite fleshless apart from the area over the left brow touched with three fingers by Our Lord Jesus Christ when he said, 'Touch me not'; and indeed, it is a relic genuine beyond all doubt and most venerable. And from the head (which is very large and has the jaw-bone intact and some of the molar teeth) and the arm-bone, as well as the things already referred to, it may readily be inferred that the Magdalen was an extremely tall woman. In the same chapel the body of St Maximin is kept in an iron chest; and one is also shown some of the blood of Our Lord Jesus Christ, which is kept in a phial, itself inside a larger bottle. This was gathered up beneath the most holy Cross by the most glorious Mary Magdalen, who in devotion always carried it about with her, and everyone in those parts maintains that it produces the spectacle of a most genuine miracle; for every year on Good Friday, the day of Our Lord's most bitter passion, it starts to liquefy and to boil so vigorously and noisily that it can be heard even from outside the chapel; and whereas normally this most precious blood is mingled with earth, owing to the way in which it was collected, and as hard as stone, now it liquefies to such an extent that it overflows from the phial into the bottle, drawing constant increase from within itself according to the mysteries inherent in the most cruel passion. But at the hour of Christ's death, all this outpouring of blood immediately flows back into

[1] More probably the Roman site was called Villa Latum or Castrum Rhodani. *Urbs Aquensis* was the Latin name for Aix-en-Provence, to which the rest of this sentence refers.

the phial and returns to its original hard state. All Provence and most of the inhabitants of the neighbouring regions flock to see this glorious and quite astounding spectacle.

The chapel is secured with several locks, and this is because before St Mary's head was so closely guarded a friar of the same order from Padua, or according to some, Naples, came to stay here and under cover of religious zeal schemed until at length he had the opportunity to enter the chapel and steal the head. But by a genuine miracle he found himself unable to remove it from the church and was forced to put it back in its place. Then, tempted by the devil, who appeared to him at that moment, he decided to carry off at least the silver, and when he had taken it he made off. The next morning the friars discovered the outrage and realizing that the culprit was the Paduan or Neapolitan friar, set out in pursuit. Finding him in a wood only a league away, unable either to make his way forward or retrace his steps, they seized him and had him put to death.

On the high altar of the church are the body of the Magdalen in a silver casket and an arm encased in silver, the thickness of the bone being visible through a small aperture where the arm is left uncovered for the faithful to kiss. And there in a glass reliquary we also saw some of the saint's hair which is lovelier than gold. It is said that only the hair that touched the most holy feet of Our Lord has survived; all the rest having turned to dust and ashes. The arm of St Maximin, and the heads of the man born blind and given sight by Christ, of the woman who said, 'Blessed is the womb that bare thee', of Sidoine and Blaise,[1] disciples of St Maximin, and of Susanna who was cured of an issue of blood are all kept on the same high altar enshrined in sumptuous, finely wrought silverwork. These saints, in the company of the Magdalen, were exposed by infidels to the perils of the deep on an unmanned vessel, so that they sank and by divine assistance finally reached Marseilles in the fourteenth year after the passion of Our Lord, as can be seen at greater length in the breviary, in the life of St Martha.[2]

There was a tablet in the church with the following lines in

[1] De Beatis has 'Ciffredo' and 'Blasio'. The former may denote Maximin's (reputed) companion Sidoine (or Sidonius), the latter appears to reproduce the French 'Blaise'.

[2] As in *Breviarium de camera secundum consuetudinem romane curie*...(Venice, 1500) where an account of the miraculous voyage (though mentioning only the Magdalen, Maximin, Martha, Lazarus and Marcellina) follows the prayers to the saint, f. 351v.

honour of St Mary Magdalen written by Messer Mario Equicola, tutor to the most illustrious Marchioness of Mantua, at the time when she visited St-Maximin as a pilgrim:

Versus endecasyllabi Marii Equicoli

Salve presidium meum
Magdalena tuo grata theantropo,
Quare perpetuum tibi
Debetur tacita laude silentium.
Cui Ferraria patria,
Estensis genitor cuy inclitus Hercules,
Mater sanguine Aragonum,
Que cum Gonzaico coniuge Mantuam
Princeps imperio regit.
Isabella Italis gloria plurima
Heic tua dum voto supplex vestigia adorat,
Orabat Marius talibus Aequicolus.[1]

November 26. We heard mass and lunched at St-Maximin, then went on to dinner at Le Luc seven long leagues away by a road that was poor in places. Le Luc is a town in the diocese of Fréjus and belongs to Monsignor de Solier, who has served as the Most Christian King's ambassador in Rome.[2] One league beyond St-Maximin is a village called Tourves, consisting of a few houses with a small adjoining quarter, through which one passes. Another league and one comes to a town with a fine suburb, called Brignoles.

November 27. From Le Luc to lunch and dinner at Fréjus, in Latin *Forum Julii*, seven long leagues distant by a road which was very poor in places. One short league beyond Le Luc is a small town

---

[1]   *Hendecasyllabic lines by Mario Equicola*

'Hail O Magdalen, my defence, who art dear to thy God-Man, wherefore perpetual silence in mute reverence is due to thee. While she who, born at Ferrara to the illustrious Ercole d'Este and a mother of Aragonese blood, is a princess holding sway at Mantua with her Gonzaga husband and to Italians is their chief glory, Isabella, knelt here in devotion before thy mortal remains, Mario Equicola prayed to thee with these words.' Thus in the version of these distichs transcribed from Equicola's *Iter* by Domenico Santoro, *Della vita e delle opere di Mario Equicola* (Chieti, 1906) 204. The text given by de Beatis lacks line 10, and has 'tanta' and 'dictis' instead of 'tacita' and 'Marius' in lines 4 and 12 respectively. (J.M.L.) The humanist scholar Equicola accompanied Isabella d'Este on a pilgrimage to the Sainte-Baume and St-Maximin as her secretary in April 1517. See above, p. 35.

[2] Palamède de Forbin, known as 'M. de Soliers', was the outstanding soldier-administrator of his clan under Charles VIII; as he appears to have died in 1508, this is perhaps his heir.

on a hill, Cannet, which is a seignory;[1] two leagues further on, a village consisting of little more than one street, called Vidauban; after another two leagues, the town of Le Muy, also a seignory; and after two leagues more, Puget, a small village one league from Fréjus belonging to the bishopric of that town.

On this day, though I do not recall the name of the town or the precise locality, I remember that we came upon a mountain which, according to local report, collapsed many years ago and buried a substantial town because of the most foul and abominable sin of sodomy;[2] for it so pleased the Lord God, who oft times in this vale of misery manifests His power and justice with a strong hand, to uphold the righteous and as an example to the ungodly. The mountain, over which we rode with great difficulty for half an Italian mile, looks almost as if it has collapsed only recently.

Fréjus is not a large city and has little of the city about it. The church is very low, dark as a cavern and, though well endowed, poorly maintained. Its bishop and permanent administrator is Cardinal Fieschi. An ancient theatre, still in quite good condition, lies a short distance outside the town; and there are also aqueducts and a number of other Roman remains, for this region was formerly much frequented and enjoyed by the Romans and for this reason was known as *provincia Romanorum*.

November 28. From Fréjus we went to eat (fastingly as it was St Andrew's eve) at Cannes, five leagues distant over mountains. A league from Cannes we crossed a river by boat: not a very wide one, but deep and of the purest water, and called the Siagne. We were welcomed with great courtesy and abundant hospitality, by the Bishop of Grasse.[3] The food was excellent and included good, large fish in plenty. Cannes belongs to His Lordship's abbey of St-Honorat, and although it consists of only a few houses, its seaside location and fine view give it great character and beauty. The Bishop has built a castle there with many comfortable apartments. Opposite the town are two islets which face one another, and on the further one, two Italian miles away, is the Benedictine monastery of St-Honorat, which has a community of twenty-four monks and an annual income of two thousand ducats. My master and some other members of our party who visited the

---

[1] I.e. independently administered. [2] Reference untraced.

[3] Agostino Grimaldi, brother of Luciano, Prince of Monaco, whom he succeeded in 1523. He had been Bishop of Grasse since 1505.

monastery with the Bishop said that it is very fine, and well fortified against the pirates and Moors who come here occasionally, and that the island is most attractive and delightful. This is where the Bishop usually spends the whole of Lent, most of Advent and the fast of All Saints. At these times he fasts continuously. And being not only of noble blood and good learning (indeed he is very learned) but a man of conscience and holy life, and extremely devout (as is apparent from his pilgrimages to St James of Galicia, to St Thomas of England, to all the sanctuaries of France and Italy, and recently to the Holy Sepulchre) he has made the monastery over to the community for them to enjoy after his death. Moreover, he already gives the monks eight hundred ducats a year for food and clothing, although with his bishopric and a number of other small livings which he holds he spends about three thousand ducats a year.

November 29. From Cannes we went with the Bishop to lunch at Antibes, which is two leagues away. This is a fine town, abounding in the most perfect muscadine grapes, and we were most hospitably received there by the Bishop's nephew, who is the *seigneur*. There is a ruined amphitheatre nearby; and two bowshots outside the town, on the road from Cannes, is a stone arch, with a stretch of broad highway well paved with massive white stones. On the arch there was an ancient inscription which I was unable to read but which said that these things were the work of Hercules who, as we read, visited those parts.

Still in the company of the Bishop of Grasse and his nephew, who is a most courteous youth of about twenty, married to a beautiful and agreeable wife (an exceptional combination), we went on from Antibes to dinner at Nice, another three leagues' journey away. One league from Nice there is a river which we forded although there was a ferry-boat. It is called the Var and divides Italy from France, or rather, Provence, which is the same thing.

Italia Bella[1]

The city of Nice is by the sea, built partly on a hill and partly on level ground, and is of considerable size and beauty. The women, too, are attractive, and their dress is rather similar to the

---

[1] De Beatis's heading.

Genoese in style. It is the common opinion that Nice [Nizza] owes its name to the fact that it is neither [ne] here [za] nor there, that is to say, neither in Italy nor in France, situated right at the frontier. For the same reason, its emblem is an eagle with one foot raised and not resting anywhere. It has a strong castle on the hill. It has good wines, citrus fruits in abundance and some of the largest lemons I have yet seen. The ruler is the Duke of Savoy.[1]

As we have repeatedly passed to and fro between province and province, I have not been able to offer separate descriptions of Brittany, Normandy, France,[2] Dauphiny and Provence, as I did in the case of Upper Germany, Flanders and the small stretch of Picardy we crossed. But now that we find ourselves back in the fair, sweet, pleasant, gentle and temperate land of Italy, I feel duty-bound to say something about these provinces. I shall be as brief as possible, weary as I am both from such a long journey and from the variety and multiplicity of customs in regions and among peoples so unlike those of Italy. And since the provinces in question are similar in most respects, I shall take them all together, distinguishing between them, however, wherever it may seem necessary, and beginning with conditions in the hostelries.

Conditions are usually good in these provinces, much better than in Germany where rooms invariably contain as many beds as can be fitted in, whereas here each room has a large bed for the master and a little one (which, too, is a feather-bed) for the valet, and there is a good fire. They also make good stews, pies and tarts of every sort. Yet whereas in Germany there are one or two tin chamber-pots to every bed (in Flanders they are made of brass and very clean), in France for want of any alternative one has to urinate on the fire. They do this everywhere, by night and day; and indeed, the greater the nobleman or lord, the more readily and openly will he do it. Good veal and beef are usually to be had, but the mutton (that is, wether-meat) is first-rate: there is no other meat, however much of a delicacy, that one would not leave off eating for a shoulder of roast mutton served, as is the custom all over France, with titbits. Partridges, pheasants, peacock, rabbits, capons and chickens are all cheap, abundant and well-prepared. There is game of every description and the

---

[1] Charles III, Duke since 1504.
[2] I.e. the 'historic' heartlands of the Kingdom: the centre and north east.

plumpest you ever saw, it being the custom never to hunt wild
animals out of season.

But of all these provinces it is France which has the best inns
and, thanks to court and aristocratic society, is the most civilized.
In all of them, especially France, window recesses, doorways and
fireplaces are commonly decorated with plasterwork. The
fireplaces in particular are richly ornate. Dress, both men's and
women's, is the same everywhere, though in France, for the reason
already mentioned, they dress more elegantly and in better quality
cloth. The women everywhere line their skirts, usually with black
or white lambswool, on account of the severe winters; and on
their heads, under their velvet or woollen chaperons they wear
linen coifs which tie under the chin and are very warm indeed.
In rainy weather, they wear a kind of small hooded cloak of camlet
which comes down to the waist. As in Flanders and Germany, they
do all kinds of work and sell all sorts of merchandise. There is not
an inn which does not have three or four chambermaids. The
women are good-looking on the whole (though less so than in
Flanders), pleasant and polite and can always be kissed as a mark
of courtesy and respect. Also, in many parts of these provinces the
women shave the men, and they do it very well, with great skill
and delicacy. Frequent banquets are another custom, and all
gentlewomen (there are always a good many present) dance with
supreme grace and a perfect grasp of the music.

Although the same language is spoken everywhere, there are
some differences of vocabulary from province to province, and
since, as I have said, the Court resides there, France proper is more
refined and politic than the rest of the country.

In general, the men are deficient in stature, and still more so
in presence, except for the noblemen, who are often well-built and
handsome. Most of the nobility bear arms, and those who do not
nonetheless live with the Most Christian King, who pays them
pensions for being in attendance at Court four months in the year.
When they have served their term, they are free to go where they
choose. But most of them go and spend their periods of leave from
court service at their castles or country houses, hunting in the
forests, living cheaply and 'saving their velvet'. The nobility are
exempt from all taxes or levies, while the peasants are in complete
subjection, more ill-treated and oppressed than dogs or slaves. Not
only noblemen but commoners, the merchants and men of every

rank and station, so be they French, are devoted to feasting and jollity, and are so given to eating, drinking and lechery that I do not know how they remain capable of doing anything worthwhile. But to conclude my remarks on the nobility, let me say that, in view of all the prerogatives, privileges and favours they enjoy, all French noblemen can be more thankful to God than those of any other part of the world. For they are certain, as gentlemen-born, never to starve nor to engage in any base occupation as most noblemen do in our part of the world. Very few Italians in fact live the life of true gentlemen, even if they have the manner and style of a gentleman.

In none of the provinces in question are the towns nearly so fine or attractive as in Germany or Flanders: they lack the fine squares and streets, the imposing houses and public buildings of those countries which, above all, are extremely well fortified, with walls and wide moats usually containing deep water from a river or a marsh. But they do often have fine churches, where divine worship is well performed; and there is not a cathedral or main church anywhere which does not have figured music[1] and more than one sung mass daily, led by six or eight choirboys who are learning to sing and who serve, tonsured like little monks, in the choir, receiving free food and clothing in return. They all have cloaks of red cloth with hoods, such as canons wear in Italy. This custom is also found throughout Flanders and in many German towns.

France consists almost entirely of plain, and so too for the most part do Brittany and Normandy, which have a long ocean coast. In Picardy, Normandy and Brittany, in addition to using farm manure, they extract from their estates a kind of earth as white as chalk,[2] and spread it over the farm-lands to fertilize them. It is found, however, only at a considerable depth. In Brittany the Bishop of Nantes, Monseigneur de Laval and many other lords and gentlemen maintain that a certain species of bird similar to the shearwater is generated from the rotting fir-wood of the masts of ships that founder off the coasts. These are variously known as *anatifes*, bernacles or *zopponi*. They cling to the wood with their beak until they are fledged and can fly. Then they emerge from the water and live on shore; and although it goes against

---

[1] 'Musica figurata', i.e. written for several parts.
[2] Marl: a readily friable form of limestone.

philosophy, which lays down that no lunged creature can live without air, vast numbers of them are to be found in those parts. Thus, in this instance, experience contradicts biological principles. These birds are the size of a large duck and most pretty creatures.[1] The Cardinal was given two by the Bishop of Nantes, but owing to negligence on the part of the carter who was transporting them in an uncovered cage they died from cold near Marseilles. The same carters came as far as Marseilles with some of our goods and a royal litter which the Cardinal had had made at Blois. There he sent them on to Rome aboard a galleon, together with upwards of two hundred and fifty dogs, which included ones of both slight and heavy build, ranging from bloodhounds to greyhounds. He had already dispatched overland to Rome twenty-eight horses - curtals, hobbies and saddle-horses – when we were at Lyons. We were also told that inside oysters caught in the ocean in the months of April and May crabs have been observed to have formed, and so they are not eaten at that time of year; and that crabs are found in the long, black sea mussels, and grubs or lice in the sea crayfish which have soft exteriors and which we in the Bari region call *salepici*.

All the provinces in question are very rich in cereals and forage, and in red cows like Germany; and there are large numbers of sheep, which yield wool of the finest quality. Yet though there is no lack of woodlands, pigs are not plentiful; but those that are to be found, are, however, extremely large, especially in Savoy, and generally pink. Pig-meat is hardly ever eaten except salted. In Dauphiny they have a large breed of cows and oxen, which are black all over with a hide like fine velvet. Around Avignon there is a type of large goat with a variegated hide and ears a span long; and not only there but throughout the provinces in question, wherever we saw goats their fleece was as fine as the wool of our sheep.

In the two provinces of Normandy and Brittany, they do not have a single vine owing to the cold winters, and instead of vineyards there are huge estates entirely planted with apple and pear trees. They extract the juice, keeping the two fruits separate, and drink it all the year round. They call this beverage cider. In

---

[1] The Barnacle or Brent Goose (also formerly called the Tree Goose) became the subject of this legendary and long-lived explanation because it was not realized that they bred outside Europe, i.e. in the Arctic.

taste it is incomparably better than beer, but it is not so wholesome. They make large quantities of it, wringing the pears and apples, when they have been well crushed, in presses, just as oil is extracted from olives. The beer is so wholesome because it is made by decoction of barley, oats and spelt in water, to which they add an infusion of hop-flowers, which are unpleasant in taste but most refreshing. The cereals undergo three decoctions, but the first is the best. The beers of Flanders are generally excellent and large quantities are produced. There they grow hops, carefully tended on stakes, in plantations just like our vineyards, and it must be said that they present a very pretty appearance. They have no other kinds of fruit apart from apples and keeping pears which grow there to perfection, especially a variety known as 'Bon Chrétien'. Since olives are not to be found in most parts, they use oil extracted from walnuts, which are plentiful. They also have some filbert or hazel-nut trees, and some plum and wild cherry trees. They derive great advantages from the many rivers which they have, all of them navigable.

The vineyards extend southwards from France, and they produce excellent red and white wines, though the latter are less common. There are a great many varieties of the red wine which they call *clairet*, and these make a most perfect drink, as light and refreshing as any I have ever tasted elsewhere. The same holds good for Dauphiny and Savoy, and for Provence where high quality figs and olives are also plentiful thanks to the mild sea air. France produces many more kinds of fruit than Normandy and Brittany but no figs. At Avignon, however, when we were there, which was in November, we ate black figs in perfect condition and a variety of hard-fleshed black grapes, just freshly picked, which would not have been better at Naples at the most favourable time of the year.

The length of the league. The Breton league is the longest, and by my reckoning is equal to four Italian miles. In Normandy, Dauphiny and Provence, and in the small part of Savoy we passed through, it was three miles, but in France only two, the French league being the shortest of all, equivalent to a league of the best going to be found anywhere else. And although everywhere difficult going or overestimation of the distance may result in one mile, league or whatever else the units may be called being greater than the last, this does not mean that the leagues of the four provinces in question and of the Kingdom of France can all be considered without distinction theoretically equal to three Italian miles.[1]

Throughout the French provinces they erect wayside crosses. But these are not crucifixes on the German pattern, nor are they so numerous. The nobility and wealthy apart, the dead are buried outside the churches, and what is worse, the graveyards are not enclosed, so that graves are scattered about the country towns and villages, albeit close to the churches, just as if they were the graves of Jews. Justice is rigorously dispensed everywhere: gallows are generally to be found at every turn, and they are always well supplied.

I shall leave out a number of other details, since they have been noted down at the appropriate places, that is, at the points where I came across them.

November 30. We left Nice after lunch and went to dinner at Monaco, which is nine miles' journey over rugged mountains without even a foot of good going. A mile from Nice is Villefranche. This too belongs to the Duke of Savoy. It has few houses, but there is a fine and famous harbour where ships are very safe – so deep that any vessel, however large, can draw right up to the steep hillside. Nevertheless, two years ago a large Genoese vessel which had put to sea with a fine array of artillery on board and a crew of over three hundred foundered in this very harbour with loss of all hands. The crow's-nest of the main mast can still be seen, sticking up about two rods out of the water. Everyone says that no other ship or vessel was ever lost in the harbour except this, which was unable to turn and went down instantly when a squall or windstorm so sudden and violent sprang up that many huge olives were uprooted. The event was considered by everyone to be a miracle, for the master and crew had long been evil-living pirates. Two miles further on is a village called Eze perched on a conical rock by the sea. This too belongs to the Duke. The whole way from Nice to Monaco we found large numbers of vanilla or carob trees, and some olives, growing all over the mountain slopes, almost down to the water's edge. Note: the southernmost Alps stretch from Nice to a point ten miles the other side of Monaco; a little further on the Apennines begin, which follow the coast as far as Genoa. After that, however, they extend across Italy.

[1] See note on p. 188.

Monaco, which belongs to the brother[1] of the Bishop of Grasse, is situated on the flat top of a round and quite high rock or promontory with sea most of the way round it. Its walls run right round the rock. They are very robust, well-designed and well-equipped with artillery. At the entrance gate (there is only one) it has a fine and extremely strong castle where there are some well-appointed living quarters. In the rock underneath are three or four artificial chambers from which artillery can be used without the slightest fear of attack. Thus by virtue of its situation and fortifications on the one hand, and of the strong garrison and lavish artillery which the lord maintains on the other (the artillery consisting of culverins, cannon and falconets, all of bronze and well-maintained) the town has been judged to be well-nigh impregnable. Some few years ago, the Genoese laid siege to it, when it was less strongly fortified than it is today, and although in large numbers were smashed and routed.[2] The lord of Monaco keeps a hundred and eighty men permanently in his pay, partly as castle guards and partly to man a very large *fusta*[3] used to intercept eastbound vessels of eight hundred *botti*[4] or less which do not put in and pay his lordship a two per cent duty.

This lord of Monaco, who acknowledges no superior, gave the Cardinal and everyone else a very kind and hearty reception. The Cardinal was accompanied as far as Monaco by the Bishop of Grasse, whom I would never grow weary of praising, being the humane, liberal and most virtuous prelate he is.

December 1. After lunch at Monaco we went on to S. Remo: twenty miles of extremely poor road and barely negotiable passes. Three miles beyond Monaco, perched on a mountain, is a castle belonging to the lord of Monaco, called Roquebrune, and two miles further on a town of his called Menton which we passed through. Halfway between Monaco and S. Remo there is a Genoese town called Ventimiglia, built on the hillside. This is large and has a broad, straight highstreet lined with big, fine houses;

---

[1] Luciano Grimaldi, Lord of Monaco, 1505–23.   [2] In 1507.

[3] An oared vessel, regularly distinguished from a galley, but equally dependent on sail for normal purposes, on oars for emergencies – as for spurting to intercept customs-dodgers.

[4] Estimating cargo capacity by 'botti', or barrels of a standard size, was the normal Italian method. For the problem involved in translating 'botti' into tons deadweight see Frederick C. Lane, *Navires et constructeurs à Venise pendant la Renaissance* (Paris, 1965) 239–43.

the rest of the town is less attractive and lies on a slope. Outside the gate on the S. Remo side is a river[1] which, though spanned by a wooden bridge and not very safe to ride across at that time of year, was being forded. For two miles after this there is a fine plain, profusely planted with vines, olives and figs; at the end of which is a little town called Bordighera, which again is Genoese and is run by a company in Genoa, similar to the *monti di pietà*[2] elsewhere, which controls the dealings of and has the income from the community. Another two miles on is a village, Roia, belonging to S. Remo and only a mile from that town. This lies partly on a hillside and partly on flat ground by the sea. Hereabouts are the finest, thickest, biggest and most productive citrus orchards I have yet seen, and enough palm-trees to supply Genoa, France, Florence and Rome.[3] They make the palm-fronds so white and tender by keeping them tightly bound all the year round. However, the fruit they yield is not good.

December 2. We left S. Remo after lunch and went to dinner at Porto Maurizio fifteen miles away. This is situated by the sea partly on a rocky height. Nine miles from Porto Maurizio is Arma di Taggia. Only a short way (less than a quarter of a mile) further on is S. Stefano and four miles beyond that S. Lorenzo: these are unwalled towns situated on the flat ground by the sea, and both they and Porto Maurizio belong to the Genoese republic.

December 3. After lunching at Porto Maurizio we went on to dinner at Alassio, fifteen miles away. The going is very poor. A mile beyond Porto Maurizio is the town of Oneglia, situated on a flat stretch of coast. It belongs to Girolamo Doria,[4] the *capitaneo* of all that part of the Riviera. Three miles further on is Diano Castello, up on the mountain, with its suburb on the coastal plain. After another mile is Cervo, which is by the sea, lying partly on a mountain-side and partly on level ground. Four miles further on is Andora, situated in a hollow on a hill, and another two miles

---

[1] The Roia.

[2] A *monte di pietà* was a loan bank with interest rates kept artificially low by government regulations favouring the needy. The company in Genoa was the Bank of St George, of great political as well as economic importance; it had encouraged settlement at Bordighera in 1470–71.

[3] While part of the frond of the European palm is edible, they were chiefly used for distribution on Palm Sunday.

[4] Of the branch of the Doria family of Genoa which had owned, and taken their title from Oneglia since the thirteenth century. They sold the town to Emanuel Philibert of Savoy in 1576.

beyond that Laigueglia, on a flat stretch of coast. All these towns are quite sizeable and belong to Genoa.

December 4. We left Alassio after lunch and went on to dinner at Finale twenty miles away. Five miles beyond Alassio is a city called Albenga, lying on level ground half a mile back from the sea. Cardinal Sauli[1] was the administrator there. It yields about seven hundred ducats a year. Two miles further on, another unfortified town called Ceriale. And after another two and a half miles there is Borghetto. These are all coastal towns and belong to Genoa. After another two and a half miles is Loano, which is only a small place, but the walled area is on the mountain and belongs to the Fieschi family. After two and a half miles more is Pietra Ligure, a walled town by the sea, and a mile beyond that, Borgio Verezzi, another small seaside town. Both belong to Genoa. We rode about ten miles on the level; the going over the rest of the way was extremely difficult, especially three miles from Finale.

December 5. From Finale to lunch and dinner at Savona, a distance of fifteen miles. A mile beyond Finale is an Olivetan monastery, called the Madonna di Finale, which is a place of pilgrimage. Finale itself lies by the sea on level ground and is not very large, but it has a castle, town walls which stretch up over the hillside, and an almost continuously built-up street running across level terrain all the way to the monastery in question. Beyond the monastery, four miles of extremely hard going bring one to a place called Vezze consisting of just a few houses on the mountain. Two miles further on is Noli, an ancient coastal city and once, in remote times, a thriving port. Now it is poor, much of it is in ruins and there is not a single ship. I heard that this was due to its being condemned by the Apostolic See, which it had opposed and rebelled against. After another two miles is Spotorno, and after three, Vado, a little seaside town.

Savona is a substantial city, gay and graced with fine streets and houses. It lies mainly on level ground by the sea, where it has a large harbour artificially formed by means of a long, wide mole, which is very fine and makes it very secure. The cathedral is situated in the highest part of the city overlooking the sea, and although it does not rise to any great height it is a big church and,

---

[1] Bandinello Sauli, created cardinal by Julius II in 1511, d. 1518.

moreover, quite beautiful and well-designed, being faced all over, inside and out, with black and white striped stonework. Inside there is a raised choir of great beauty, decorated with little columns of brass which enclose it all the way round, and over the altar a large, beautiful and sumptuous image painted on a panel. Beneath the choir is a vaulted chapel, supported by columns, which is very lofty and beautiful: an open gallery runs round the outside, offering a magnificent view out over the sea. This church was built by Pope Julius II of most happy and glorious memory, who as a cardinal was bishop of Savona.[1] In front of the church extends a fine brick-paved piazza, overlooked by a most stately palace. This is well appointed and maintained. It has a very well-designed garden, and decoration consisting of paintings and of ornaments entirely in marble. It too was built by His Holiness, Pope Julius, at the time of his cardinalship. It has a central courtyard completely surrounded by arcades which are very lofty and graceful. Here the Cardinal was given lodging by the archbishop of Avignon[2] and received with the lavish and excellent hospitality which it is the Archbishop's custom to give, for he is a most refined and liberal prelate. In front of the steps leading up to the cathedral portico there is a square design in the paving of the piazza, of the same width as the steps, and made like mosaic but using small natural pebbles of various colours which are found naturally in the sea. It shows the city's coat-of-arms, which consist, if I remember rightly, of white and red bars surmounted by a black half eagle with outstretched wings and the Fregoso device edged with black and white;[3] and below the arms are the following lines of verse in fine antique lettering also done in mosaic:

Verses

Hoc Domine rerum casus servata per omnes
Stravit opus, meriti parva Saona memor.[4]

In the same city the aforementioned Pope Julius of happy memory began a great palace to the glory of his native city and

[1] From 1499 to 1502. The cathedral was destroyed by the Genoese in 1542 and rebuilt from 1589. The palace (Palazzo Della Rovere) was designed (1493–6) by Giuliano de Sangallo. Subsequent alterations have left little of his work visible.

[2] Orlando de Carette, Archbishop from 1513 to 1527.

[3] De Beatis's memory was accurate. These were the arms of Savona, and the Fregoso device had been included to commemorate the influence of this Genoese family there.

[4] 'This work, O Lord, little Savona, preserved through all vicissitudes, laid out mindful of Thy goodness to her.'

family. This, though unfinished, is a considerable structure: all the cellar vaults are complete, and a number of vast, sumptuous ground-floor apartments have been built. The city is entirely surrounded by fine suburbs and further out, on the estates, has many fine country-houses for the enjoyment of its citizens. The Archbishop of Salerno[1] came here with two galleys from Genoa in order to meet the Cardinal, but the unfavourable weather (a severe storm blew up) made the sea journey impossible, and my master left for Genoa by land, accompanied by the Archbishop, in driving rain, on the day indicated below.

December 8. From Savona, where my master breakfasted before day as he had not dined the previous evening, we went to dinner at Genoa. This is a journey of thirty miles, and the road extremely poor. Two and three miles respectively beyond Savona are Albisola and Celle, small seaside towns. Two miles further on is Varazze, a walled town by the sea. Arenzano is another three miles' journey, Voltri five: these are two large, prosperous townships. From there onward the road is built up all the way to Genoa. After five more miles there is Sestri, after two Cornigliano, and after two more S. Pier d'Arena where Genoa builds all her carracks. At that time, there were two huge new ones about to be caulked and launched, one of 2200 *botti*, and the other of 4000 *botti*, we were told by the builders.

Over this whole stretch of the Riviera, one is riding along very rugged mountain coastline, and even where gradients are not steep one finds paths and tracks that are so narrow and so precipitously perched at an immense height above the sea that to ride along them is the greatest danger in the world; and indeed they are ridden along only very seldom. Most of the towns are situated on level ground by the sea, and the few that are on the mountains (which in some places come right down to the water and in others do not) have their suburbs down by the sea, where the climate is so delightful and where crops (except grain) are so plentiful that it is like an earthly paradise. Yet this route is such that on one particular day's journey of only fifteen miles the horses had to be shod four or five times. We found olives, vines and figs in abundance, and other fruits as well, all the way along this coast, and the weather was remarkably mild and temperate. As the

---

[1] Federigo Fregoso, brother of the Doge of Genoa, archbishop 1507–33.

vineyards lie on the steep hillsides, walls are built in step-like series to prevent the rain from washing them away.

The city of Genoa lies by the sea in the form of a curve: hence the notion, entertained by some uneducated people, that the name Genoa comes from *genu*.[1] It is a very populous, fine city. The streets were built narrow from the outset, to make them easier to defend against the Moors and pirates who used to invade it; but the houses, which are all very tall and imposing and extremely well designed, make them seem much narrower than they really are. The greater part of the city is situated on hills, and the walls stretch a long way and encompass several hills and valleys, running in and out in a most curious fashion. The castle stands within the city on a hill close to the very fine church of San Francesco, which was built by the grandfather of the reigning doge, Ottaviano Fregoso. This castle can do the city great harm and is in the hands of the French.[2] But the Lanterna could do far more, because Genoa is essentially a port, and since no vessel whatever could enter the harbour without its permission, the Lanterna was a bridle on the city, and a very harsh one indeed. The Lanterna was a castle built by King Louis of France on a low rock which projects from the sea for some way, and it hangs like a falcon over the harbour and the part of the city situated along the shore. It is called the Lanterna because at one time there was a lighthouse with a lantern lit at night to show sailors the way into the harbour. The aforementioned Doge, being the loyal son of Genoa he is, had the fortress completely destroyed before surrendering it to the French, pretending that he was powerless to resist mob violence.[3] The harbour faces westward and is formed by means of an artificial mole running a good way out into the water. Large sums are spent every year in repairing this mole so as to prevent it from

---

[1] De Beatis spells the name Genua. Cf. Grassetto (op. cit. on p. 35, 60): '*Et ista dicesi da Genuo figlio de Saturno, condita e nominata, altri da Genuino, uno di compagni di Phetonte, alguni a Jano de Italia primo re... et altri dal genochio l'ano nomata, perchè in tal forma quasi genu Italiae sita ene.*'

[2] Apart from brief republican interludes, Genoa had been controlled by France since Louis XII's invasion of Italy in 1499. After the defeat of the French at the battle of Ravenna in 1512, the city resumed its independence, but in the shadow of a French garrison which remained in the fortress. Ottaviano Fregoso (or Campofregoso) became doge in 1513 with, from 1515, French support. He died in 1524. He, like Lodovico Canossa (see note, p. 106), is one of the speakers in Castiglione's *The Courtier*.

[3] Ottaviano Fregoso destroyed in 1515 the fortress which Louis XII had had built in 1507 on to the lighthouse tower, or Lanterna.

collapsing, for the waves batter it very hard indeed. At the time of our visit, there were ten ships in the harbour.

The cathedral is large but hardly adequate for a city the size of Genoa. It is situated on high ground a fair distance from the sea. In the sacristy on December 11, my master and the rest of our party saw the Holy Grail, the bowl from which Christ ate with his disciples. The Doge, his brother the Archbishop of Salerno and many other noblemen were present, and two decrees were issued there in the name of the Doge: one forbidding anyone, under pain of death, to carry arms in the sacristy, the other imposing the same penalty for throwing anything through the window, since this might damage the aforesaid vessel. This is made of smooth and extremely transparent emerald.[1] It has six sides on the outside (each of them over a third of a span across), two small, round handles and a base of very fine workmanship. The interior, on the other hand, is quite smooth and without faces. The bowl is displayed at the top of a cabinet which has a window high in either side so as to show off its perfection; and we were told by our hosts that it is kept in this cabinet, which locks with twelve keys, because when, as was formerly the case, it was kept under only two keys, which were in the hands of citizens, one of the latter was secretly approached by the Venetian *signoria* and promised many thousands of ducats if he would put the bowl in their hands, and he covertly went through with the intrigue to the point of being sent an imitation bowl to substitute for the real one. But being a virtuous and upright citizen, he reported the whole affair, so that precautions should be taken for the future. And so the twelve keys were ordained. My master climbed up and handled the bowl, judging it to be a perfect and quite priceless emerald. Cardinal d'Este was of the same opinion when, on a visit here five or six years before the Cardinal, he adroitly brought an expert jeweller of his on to the cabinet, where none but high officials normally ever climb, and had him test it with his graver. They said that the ashes of St John the Baptist, which they preserve with due veneration, had come to them from the east with this basin.

The *palazzo del comune*, where the Cardinal lodged with the Doge and the Archbishop of Salerno, is an ancient affair with extensive living quarters, situated near the cathedral. In front of

---

[1] It is of green first century Roman glass.

it is a large piazza with arcades running round it and over them rooms where the Ducal Guards are quartered. Four streets, barred with double gates, lead into the square. Formerly they had single gates, and the reason for doubling them was that one night about ten years ago Signor Girolamo Adorno, an opponent of the Fregoso family, entered the city with a large body of soldiers, including a number of Neapolitan gentlemen, and with the complicity of his faction, and launched an attack on the gate so fierce that had not the Doge been there to get up in his nightshirt, seize sword and buckler and repel the enemy the palace would have been taken and the Doge with all his confederates and supporters would have come to grief. The gates consist of a single door of massive intersecting beams and are kept locked with keys normally guarded night and day by the Ducal guard, to prevent horsemen and troops from entering the square and breaking into the palace where the head of the reigning faction always resides and which serves as a castle; and it was to make the gates easier to guard and defend that, as I have said, they were doubled, with a space of more than ten paces between each pair. Note: the original gates are situated just where the streets open on to the square.

We stayed here at Genoa for four whole days and were entertained with great kindness and hospitality. The Archbishop always ate with the Cardinal, as the Doge was keeping Advent and fasting every day. The latter is truly a man of great valour and magnanimity as he showed in the way he treated his opponent, Girolamo Adorno, on the night I have just described, for Adorno was taken prisoner with a serious wound, and although the Doge himself had had his left hand badly injured by gunshot in the same fighting, he had him treated and looked after the whole time, constantly visiting him like a true brother, and when he had recovered, not only spared his life but gave him thousands of ducats and other gifts and sent him away, providing him with an escort until he had reached a safe place. But he has many other fine qualities; indeed, he is so virtuous, learned, just, liberal and noble that I judge him worthy of all honour and happiness.

At Genoa we ate a variety of pear which grows along the coast and which they call a bergamot. This is not very large and has a tough, wrinkled skin, but the flesh is tender. As winter pears go it is first-rate. The city manufactures high-quality velvets on a large scale (the black weaves costing from eight to ten gold ducats per rod), and it is the same with all the other skilled crafts, particularly the making of delicate, cleverly-wrought ornaments of coral and of shells, which are not as fragile as coral, though they belong to the same species; there are black ones, tawny ones, grey ones and many other colours. They are taken at sea off the coasts of Sardinia.

In Genoa it is the custom for the men of the same family, so as to be united and not lead separate lives, to live in adjoining houses in the same locality, where they have piazzas in which they constantly gather and enjoy each other's company. I do not, of course, mean that all the families of Genoa have this amenity, but only the ones that are great and rich, such as the Spinola, the Doria, the Lomellini, the Sauli, the Grimaldi and a few others of similar standing, who give these piazzas their family names, viz. *piazza Spinola, piazza Doria*, etc. The women are generally tall and endowed with fine teeth and really golden hair, which some wear loose and some fasten up in a special style which looks very attractive. They do not wear veils or headgear of any kind, except cords and other gold ornaments which are very common, and when they do not have fair hair naturally, they wear a wig and lavish the utmost care upon it. The matrons wear a black stole over their shoulders which is made from a full width of taffeta and reaches right down to the ground. When they keep vigil by the dead and wear mourning, they have a white linen one. And certainly, in the city itself, as distinct from the Riviera, where they are as plain as can be, the women are generally speaking the most beautiful, sturdy and graceful in Italy, though there are some beauties at Savona as well. But they have already started to abandon their traditional costume and nearly all dress in the Spanish style and follow every other flirtatious and wanton fashion. At various times of the year they hold evening parties at the houses of different noblewomen. Many young men and women attend, and one stays, if one is minded to do so, until the fifth or sixth hour of the night. Besides, the women commonly stay out in the streets, even in winter unless it is raining, until four, five or six o'clock, as the case may be, conversing together with the young men of the city, for they do not readily get involved with strangers.

December 14. We left Genoa after lunch and went to dinner at Voltaggio, twenty miles away. First we had to ride back to S. Pier d'Arena before setting out on our road. Once away from the coast we came upon more than five spans' depth of snow (which continued all the way to Milan) and such extreme cold that our boot soles froze to the stirrups and we could not free our feet. Along the route there were four or five small towns, two of which belong to the Spinola. The Doge sent some of his men on ahead of us as far as Voltaggio (a castle of little account) where they found us good food and lodgings.

December 15. From Voltaggio to dinner at Alessandria della Paglia, a distance of twenty-four miles. Fifteen miles[1] beyond Voltaggio is a fortified town called Gavi, the Genoese frontier post. This is a substantial place, situated on level ground with a castle on the nearby hill two stone's throws away, and it is heavily garrisoned. There are many small towns on the way to Gavi which belong to the Spinola, and similarly many on the way to Alessandria which belong to the Visconti, and although some of them were walled, the houses are generally built of brick.

Alessandria is a large, level city, but very depopulated because of its party struggles and because it has been sacked several times of late.[2] Half a mile from the gate one enters if coming from Genoa there is a river called the Bormida, which was difficult to ford at this time of year. At the same gate stands a fortress which has wet moats and is of considerable strength.

December 16. From Alessandria after lunch to dinner at Casale, which is twelve miles distant. Just outside the city gate we crossed a fine stone bridge spanning the river Tanaro, beyond which there is a large, fine suburb with a broad street flanked by magnificent palaces. Five miles from Alessandria there is a place which is called Castelletto Monferrato, and two bowshots away San Salvatore, a considerable walled town with a large suburb, though its houses are mostly built of earth. This and a number of other small towns belong to the Marquis of Monferrat.[3]

Casale is a city lying on level ground. Its site and its very well-designed walls give it great defensive strength, and it is well

---

[1] A mistake: Gavi lies only a quarter of the distance from Voltaggio to Alessandria.

[2] Notably in 1499 during Louis XII's invasion of Italy, but it suffered on other occasions as being an essential strategic centre both to the Milanese and the French.

[3] William VIII, died in 1518.

equipped with artillery. It is graced with fine piazzas and palaces, including the one – very sumptuous and well designed – that belongs to the Gambera[1] who was chamberlain at the court of Pope Innocent VIII of happy memory. The whole city is paved, and although it was not at its best with everything under snow, one could see from its situation and broad streets that it must have beauty and charm. The Cardinal lodged with the aforementioned Marquis at the castle, which is a fine, strong and very commodious building. Here we relaxed for two days and were generously entertained by the Marquis and his French wife.[2] The latter is Cardinal Lanson's sister and is of great beauty and grace. The Marquis himself is a most courteous and affable young man of about thirty-six (though he suffers from a leg ailment and could not much enjoy himself) and there is no doubt that he has a fine household, for in addition to Master Andrea Cossa,[3] who is quite exceptional, he has many well-to-do nobles, gentlemen of merit who would be a credit to any great prince. The palace is finely decorated, and life there is very opulent. The marquisate normally yields revenues of sixty thousand ducats a year, or so they said. Here we saw the child wife[4] of Federico Gonzaga, the Marquis of Mantua's son. She is about nine years old and very pretty. We also saw a first-rate stable: very well provided with stalls and boxes and housing fifty-five horses. In two other stables there were thirty-five more. Most of them were fully-grown steeds or four- to five-year-old colts: saddle-horses, curtals, Frisians, jennets and Turkish.

December 19. From Casale we went to dinner at Vigevano, a distance of twenty miles. Four miles beyond Casale we ferried across the Po, which flows within a bowshot of the town, and a mile further on we crossed back again, still by ferry, though the river-port was frozen over owing to the extreme cold and we had to wade ashore up a break in the ice. Seven miles from Vigevano we came to a fortified town called Mortara belonging to the Duchy of Milan. On the way there are a number of small towns which belong to noble families, one of them to the Gallarani.[5]

December 20. From Vigevano, the fortified town belonging to

---

[1] Bishop of Cavaillon, Vaucluse.
[2] Anne, daughter of Réné, Duke of Alençon.   [3] Untraced.
[4] Margherita Paleologo di Monferrato. Federigo became Marquis in 1519.
[5] I.e. Gallerani. The best known member of this family is Cecilia, mistress of Ludovico Il Moro and painted by Leonardo.

Gian Giacomo Trivulzio,[1] which has an income of twenty thousand ducats a year, we went to dinner at Milan, a distance of twenty miles. Seven miles beyond Vigevano is Abbiategrasso, a sizeable fortified town which also belongs to the Duchy of Milan. Two miles beyond Vigevano we ferried across the Ticino. An artificial canal of considerable breadth runs in a straight line from Abbiategrasso to Milan, with many houses on either bank. They call this the Naviglio,[2] and its water is drawn from the Ticino, a distance of twenty miles from Abbiategrasso. Yet there is another very large canal which runs into Milan, from Lake Como.[3] This great city derives untold benefit from its canals.

As it has not been my intention to give detailed descriptions of the cities and towns of Italy (though I have written at length about Genoa, because less frequented than other cities and set apart from their customs), in the case of Milan I shall merely say that, after viewing it carefully from the top of the cathedral tower,[4] in my opinion it is no smaller than Paris, particularly in circuit. It has a great cathedral and a great castle, which is undoubtedly the biggest in Italy and perhaps in Christendom; and as far as fortresses built on level ground go, it is certainly the strongest one can imagine, with all its array of wet moats, its massive walls designed on a vast scale and its many underground chambers and counter-mines. The castle also has the *Rocchetta*[5] and it is so well equipped with artillery and munitions (as we saw in detail one day when the Cardinal was invited to lunch by the commander) that all the rest of Italy would not, I believe, be capable of creating its equal in a hundred years. The more one has considered it and examined it at first hand, the more it stirs one to anger and detestation against the man who came forth and surrendered it to the French.[6]

[1] Milanese exile, Commander-in-Chief of the French army which took Milan in 1499. Led the French opposition to Julius II during the Ferrara campaign in 1510–11, at which time the Cardinal of Aragon was with the Pope. Died 1518.

[2] The Naviglio Grande.

[3] The Martesana. Leonardo da Vinci, when resident engineer to Ludovico Sforza, was among those who worked on the construction of this canal.

[4] De Beatis has 'campanile'. He presumably means the octagonal *tiburio*, the cathedral's highest point (but never used for bells) which had been built *c.* 1490–*c.* 1505.

[5] An older fortification, incorporated into one of the corners of the *Castello Sforzesco*.

[6] When Ludovico Il Moro was forced to withdraw from Milan in 1499 in the face of Louis XII's advancing army and of unrest within the city, he entrusted the castellanship of the *Castello*, which was considered impregnable, to his friend and agent Bernardino da Corte, who betrayed it to the French ten days later. This act of treachery quickly became notorious, and was cited as an example of how unwise it was to trust overmuch in fortifications by Machiavelli in *The Prince* (ch. 20) and the *Discourses* (bk. ii, ch. 24).

181

In Milan we lodged at the monastery of Sant' Antonio, where not only the Cardinal but all the rest of us were honourably received by the abbot, Cardinal Trivulzio's brother, who is a most courteous and refined person. We stayed there for ten days, and as well as receiving visits, banquets and marks of high esteem from the Master of the Horse,[1] the archbishop of Vienne[2] and all the lords and noblemen who were in Milan at that time, the Cardinal was visited constantly, and shown much kindness and respect and great favour, by Monseigneur de Lautrec, Governor General of the State of Milan and of all pensioners of the Most Christian King in Italy.[3] The day but one before our departure, the Cardinal held a tournament on the open space in the *Castello*, attended by many ladies in carriages.[4] This was more notable for pageantry than for prowess, for although it included single combat with sharpened swords, not only was there not a single casualty or wound, nor any honourable thrust, but most of those who jousted were mere tiros, new to the exercise, and did not engage their opponent. The floats were quite magnificent, graced as they were not only by honest gentlewomen in all their finery but also decorated with gold trimmings and covers made from silks or brocades of various colours, and drawn by fine, splendidly caparisoned horses. In the evening the Cardinal gave a most lavish and stately banquet where he was staying. It was attended by about forty gentlewomen who, if not beautiful without exception, were all nonetheless richly and gracefully attired.

At the Dominican convent of Santa Maria delle Grazie, which was built by Signor Ludovico Sforza and is extremely beautiful and well cared for, we saw in the friars' refectory a Last Supper painted on the wall by Messer Leonardo Vinci, whom we had met at Amboise. This is most excellent, though it is starting to deteriorate: whether because of the dampness of the wall or because of some other oversight, I do not know. The figures in the painting are portraits, from life and life-size, of various court personalities and Milanese citizens of the time.[5] At the same church we also saw a sacristy extremely rich in brocade vestments, which were likewise ordered by the late lamented Signor Ludovico.

[1] See p. 135.
[2] Alessandro Sanseverino. Died 1527.   [3] See note, p. 107.
[4] 'Carrecte' again, perhaps here in the sense of carnival floats.
[5] The Last Supper was commissioned by Ludovico Sforza (date uncertain, but it was nearly finished in 1497). Its early deterioration was probably due to Leonardo's use of an untried technique. For de Beatis's comment on 'portraits' see p. 47.

December 30. From Milan after lunch to the Certosa di Pavia, fifteen miles away. This monastery does not have such extensive living quarters as the Grande Chartreuse in Dauphiny, but is much finer and better planned as regards cloisters, accommodation for both monks and lay brothers, and other necessary amenities. In addition to this it has the finest, loveliest and most splendid church we have seen anywhere in our journey. This applies equally to the body of the church and to its chapels. The former has a most beautiful floor and is rich in marble decoration, excellent paintings and ivory ornaments, particularly the image over the high altar and two richly-carved vessels of considerable size in which relics are preserved. The chapels are very numerous and run the whole length of the building on either side, shut off from the body of the church by heavy brass grilles. There are also doors which communicate between one chapel and the next, and they are as well finished with altars, altarpieces and ornaments as any we have yet seen. The first two chapels are entered by doors opening into the crossing which is near the choir. The façade, which is not yet finished, is made in black and white marble with many reliefs and both round and rectangular panels in porphyry and serpentine, all of first-rate workmanship. For a church façade it is most sumptuous. A great courtyard stretches in front of it and at the far end is an entrance building with fine rooms, lofty arcade and an ornate and imposing gate.

This monastery was founded by the most excellent Signor Galeazzo Visconti of happy memory, Duke of Milan, who lies buried in the church, to the right before you enter the choir, in a very fine marble tomb. This has upon it a life-size relief effigy of him, with a sparse beard consisting of just a few long, curly hairs, in the strangest fashion nature could ever produce, and indeed from the appearance of this statue he would not seem to have lived to be over thirty.[1] The Duke endowed the monastery with an income of seven thousand ducats, partly for the sustenance of the monks and partly for the construction and necessities of the church and for almsgiving to the poor. But the estates left for this endowment have been added to, and the monastery at present enjoys an income of over sixteen thousand ducats. It has a large community of monks.

December 31. We set out after lunch from the Certosa, where

[1] Gian Galeazzo Visconti, born 1351, died in 1402. His tomb was not constructed until 1497.

we had been lodged very comfortably and treated with great kindness, and went on to Pavia five miles away. On leaving the Certosa we immediately entered the great park and from there passed into the small park,[1] and this brought us all the way to Pavia. Though now in a state of neglect and decay, these parks still clearly show that they were once worthy of a King.

Pavia is a large city built, like most others in Lombardy, on level ground. It has a fine castle notable less for its defensive strength than for its apartments, which are spacious and magnificent. On a square in front of the cathedral, which is very small, dark and cavern-like, there is a metal equestrian statue standing on a finely wrought marble plinth or base, in the same posture as the one at St John Lateran in Rome.[2] It is very old and handsome, but small. They say that it was formerly at Ravenna and was brought to Pavia by the Goths.

Past one of the city gates flows the Ticino, which is spanned by a great roofed stone bridge. In a large chapel or sacristy at the Augustinian friary there is a great monumental sarcophagus or tomb of marble. This stands about four spans away from the wall and has a depth of three feet, with all the sculpture it carries and the innumerable delicately carved figures that encrust it. Above all, the marble has such polish and lustre as to pass for alabaster. No modern master can achieve such an effect. The experts consider this tomb to be one of the most beautiful things in Italy, or indeed anywhere, for there is no need to take the foreigners into account: what cannot be found in Italy will never be found anywhere.[3] There is a relief of the glorious saint in an embrasure which is framed by a little arch spanning the tomb from one side to the other. Some say that his body is in this cantharus, others, inside the altar of the crypt or vaulted chapel under the choir of the main church, which is served by the Augustinian friars.

January 1, 1518. From Pavia we went to dinner at Ospedaletto twenty miles away. Three miles before reaching our destination we passed through a port on a smallish river called Lambro, by antiphrasis for it is extremely muddy.[4] Here we stayed the night

---

[1] These parks were hunting preserves of the Dukes of Milan. The battle of Pavia, at which Francis I was taken prisoner by the Emperor Charles V in 1525, was fought in the small park, near the Castello.

[2] The statue of Marcus Aurelius, moved to the Campidoglio in 1538. The Pavia statue appears to have perished.

[3] The fourteenth-century Arca di Sant'Agostino in S. Pietro in Ciel d'Oro.

[4] *Ambra* = amber.

at a monastery of the order of St Jerome (to which Ospedaletto itself belongs) where we were most comfortably accommodated: a very fine monastery with a large community of friars. The living quarters include a square block with four rooms per floor, one in each corner with its own privy, leaving a small cross-shaped hall in the middle, which has three barred windows and a door, a centre cupola or spined vault, and intersecting barrel vaulting on the two floors of the block. In addition it has cellars, vaulted throughout, with four thick pillars which support the vaults of both the floors above. My master took drawings of this block or annexe, and indeed without such drawings it is extremely difficult to show the reader by means of a description, however precise, all the convenience and genial design of the building.

January 2. From Ospedaletto to dinner at Cremona, a distance of twenty miles. After ten miles, at Pizzighettone, a fortified town belonging to Signor Teodoro Trivulzio,[1] we ferried across the Adda, and aboard the boat were treated to a ready-made lunch by Master Jacopo Cippella, a papal courtier and a native of Pizzighettone, which is extremely strong by virtue of the river which flows round it.

January 3. As we reached Cremona late in the day and set off again early the next morning, no account of the city can be given except of the part we rode through, which is very fine and has an extremely high tower. From Cremona we went to lunch at Pieve S. Giacomo, a distance of eight miles, together with the Bishop of Nice,[2] who accompanied the Cardinal from Milan to Mantua. From there we went on to supper at Bozzolo, a distance of sixteen miles, making a day's journey of twenty-four.

We spent a whole day at Bozzolo. This is an unwalled town, but there are some fine palaces, especially the apartments at the castle, where Signor Federico Gonzaga and his wife, Signora Giovanna Orsini, the Cardinal's niece, live very comfortably. Signora Camilla, the sister of Signor Federico, came over from Gazzuolo. She is as noble a lady – affable, beautiful, virtuous and musical – as any gentlewoman in Lombardy; and indeed were I to say she surpassed all others I should not be telling a lie.[3]

---

[1] 1474–1551, fought for the Aragonese in Naples and went into exile with them in 1495; then joined the French and in 1516 became Venice's captain general.
[2] Girolamo Aragi, bishop, 1511–42.
[3] Federico, son of Gianfrancesco Gonzaga, Prince of Bozzolo, died in 1528; Camilla, his youngest sister, married Alfonso, Marquis of Tripalda.

January 5. Leaving Bozzolo after lunch with Signor Federico and his aforementioned wife and sister, the Cardinal went on by carriage to dinner at Gazzuolo, seven miles away, where we found Milady Antonia del Balzo,[1] sister of Queen Isabella[2] and the mother of Signor Ludovico, Signor Federico and Signor Pirro Gonzaga, and also of the Marchioness of Bitonto[3] and of the Countess of Colisano;[4] and although Signor Ludovico was at Casalmaggiore, which he has recently purchased, his wife and daughters were there at Gazzuolo, and they are very lovely. The eldest daughter, an accomplished and charming person, is already married. Here we halted overnight, there was splendid and prolonged dancing, and we received great kindness and hospitality.

January 6. From Gazzuolo after lunch to dinner at Mantua, a distance of twelve miles. A stone's throw from Gazzuolo, which is not so populous as Bozzolo, we ferried across the river Oglio which flows in front of the castle.

Mantua is a city which not only the student of poetry, mindful of the great poet[5] it has produced, but every noble spirit must needs revere, commend and extol to the skies. And I especially am in duty bound to love, exalt and hallow it. But since the feeble powers of my wit do not suffice to conceive, let alone express, all the praise it would deserve, I shall simply say that I delight in it as in no other city in Lombardy: for here one sees so many valiant captains of the House of Gonzaga; here one sees so many fair and virtuous ladies (above all the most illustrious and most excellent Marchioness, from whom I pass on in silence, reverently kissing her hand, since to speak of her requires more than mortal powers); and lastly one sees here all the nobility and virtue of Italy gathered together.[6] And let me briefly conclude by saying that although the city is compassed about with lakes and founded on water, within it (a veritable miracle of nature) one neither feels nor sees aught but sweet fire, flames and ardent courtesy.

---

[1] Died 1538; wife of Gianfrancesco Gonzaga, Prince of Bozzolo.
[2] Widow of King Frederick of Naples. See note on p. 114.
[3] Dorotea Gonzaga, wife of Gianfrancesco Aquaviva, Marquis of Bitonto.
[4] Susanna Gonzaga, wife of Pietro di Cardona, Count of Colisano.
[5] Vergil.
[6] Only the letter to Isabella d'Este quoted on p. 2 supports de Beatis's contact with and, possibly, previous residence at the court of Mantua, but the Cardinal of Aragon was an old friend as well as a distant relative, and de Beatis could have been with him on previous visits. The adulatory tone reflects that of Equicola's verses (see p. 161).

At Mantua we were guests of the Marchioness at the castle, and we stayed for twenty days with all the customary hospitality, with dancing and festivities, and in one long round of pleasures. Here, too, one day there was a tournament, and the most illustrious Signor Federico Gonzaga, eldest son of the most excellent Marquis, and all the other lords and gentlemen, in spite of their youth, jousted valiantly and acquitted themselves extremely well.

January 26. The Cardinal set out from Mantua by water with most of his retinue (for those who were so minded had set out overland the previous day) and in the evening, at one o'clock of the night, we reached the illustrious city of Ferrara. On this day we sailed fifty miles.[1]

Since Ferrara is so well-known and celebrated both in its own right and for the virtue and greatness of its lord the most excellent Duke[2] and of the most illustrious and reverend Cardinal d'Este his brother,[3] and also in order to avoid entering into the misfortune and misery of that most unhappy queen, Isabella, and of her most illustrious son and daughters, who reside there, I shall not attempt to give an account of that city, but bring the present itinerary to an end here in the place from which I began to describe it. After halting for twenty days at Ferrara with an attack of gout, my master set out for Rome, and by the grace of God arrived there, with the whole party alive and well, on March 16, 1518.

Postscript [4]

The company of my most illustrious and reverend lord consisted of ten gentlemen, each with a valet, and included his doctor, the Bishop of Anglona,[5] and the Reverend Fra Annibale Monsorio, Abbot of Avanzo, his major-domo; there were two harbingers,

---

[1] N. 2 has: 'xxvj. We went from Mantua by water (having first sent the animals and part of the household by land), embarking on the [river] Mincio to get in the same day to Ferrara, which we reached by two hours after nightfall. As the excellencies of his city and the virtue and valour of the Duke are well known to everyone, and also in order to avoid bringing to my mind the Queen Isabella, the more unhappy for being so good, who lives there, I shall make no more mention of the place. But as this journey began here, here I have designed to end it, so in conclusion I state that from this city monsignor set out for Rome in the second week of Lent and reached there on March 17 [sic] without any accident or illness having affected him or his party.'

[2] Alfonso I d'Este, Duke from 1505 to 1534.

[3] Ippolito. See note, p. 69.

[4] 'Continua' in Pastor's ms. and N. 1.

[5] Giovanni Antonio Scotti, Bishop of Anglona and Tursi from 1511. Died 1528.

two cooks, a comptroller, an interpreter, two grooms and three stable hands, all on horseback; the latter were leading three fine saddle horses by hand, for the person of the Cardinal, and two mules, one carrying the candlesticks and some silver in two panniers and the other a portable bed very conveniently packed in two small bundles. Thus in all, including the animals we were leading, there were about thirty-five mounts in the party until we reached France. From there onwards, with musicians and mountebanks whom the Cardinal brought back to Italy for his service and pleasure, the number rose to over forty-five. The Cardinal always went incognito and never wore his robes except at the courts of the Catholic and Most Christian kings. However, when we were travelling, he like all the rest of us wore a habit of pink silk with sashes of black velvet. The servants were dressed in the same colour and manner but without velvet sashes.

In the course of our travels, from leaving to getting back to Ferrara, we rode in all a distance of 476 Italian miles and (including travel by water) 201 German miles which, on the basis of five Italian miles to one German mile, make 1,005 Italian miles. We also travelled 565 leagues, which, at three Italian miles per league, amount to 1,605, giving a grand total, in Italian miles, of 3,176.[1]

[1] Checked against kilometres the 'Italian mile' used by de Beatis fluctuates in value from 1·46 to 2·05; it averages (over twelve measured stretches) 1·79 km. De Beatis puts the German mile at five Italian miles: 8·95 km. Averaging from the stretches Landsberg–Augsburg, Nördlingen–Ravensberg, Worms–Jülich we get 7·72 km. (variations from 6·33 to 10·75). From Diest he changes from German miles to an unspecified league. Fifteen measurements in the Low Countries give an average of 6·04 km. to the league (variations from 5·00 to 8·00). In speaking of the leagues used in measuring his distances in France, de Beatis remarks that the Breton league is equal to four Italian miles; adopting his mile, this would give 7·16 km., but measuring his route from St-Lô to Nantes gives an average of 5·10 km. based on variations between 4·4 km and 5·85 km. per league. In Normandy, Dauphiny and Provence he puts the league at three Italian miles; this would give 5·37 km., but over the route Calais–Neufchâtel-en-Bray it averages 4·70 km. (variations from 4·08 to 5·28) and over the route Sorgues–Cannes it averages 5·85 km. (variations from 4·75 to 7·00, omitting an exceptional 8·30 between Auriol and St-Maximin). For 'France' proper he puts the league at two Italian miles; this would give 3·58 km., but on the route Rouen–Paris–Rueil it averages 5·35 km. (variations from 4·58 to 6·83). Thus, averaging the 'French' leagues at 5·25 km. we get the following distances to bear in mind when reading his narrative or the Itinerary:

	Km.	statute miles
Italian mile	1·79	1·11
German mile	7·72	4·79
Low Countries league	6·04	3·75
French league	5·25	3·26

In his summary of distances covered there are some minor discrepancies between the figures and the distances he gives day by day in the text (485 Italian miles, 194 German miles, 570 leagues). Also, 1,605 is an arithmetical mistake for 1,695. (N.I. has a grand total of 3,161). Using our average values, the distance covered in modern terms was 5,451 km. or 3,387 miles.

To this should be added the journey from Rome to Ferrara and back, a distance of some 400 miles.

The present transcription was finished at Molfetta by me Don Antonio de Beatis on 29 May[1] in the year of Our Lord 1521.

[1] The fuller of the two Naples mss. has '21 August'.

Itinerary and distances

Date	Place	Distance (see note on p. 188)
May		Italian miles
9	Ferrara to Melara	30
10	Verona	33
11	Borghetto	24
12	Trent	25
		German miles
13	Salorno	3
14	Bolzano	4
15	Chiusa	4
16	Eisack	4
17	Steinach	$5\frac{1}{2}$
18	Innsbruck	$3\frac{1}{2}$
21	Seefeld	3
22	Partenkirchen	6
23	Rottenburg	4
24	Landsberg	5
25	Augsburg	6
27	Donauwörth	6
28	Weissenburg	4
29	Nuremberg	7
June		
1	Gunzenhausen	6
2	Nördlingen	5
3	Lauingen	5
4	Ulm	6
5	Biberach	4
6	Ravensberg	4
7	Constance	4
10	Schaffhausen	4
11	Laufenburg	4
13	Basel	4
14	Strasbourg	20
17	Rastatt	6
18	Speyer	3
23	Worms	6
26	Mainz	7
27	St Goar	8
28	Bonn	12
29	Cologne	4
July		
1	Jülich	6
2	Maastricht	8
		Leagues
3	Diest	7
4	Louvain	4
5	Antwerp	8
10	Bergen op Zoom	6
11	Veere	8
12	Middelburg	1
22	Dordrecht	18
23	The Hague	6
24	Workum	12
25	Breda	7

Date	Place	Distance
		Leagues
27	Antwerp	8
29	Malines	4
30	Brussels	4
31	Ghent	10
August		
2	Bruges	8
3	Nieuwpoort	7
4	Gravelines	8
5	Calais	3
8	Boulogne	7
9	Montreuil	7
10	Abbeville	10
11	Blangy-sur-Bresle	6
12	Neufchâtel-en-Bray	6
13	Rouen	[no distance given]
September		
		Leagues
3	Pont-de-l'Arche	3
4	Gaillon	4
7	Mantes	8
8	Paris	12
12	Montfort-L'Amaury	11
13	Rueil	13
14	Chambrais [now Broglie]	13
15	Lisieux	6
17	Ste-Barbe-en-Auge	6
18	Caen	7
19	Bayeux	7
20	Neuilly-la-Forêt	7
22	St-Lô	6
23	Villedieu	7
24	Mont-St-Michel	7
25	Bazouges-la-Pérouse [?]	7
26	Rennes	7
28	Bain-de-Bretagne	7
29	Nozay	7
30	Nantes	8
October		
3	Ancenis	7
4	Angers	10
5	Le Verger	4
6	La Flêche	6
7	Sonzay	10
8	Tours	6
10	Amboise	7
11	Blois	10
13	Romorantin	8
14	Bourges	15
15	Dun-le-Roi [now Dun-sur-Auron]	7
16	Cosne d'Aumance	11
17	Varennes-sur-Allier	11
18	St-Germain l'Espinasse	11
19	Tarare	8
20	Lyons	6
26	Bourgoin	6
27	Aiguebelette	7

Date	Place	Distance Leagues
28	Chambéry	2
29	La Grande-Chartreuse	5
30	Grenoble	5
31	St-Marcellin	7
November		
1	Valence	8
2	Montélimar	7
3	Bollène	5
4	Sorgues	5
7	Avignon	2
20	Arles	7
21	Salon-de-Provence	7
22	Marseilles	8
24	Auriol	5
25	St-Maximin-la-Sainte-Baume	5
26	Le Luc	7
27	Fréjus	7
28	Cannes	5
29	Nice	5
		Italian miles
30	Monaco	9
December		
1	San Remo	20
2	Porto Maurizio	15
3	Alassio	15
4	Finale Ligure	20
5	Savona	15
8	Genoa	30
14	Voltaggio	20
15	Alessandria	24
16	Casale Monferrato	12
19	Vigevano	20
20	Milan	20
30	La Certosa di Pavia	15
31	Pavia	5
January 1518		
1	Ospedaletto	20
2	Cremona	20
3	Bozzolo	24
5	Gazzuolo	7
6	Mantua	12
26	Ferrara	50

[Rome reached, after no more descriptions, on 16 March.]

BIBLIOGRAPHY

EUROPEAN TRAVEL NARRATIVES UP TO 1521

Anonymous Milanese. 'Account of a journey through Europe in 1516–1518 [recte, 1519]'. British Museum. Add. MSS. 24180.

Bartholinus Riccardus. *Odeporicon idest itinerarium Reverendissimi in Christo patris et Dñi. D. Mathei Sancti Angeli Cardinalis Gurcensis...* Vienna, 1515.

Beatis, Antonio de. *De Reise des Kardinals Luigi d'Aragona durch Deutschland, die Niederlande, Frankreich und Oberitalien, 1517–1518. Als Beitrag zur Kulturgeschichte des ausgehenden Mittelalters veröffentlicht und erläutert von Ludwig Pastor.* Freiburg in Breisgau, 1905.

Beatis, Don Antonio de. *Voyage du Cardinal D'Aragon en Allemagne, Hollande, Belgique, France et Italie 1517–1518.* Tr. Madeleine Havard de la Montagne. Paris, 1913.

Butzbach. *The autobiography of Johannes Butzbach a wandering scholar of the fifteenth century.* Tr. R. F. Seybolt and P. Monroe. Ann Arbor, 1933.

Casola. *Canon Pietro Casola's pilgrimage to Jerusalem in the year 1494.* Tr. and ed. M. Margaret Newett. Manchester, 1907.

Dürer. *Diary of Dürer's journey to the Netherlands, July 1520–July 1521.* Tr. in Conway, William Martin. *The writings of Albrecht Dürer.* New York, 1958.

Equicola, Mario. *De Isabella Estensis iter in Narbonensem Galliam.* N.p., ?1517.

Franceschi, Andrea de'. *Itinerario de Germania...* [1492]. Ed. Enrico Simonsfeld. *Miscellanea della R. Deputazione Veneta di Storia Patria.* 2nd Ser. vol. ix, 1903, 275–345.

Franciscus, Andrea. *Two Italian accounts of Tudor England.* Ed. C. V. Malfatti. Barcelona, 1953.

Grassetto. *Viaggio di Francesco Grassetto di Lonigo lungo le coste Dalmate-Greco-Venete ed Italiche nel anno MDXI e seguente.*

Miscellanea della R. Deputazione Veneta di Storia Patria. 2nd Ser. vol. iv, 1886.

Guicciardini, Francesco. *Diario del viaggio in Spagna*. Ed. Paolo Guicciardini. Florence, 1932.

Harff. *The pilgrimage of Arnold von Harff, Knight, from Cologne, through Italy, Syria, Egypt, Arabia, Ethiopia, Nubia, Palestine, Turkey, France and Spain, in the years 1496 to 1499*. Tr. and ed. Malcolm Letts. London (Hakluyt Society, 2nd Ser. vol. 94), 1946.

Lalaing, Antoine de. *Relation du premier voyage de Philippe le Beau en Espagne, en 1501*. Ed. M. Gachard. *Collection des Voyages des Souverains des Pays-Bas*. Brussels, 1876.

Lannoy, Ghillebert de. *Oeuvres*... Ed. C. Potvin. Louvain, 1878.

Le Bouvier. *Le livre de la description du pays de Gilles le Bouvier*. Ed. E.-T. Hamy. *Recueil de Voyages et de Documents pour servir à l'histoire de la Géographie*. Vol. xxii, 1908.

Le Saige, Jacques. *Chy sensuyvent les gistes, repaistres et depens que... ay faict de Douay à Hierusalem*... Cambray, 1520 (?).

Lopis Stunica, Jacobus [= López de Stuniga, Diego]. *Itinerarium ab Hispania usque ad urbem Romanam*.... Rome, 1521.

Münzer. 'Le voyage de Hieronimus Monetarius à travers la France (1494-5).' Ed. E. Ph. Goldschmidt. *Humanisme et Renaissance*, 1939, 55-75, 198-220, 324-48, 529-39.

Münzer. 'Jérôme Münzer et son voyage dans le midi de la France en 1494-1495.' Ed. Eugène Déprez. *Annales du Midi*, 1936, 53-79.

Rozmital. *The travels of Leo of Rozmital through Germany, Flanders, England, France, Spain, Portugal and Italy 1465-1467*. Ed. Malcolm Letts. Cambridge, Hakluyt Society, 1957.

Sanudo. 'Frammenti inediti dell'itinerario in terraferma di Marin Sanudo.' Ed. R. Fulin. *Archivio Veneto*, 1881, 1-62.

Sanudo, Marino. *Itinerario per la terraferma veneziana*. Ed. Rawdon Brown. Padua, 1847.

Tafur, Pero. *Travels and adventures 1435-1439*. Ed. Malcolm Letts. London, 1926.

Tolmezzo, Francesco Janis da. *Viaggio in Spagna* [1519]. Ed. R. Fulin. *Archivio Veneto*, 1881.

Vandenesse, Jean de. *Journal des voyages de Charles-Quint, de 1514 à 1551*. Ed. M. Gachard. *Collection des Voyages des Souverains des Pays-Bas*. Brussels, 1874.

Vettori, Francesco. *Viaggio in Alemagna.* In *Scritti storici e politici,* ed. E. Niccolini. Bari, 1972.

Vital, Laurent. *Premier voyage de Charles-Quint en Espagne de 1517 à 1518.* Ed. L. P. Gachard and C. Piot. *Collection des voyages des Souverains des Pays-Bas.* Brussels, 1881.

INDEX

Note: the forms of place-names used by de Beatis are in square brackets